HEMINGWAY
at WAR

HEMINGWAY
at WAR

Ernest Hemingway's Adventures as a
World War II Correspondent

TERRY MORT

PEGASUS BOOKS
NEW YORK LONDON

HEMINGWAY AT WAR

Pegasus Books Ltd.
148 W 37th Street, 13th Floor
New York, NY 10018

Copyright © 2016 by Terry Mort

First Pegasus Books cloth edition December 2016

Interior design by Maria Fernandez

Library of Congress Cataloging-in-Publication Data is available.

ISBN: 978-1-68177-247-9

10 9 8 7 6 5 4 3 2 1

Printed in the United States of America
Distributed by W. W. Norton & Company

To Jon Otto and Sam Griffiths, my friends in all weathers,
and two thirds of the estimable Tuna Boys.
Long may they prosper.

HEMINGWAY
at WAR

INTRODUCTION

R eaders interested in Ernest Hemingway know that he has been the subject of a number of comprehensive biographies and memoirs. There is hardly a need for another. Nor is this book intended to be one, although some of his personal history is revisited to provide context to his adventures as a war correspondent in World War II. Hemingway had a talent for being at the center of important events. Those events—and some of the people connected with them—are a large part of this story. He was with the Allied landings on D-Day. He flew with the RAF on at least one bombing mission. He flew with them during an attack of V-1 flying bombs. He operated with the French Resistance and the US Office of Strategic Services (OSS) as the Allies advanced to Paris. And he was present and indeed active during the horrendous carnage of the battle for the Hürtgenwald in Germany's Siegfried Line. As such he provides a useful lens to examine these events and also some of the people, both the troops who fought and the civilian journalists who covered the fighting. Inevitably and understandably, his exposure to people and events affected him deeply—and affected his journalism, and later his fiction. This book attempts therefore to place him in the context of this history and in so doing expand understanding of those events and their effect on him, personally and professionally.

CHAPTER ONE

"There is no pain compared to that of loving a woman who makes her body accessible to one and yet who is incapable of delivering her true self."

—Lawrence Durrell

Lawrence Durrell was plainly a little overwrought when he wrote those lines. Probably, he really didn't mean it. There are quite obviously many worse pains that humans suffer. Those who experienced the grotesque cruelties and disasters of the Second World War knew that—and some dwindling few still know that—all too well.

But there is at least a whiff or two of truth there, as the relationship between Ernest Hemingway and Martha Gellhorn illustrates. Their relationship influenced their subsequent careers and reputations, so it is more significant than the simple story of one writer's love for another, however painful and unsatisfying that became. It became a story of marital conflict in the context of global conflict between nation-states that were fighting for survival—and races that were enduring genocide. And it is also the story of the men and women who went to the war to report it.

In the spring of 1944 Ernest Hemingway went to Europe on assignment from *Collier's* magazine. As a war correspondent, he was obviously a little late in arriving. Why did he finally decide to leave his comfortable home in Cuba? He disliked the bureaucracies involved in journalism, the military censorship, the competitive nature of journalists scrambling to meet deadlines and beat their rivals. Why should he enter the rat race? He was a writer of fiction, primarily, and defined himself that way. He considered himself an artist, and rightly so; these others were mostly just reporters. Some were good writers of the news, some less so. But news was different from fiction. Different from art. It was the difference between photography and painting. Now and then the two might overlap, but not often. What novelist with his reputation would enjoy simple reporting—a narration of carefully massaged facts mixed with homey references to individual soldiers? Besides, he wanted to live his professional life as a lone wolf, not as a cog in an information engine—especially one that was highly regulated. Working for the weekly *Collier's*, he would not be in the business of scrambling for up-to-the-minute reports—a cross that many of the lesser-known journalists would carry. He was there to write features and opinion columns, not straight news stories. He would later say he only did enough to avoid being sent home. He knew he would be under the thumb of military censorship—something that he understood was necessary but still by definition irksome to a creative writer. He had been a war correspondent before, but the circumstances were different in the earlier conflicts he covered. In those days, journalism was a means to an end, both financially and artistically—a way of honing his craft. And that had worked. But things were different now. His novel,

For Whom the Bell Tolls, had been a massive success. And he was in his midforties, a time when he might have been forgiven for wanting to relax and enjoy his success. What's more, by definition, going to the war would distract him from his real job, creative writing. It was not just a matter of time away but also of possible contamination of the quality of his work. As he said in his 1958 interview with the *Paris Review*: ". . . journalism, after a point has been reached, can be a daily self-destruction for a creative writer."[1]

Given all these objections, why did he go?

While the answer to that question does not end with Martha Gellhorn, it certainly starts with her.

❖

It would have been easy to fall in love with Martha Gellhorn. Lots of men did. It would have been less easy to *be* in love with her. Lots of men found that out. One of them was Hemingway, her first husband, though not her first lover. Martha was Hemingway's third wife and the only one of his four wives who had anything like a distinguished career. A successful journalist and writer, she was also the only one of the four who was glamorous, beautiful, and fiercely ambitious. And unlike the other three she was never willing to make marriage her first priority; she had another raison d'être. Or perhaps more than one.

In the early stages of her career Martha Gellhorn believed that journalism could actually have an impact on the culture, could create the kind of social and political change she believed was necessary. "I believed that if everyone knew the truth, justice would be done."[2] Later she came to doubt, but that would come after years of work during which she became more and more embittered and cynical about the western nations' institutions and especially about America's politics, culture, and economics. The Spanish Civil War had a lot to do with that. But when she met Hemingway for the first time, she was still pretty much a true believer. She had worked for the Roosevelt administration writing articles on the condition of rural workers in the South. The misery that she encountered and chronicled fanned her already well-stoked indignation over the country's economic and social structures, and their corresponding inequalities. Describing a Depression-era mill town she wrote: "It is probable—and to be hoped—that one day the owners of this place will get shot and lynched."[3]

Martha's brand of journalism, especially when politics were involved, was frankly and unashamedly tendentious. If the facts did not fit her version of what to her was the correct narrative—i.e., the truth as she perceived it—she had no qualms about ignoring or adjusting them. In one early and notorious example, she wrote about a lynching in the South as though she had been there, even though she heard the story secondhand from a dubious source. (It's probably unnecessary to say that the victim in this story was a rural black man, not a factory owner.) Afterward she said, "The point is, that article was a story. I am getting a little mixed up around now and apparently I am a very realistic writer (or liar) [sic] because everyone assumed I had been an eye-witness to a lynching whereas I just made it up."[4] In her view, exposing the evils of white supremacy and the lynching of blacks in the South justified mixing fact with a generous dollop of fiction. No doubt there were others then, and now, who would agree. Nor did she bother to correct the record when the story was reprinted later. She never really knew whether the lynching even happened. But of course there were other lynchings that really did happen, so to Martha in this case, fiction versus fact was a distinction without a difference.

She met Hemingway, perhaps accidentally, in Key West in December 1936. She, her mother, and her brother walked into Sloppy Joe's Bar, and Martha, at least, made an instant impression on the rather unkempt writer sitting at the bar. Martha was wearing a black dress that flattered her slim figure, and she was then, and always would be, well aware of the effect she could produce. Hemingway later said, admiringly, that Martha's legs "began at her shoulders."[5] Martha's long blond hair fell casually around her face and neck in a way that was dramatically different from the dark, close-cropped coif of Hemingway's current wife, Pauline—dramatically different and for that reason, perhaps, particularly alluring. Martha was twenty-eight, at her physical peak. She was also a published author—of a novel and a book of stories based on her work with the Roosevelt administration. The prestigious *Saturday Review of Literature* magazine had featured her on their cover. So while she admired Hemingway's writing, she was not a starstruck fan. She could legitimately consider herself professionally in the game. Possibly, Hemingway found that appealing too. He was always attracted to people who were good at things, especially the things that mattered to him.

It was never clear whether Martha went to Sloppy Joe's looking to meet Hemingway. It was his known hangout, and probably not quite the sort of place a well-brought-up woman would think of taking her mother, despite the fact that her mother, Edna Gellhorn, was no shrinking violet and had long been active in feminist politics in St. Louis. Regardless of Martha's intentions, she did arouse Hemingway's easily aroused attention, and the two became friendly that very afternoon.*

Things moved rather rapidly as Martha extended her stay in Key West and ingratiated herself with Pauline in much the same way that Pauline had become friendly with Hemingway's first wife, Hadley. No fool, Pauline's antennae began to quiver, but she held her peace for the time being. Two weeks after their first meeting, Hemingway followed Martha to Miami, where they had dinner together. He then

---

* Hemingway's susceptibility may well have been enhanced by his relationship with Pauline. Pauline had already had two children and was advised against having more. As a devout Catholic Pauline allowed no traditional birth control and reportedly limited Hemingway to the coitus interruptus method—a method he later said ruined their marriage. It should be said, however, that Hemingway generally tried to shift the blame for a failing marriage from his own wanderings to the wife of the moment. Pauline's condition, therefore, ultimately became a convenient rationalization.

went to New York for a number of business meetings, while she visited her mother in St. Louis. While in New York, Hemingway made arrangements to cover the civil war in Spain, as a correspondent for NANA—the North American Newspaper Alliance. He would later submit articles for the magazines *Ken* and *Esquire*, although he greatly preferred fiction to journalism. He cared deeply about Spain and the disaster that was unfolding there. In a matter of weeks he was ensconced in Madrid's Hotel Florida. He was there to tell Spain's story—the story of a complicated, desperate war that his side would end up losing. The tragic violence and the body counts of the innocent on both sides would become part of the novel he would eventually write. It was a story that, for him, was best expressed in fiction. A novel allowed disparate points of view and could illustrate the fact that, when a fascist politician is thrown over a cliff by a mob of enraged and vengeful peasants, the politician still suffers the horror of the event and seconds later lands on the rocks below, his only life extinguished, and painfully. Then, too, the scene of El Sordo, isolated with his little band on a mountaintop, watching their doom arrive in the form of Nationalist airplanes, was a useful symbol of mechanized war versus vulnerable but valiant humans—a literary *Guernica*. This scene, indeed the entire novel, contained as much, or maybe more, truth about the war, and by extension the human condition, as any newspaper report. Besides, given the partisan reporting on both sides of the war, it's fair to say that the novel was a better way—perhaps the only way—to express the complexity of the truth. The disinterested good guys were in short supply on all sides in this dreadful war. There were only a few the likes of George Orwell. Or Hemingway, even though some of Hemingway's reports have been criticized as propaganda. Hemingway's more nuanced view of the hideous war would emerge in *For Whom the Bell Tolls*. Both writers, arguably two of the finest of the century, favored the Republican side, but neither turned a blind eye to the government's flaws, missteps, and atrocities. At least, not always. As for the objectivity of the press Orwell said: "No event is ever correctly reported in a newspaper, but in Spain, for the first time, I saw newspaper reports which did not bear any relation to the facts, not even the relationship which is implied in an ordinary lie."[6]

Martha arrived in Madrid soon after Hemingway. Relentless and courageous as always, she survived a rugged trip across the Pyrenees from France, through Barcelona, Valencia, and into Madrid, which at the time was being assaulted from three sides by Francisco Franco's rebel army. Most likely it was then that Hemingway and Martha began their love affair in earnest. And though the affair was part of the reason she came there, her primary reason was to cover the war for *Collier's*. In other words, Hemingway or not, Martha would undoubtedly have found a way to come to Spain anyway. Things did not start off on the best foot, for when Martha initially met Hemingway at the Gran Via Hotel where Ernest was having dinner, he said: "I knew you'd get here, daughter, because I fixed it so you could."[7] That raised her hackles a bit. His habit of addressing young women as "daughter" was annoying, and more than a little odd, but more importantly he had done nothing to help her get to Spain. She undoubtedly, and rightly, felt that her exertions and the risks she had taken were being slighted. It was early in their relationship, though; things that would eventually become significant affronts could still be overlooked. He was still the bright star; she was still a rising star. She joined him in the Hotel Florida. When the hotel was shelled by Nationalist rebels, she and he were seen emerging from the same room and heading for the shelter. Their affair was no secret to the other western journalists in Madrid.

During his four trips to Spain Hemingway not only wrote about the war and saw it firsthand from the front lines, but also helped produce a propaganda film. Ultimately called *The Spanish Earth* the film would be shown in the United States, at the White House and in Hollywood, particularly, in order to raise funds for the beleaguered Republic. Martha would help with some of the postproduction, inserting sound effects into a film that had no ambient sound, because of the danger and difficulty of transporting bulky recording equipment to the combat zones. Orson Welles was originally signed to do the voice-over narration, but no one seemed to care for his reading. Hemingway's criticism of Welles's performance was graphically obscene.* In the end, Hemingway capably recorded the voice-over of the script he had written for the film. The film's director was Joris Ivens, a Dutch filmmaker and enthusiastic communist propagandist. Hemingway did not, and never would, share Ivens's politics, but the two men did share a devotion to the Republican cause and a willingness to expose themselves to front-line combat in order to make a useful film. (John Dos Passos was also involved in the planning and production of the film.) Hemingway cared about Spain and the Spanish people, regardless of politics, and there was little choice but to align himself with the largely leftist movements that were fighting the Nationalists, who were supported by Fascist Germany and Italy. On the surface this was an either/or war; beneath the surface it was far more complicated—as Hemingway would depict in his subsequent novel.

Hemingway's articles for NANA had a level of authenticity that would not always be present in his later work in World War II. Some of them did, anyway. While acknowledging that some of his thirty total dispatches were "poorly done, trivial or incoherent . . . Some were masterpieces of characterization, of analysis, of description, or just plain factual reporting. A half dozen of these dispatches can stand up to the best reporting of the Spanish Civil War."[8] But not everyone agrees. Critic and biographer Scott Donaldson writes: "Phillip Knightley was still more critical in *The First Casualty*, his authoritative study of war correspondence in the twentieth century. Hemingway's reporting was 'abysmally bad,' Knightley maintained, citing in particular, 'his total failure to report the Communist persecution, imprisonment, and summary execution of "untrustworthy

---

* He said in effect that whenever Welles said the word "infantry" it sounded like a fellator swallowing. Of course, his actual language was more colorful.

elements" on the Republican side.' Knightley believed Hemingway failed his obligations as a reporter by salting away such material for use in *For Whom the Bell Tolls*. "For a novelist," he commented, "this was understandable. For a war correspondent, it was unforgivable."[9] Still others regarded his work more charitably, saying in essence that it was uneven—sometimes quite good, other times more like propaganda.

This kind of criticism would reappear in reaction to Hemingway's World War II stories for *Collier's*—but for different and nonpolitical reasons.

It is sometimes difficult to assess the quality of war reporting, since it was invariably subject to censorship. Evading censorship that was too restrictive was a constant battle for writers. In one case, Frederick Voigt, from the *Manchester Guardian*, wanted to write about mass reprisals and executions in Madrid, and knowing that the story would not pass the Republic's government censors, he asked Martha, who was planning a trip to Paris, to take a "carbon" of the story. Hemingway heard about the proposal from Martha, suspected something unusual, and opened the sealed envelope. He discovered an original text that had not been cleared by the censors. He and Martha were furious, since the stunt put Martha in danger of being arrested as a spy. This was no idle risk—both sides were untroubled by rules of law, or even decency, in their use of the firing squad. Besides, Hemingway and other journalists maintained that there had been no such mass reprisals. Or at least there hadn't been any recently. To report such atrocities, even if true, would be damaging to the Republic's cause. That, in turn, would damage their ability to raise funds among sympathetic western donors. Worse, it would provide some cover for American and European governments that wanted to maintain a position of neutrality, which meant they could avoid providing money and arms to the struggling Republic. Nor would it be necessary for France, Britain, and the United States to choose sides in a war that was widely understood to be between fascism and communism—although the truth was, as usual and as mentioned, far more complicated. In a battle between the twin evils of the twentieth century, no western government saw a reasonable alternative to neutrality, even assuming domestic politics did not matter, which is always an absurd assumption.

The tendency of western journalists to downplay Republican atrocities and failures fits nicely with Martha's attitude toward journalism; she was outspoken in her impatience with what she called "that objectivity shit."[10] Unblushing advocacy was not only acceptable, it was a virtue—not just for columnists who were paid to express an opinion, but also for reporters who were paid to report the facts, in theory dispassionately. She was not alone, for the Spanish Civil War was one in which much of the western press—especially those who were covering the war from Madrid—sympathized with the beleaguered Republican government that was fighting a losing battle against Franco's Nationalist rebels. The rebels, supported by Nazi Germany and Fascist Italy, were better equipped and generally better led than the ragtag Republican army that was hamstrung by a toxic mixture of differing—and squabbling—political ideologies. The Republicans, who were supported erratically by the Soviet Union, were a sympathetic underdog, and there was a clear-cut drama between good and evil, or at least so it seemed to Martha and her colleagues. What's more, the political demographics appealed to left-leaning journalists, for the Republic was supported by a motley collection of workers, unionists, anarchists, socialists, and communists of both Trotskyite and Stalinist persuasions. The Nationalist rebels on the other hand were supported by much of the professional army, the Catholic Church, and its militant lay supporters (the "Carlists"), a fascist political movement known as the "Falange," royalists, and the large land and factory owners. It was the classic confrontation between the oppressed and the oppressors, or at least it could easily be framed that way. And it was. Consequently, sympathetic western journalists were reluctant to report failures and atrocities committed by "their" people in the larger interests of the cause. Martha and her colleagues were not reporters so much as chroniclers of a gradually unfolding tragedy, and they felt themselves part of the fight, not mere dispassionate observers. They felt the exhilarating sensation of comradeship and shared danger (danger that was very real, to witness the shelling of Madrid in general and the Hotel Florida in particular), all in the name of a cause they considered noble. And it was a cause in which the moral nuances and inconsistencies could safely be ignored in the enthusiasm of righteous belief. Psychologically, they weren't very different from the thousands of European and American volunteers who flocked to the Republic's standard in the International Brigades. (The American Abraham Lincoln Brigade is perhaps the most famous of these. But there were many others, including a German brigade made up, obviously, of anti-Nazis.) As Martha's and Hemingway's friend and fellow journalist, Herbert Matthews said "good journalists should write with their hearts as well as their minds." Matthews also wrote: "I know as surely as I know anything in this world that nothing so wonderful will ever happen to me again as those two and a half years I spent in Spain . . . It gave meaning to life." [11] Matthews was there on behalf of the *New York Times*. While Matthews et al. were finding meaning in their lives and writing with their hearts, a quarter million civilian Spaniards on both sides of the conflict were finding their graves—through terroristic reprisals and mass political assassinations.* Martha agreed with the conventional journalistic wisdom: "Spain was where our adult hope was (the sum total of the remaining hope of youth with a reasoning and logical hope of adults) . . . Spain was a place where you could hope, and Spain was also like a vaccination which could

---

* Antony Beevor writes that the Nationalist rebels murdered somewhere in the region of 200,000 Republicans and assorted sympathizers, while the Republicans murdered something like 38,000 Nationalists—mostly in the initial stages of the war. These deaths are separate from combat casualties (*The Battle for Spain*, pp. 81–94). Estimates of combat deaths hover around 200,000, with a slight advantage to the Nationalists.

save the rest of mankind from some fearful suffering. But no one important cared."[12] Not everyone saw the conflict as a morality play. In fact, dispassionate observers saw that the two sides both embodied dangerous evils. George Orwell, and Hemingway ultimately, both arrived at the same conclusion. It was, as is often the case in politics, a matter of choosing the lesser of two evils. But only up to a point. The "political commissar" of the International Brigades was the murderous and marginally insane French communist, André Marty, a man who saw spies and traitors wherever he looked and who admitted after the war to having ordered five hundred of the brigaders shot for various flimsy reasons. As Antony Beevor writes: "Marty preferred to shoot anyone on suspicion, rather than waste time with what he called 'petit bourgeois indecision.'"[13] Hemingway portrayed him for the madman he was in *For Whom the Bell Tolls*. It was part of his clear-eyed vision of this evil war—on both sides—and a clear distancing from the cheerleaders on the journalistic left who chose to turn a blind eye to the Republic's atrocities in general and the communist evil in particular.

The western journalists in Spain, regardless of their lack of objectivity, were right about one thing—the war there was a rehearsal for a wider conflict in which fascism would be the sinister and powerful enemy. If that enemy could be stopped in Spain, the journalists believed, there might be hope for the world. But of course it was not stopped in Spain, could not have been, and observers like Martha—for all their partisanship—understood that their cause was lost and that even worse nightmares were about to begin. The needless bombing of civilians in Guernica (by German planes flown by German pilots), the indiscriminate shelling of Madrid, the continuing mass executions and rapes committed by the Nationalist rebels, many of them professional Moorish soldiers drawn from the North African colonies—all revealed that an unthinking beast had been released and was "slouching toward Bethlehem," already born. Nourished by victory, the beast would grow. The rebel generals were not simply interested in winning; they wanted a political cleansing, a "*limpieza.*" That meant eradication of all democratic/liberal/socialist/ communist/anarchist activity or sentiment. Cleansing would not come through some reeducation or indoctrination scheme—or even political argument—but rather from the barrel of a gun. People in captured villages and cities were slaughtered. In one representative incident, pregnant women who happened to be living in a Republican district were taken out of the hospital and killed. The tide of rape and murder moved toward Madrid. The Republic and its supporters would be buried together in a mass grave. And aiding and abetting the destruction of the Republic were Adolf Hitler and his swaggering henchman, Benito Mussolini—though it is interesting to wonder if the far-from-stellar performance of Italian troops raised in Hitler's mind a soupçon of doubt about his ideological and military ally. It should have.

Western governments including the United States maintained a neutral stance. Lurid reports of anticlerical Republican attacks on the Church—of nuns being raped and priests murdered, churches burned down with parishioners inside—incensed the powerful American Catholic Church. There was widespread Republican feeling that the Catholic Church was involved in the oppression of the peasantry and was therefore a legitimate target. And the fact that the Republic was being supported by the atheistic Soviets—with weapons and some advisors in the field—deepened the suspicion of the Republican cause in the United States. Hemingway, to his credit, would address the poisonous politics of both sides in *For Whom the Bell Tolls*—a novel that would be attacked in both the fascist and communist press (including American communist newspaper the *Daily Worker*), whose criticisms justified Hemingway's contempt for politics in fiction and of writers whose novels were little more than political screeds. He had a clear understanding that fiction can be truth, but that political agendas and orthodoxy rarely, if ever, are. He had been to Spain and seen the beast; he had no real interest in political orthodoxies and zealotry that, he understood, were part of the problem, and not anything like the solution. Nor was he ever a joiner in the sense that many were; he did not derive self-fulfillment and a warm glow from the abstract idea of comradeship. His "comrades" were individuals whom he chose, and no others. And it had nothing to do with their politics. Nor did the rhetoric of politics appeal to him. Famously, he wrote that the words used by politicians to inspire the masses paled to insignificance compared to the realities of war. "Abstract words such as glory, honor, courage or hallow were obscene." If a Nationalist artillery shell landed in the street outside the Florida Hotel and killed a grandmother walking with her grandson, there was no Hell too deep for those who fired it. And no Hell too deep for those who retaliated in kind. The grandmother may have been a Republican or an anarchist or a communist, but that did not matter, because now she and her grandson were nothing. You see these things firsthand, and you lose your belief in speeches, pamphlets, and manifestos. And in the very idea of an orthodoxy. He went along with the Republic, because he believed in antifascism. Beyond that, when it came to politics, not much. Dead bodies, who got that way because they believed different secular religions, were still and eternally dead, often by the accident of simply being in the wrong place.

It was in Spain that Martha lost her belief, too—her belief in the efficacy of journalism. "And of course I do not believe in journalism. I think it changes nothing."[14] Perhaps, but her loss of belief did not prevent her from writing nonfiction and fiction for the rest of her long life. While she came to doubt the wider impact of her work, she never doubted the necessity of doing it—for her own emotional and mental stability. Work was always the most important thing to her, an end in itself. As her biographer Caroline Moorehead wrote: "'*Travail—opium unique.*' The welcome stupor of hard work was a message she never forgot, however happy or preoccupied. Nothing in her later life would ever equal its unique gift of conferring forgetfulness."[15] Nor did her acceptance of journalism's impotence dampen the sense of outrage over social injustice that was a constant element of her worldview. She was on the left all her life, a disciple of Eleanor Roosevelt (about whom Martha said, "She gave off light"[16]) and a supporter of the New Deal's intentions, however objectively inept or counterproductive the policies. As she wrote to her journalistic colleague and post-Hemingway lover, Bill Walton, "It does not matter in the least that communism does not work, nor bring economic justice and happiness; hope in the unknown is always powerful if the known is dreadful."[17] This level of political cynicism is stunning or sophomoric, or both. (Apparently, she was unaware of the Aesop fable of King Stork, whose subjects desired order, but not the terror it brought.) And by choice she lived outside the United States much of her life, because she hated the values and culture of Middle America, hated the Babbitts, their way of life, their beliefs, and their political representatives: "I have never feared Communism in the US but have always feared Fascism; it's a real American trait."[18] Apparently to Martha, the members of the VFW, the Rotary clubs, and the like were only lacking a charismatic leader with a funny moustache to incite them to don black shirts and march by torchlight. She wrote this in 1964, not quite twenty years after the United States and its allies had spent hundreds of thousands of lives and billions of dollars to destroy the fascism that she seemed to think was lurking within every American town hall meeting and in the very corridors of the Pentagon and Congress. She was hardly the only one of her time and leftist political views to lump all who disagreed with her under the rubric "fascist." But her use of the word recalls Orwell's percipient observation that "thought can corrupt language, but language can also corrupt thought."[19] How Martha and those like her could conflate the perhaps bland and narrow cultural conservatism of Middle America with the murderous totalitarian Nazi Germany, or even Mussolini's inept Italy, beggars belief. But Martha was good at hating; it was a facet of her unquenchable indignation, her primary emotion. As Orwell also pointed out, however, such inaccurate and flabby usage of the word *fascist* rendered it ultimately meaningless—an all-purpose term to denote something vaguely undesirable.* It is like the word *racist* today—so scattered around as to be almost useless as a conveyor of meaning; it has descended to the realm of political or personal insult.

Martha's enduring political sensitivities were in fairly sharp contrast to Hemingway's. As mentioned, he was always a reluctant and essentially uninterested participant in the politics, especially of the left—the politics that dominated contemporary writers and political activists. Yes, he gave a nervous speech to the Writers Guild and said all the right things—some of which he actually may have believed. But he was not in any way sympathetic to the thirties' zeitgeist. Irving Stone once asked Hemingway why he never wrote about American culture. Hemingway replied that there was very little going on. Stone responded with a recital of Roosevelt's social and political programs, implying that these were worthy of a novel. "Not my kind of material," said Ernest.[20] Whereas Martha regarded the Roosevelts—and especially Eleanor—as candidates for secular canonization, Ernest was unimpressed and thought the president was "sexless and even somewhat womanly in appearance, like a great woman Secretary of Labor."[21] More importantly and perceptively, Martha wrote in 1940: "He [Hemingway] protects himself from anything and everything, takes no part in the world, cares about nothing except what he is writing."[22] For an artist, that would seem to be a good, perhaps even the only, code. To paraphrase what Hemingway said on political writing, if you read *War and Peace* today you would have to skip over

---

* Observers of the various political and social upheavals of the twentieth century will recognize the offspring of Martha, Matthews, et al. Few among the western reporters were endowed with the truth telling ability of George Orwell, who literally fought and was wounded for the Republican cause but who was not blinded to the depredations of the Stalinists who supported the Republicans with some equipment and men in exchange for the Spanish gold reserves. And if it seems inconsistent for a communist to be making a profit on arms sales, well, no one considering the world of realpolitik should expect consistency or be surprised at hypocrisy. Certainly not from Stalin.

the big political thought-pieces that Tolstoy thought were the finest parts of the book.[23] And in his 1958 *Paris Review* interview he said: "All you can be sure about in a political-minded writer is that if his work should last, you will have to skip the politics when you read it."[24] The justly forgotten political novels of the thirties are more than enough proof of Hemingway's perception. *The Grapes of Wrath* is perhaps the only surviving representative, and it is a novel that a college student could read and admire but, retuning to it some years later, probably not get through it. Interestingly, even Martha dismissed the book when it was published.

On the other hand, Hemingway was deeply committed to the Spanish Republic's side of the war—not to its bewildering array of squabbling parties, but to its antifascist role. So Martha's criticism of his lack of political awareness was not quite fair, if it is even relevant today. But he was never interested in the leftward movements in the United States, nor was he interested in writing a "proletarian novel." The closest he came was with *To Have and Have Not*, which is generally regarded as less successful than his three major works. And yet the hero is no passive victim of the system; he is someone who asserts himself and, like the torero in "The Undefeated," dies but does not suffer defeat. The contrasted "haves" are pathetic sybarites, more or less cartoons. Who, then, are the real Haves and Have Nots? Who then has what a person must have? Money can be easy to come by, especially and obviously when it's inherited; integrity is not. Hemingway based his main character on his friend who owned Sloppy Joe's and who fished with Hemingway, and the writer clearly thinks that the accomplished, self-sufficient fisherman (and dodgy character) was worth more than the vapid yachtsmen who appeared to have it all—but who didn't have what mattered. There is very little, if anything, about thirties politics in that. That is a try for the universal. And while some might say that Harry Morgan's last words ("a man alone ain't got no bloody fucking chance") is a call for comradeship and political solidarity, it's more likely that Hemingway is saying that the man alone, the individualist, is increasingly at the mercy of forces beyond his control, including political orthodoxies. Hemingway could see those forces gathering strength. It was 1937.

❧

While Martha may have loved Hemingway at the beginning of their relationship—and she said she did—the idea of being married to him, or anyone else for that matter, was distasteful to her. "I do not enjoy shared daily life, and think marriage the original anti-aphrodisiac. I like excitement from men, all the kinds there are; and you can't get that Sunday through the next Monday."[25] And there was something else—despite saying that she enjoyed all kinds of excitement from men, she did not particularly enjoy sex. Even in the early days of her affair with Hemingway, when excitement and passion should have been at their height, she said she went to bed with him "as little as [I] could manage," and that her "whole memory of sex with Ernest [was] the invention of excuses and, failing that, the hope that it would soon be over."[26] While some unappreciative critics of Hemingway might gleefully say that her reactions were a commentary on his lack of skill in the bedroom—or worse—Martha makes clear elsewhere that few, if any, of the many men in her life, before or after Hemingway, were able to arouse her physically. As she said about her first lover, Bertrand de Jouvenel: "Physically, for me, it was nothing, ever."[27] And further: "I know there are two people in me. But the least strong, the least demanding is the one that attaches itself to another human being. And the part of me that all my life I have shaped and sculpted and trained is the part that can bear no attachment, which has a ruling need of *eloignement* [detachment, remoteness], which is really untamed, undo-mesticated, unhuman . . . Since I was a child people have wanted to possess me. No one has."[28]

Despite these reservations, she much preferred the company of men. She liked being a part of their world. For allowing her in and accepting her both personally and professionally, she felt it was only fair to reward them with herself, if they were interested, and they always were: "So some men gave me that, company, laughter, movement, the sense that life was an open road and you could run very fast on it, and then they wanted me. And then, I think, I paid my debts. I returned quid pro quo. I had had my pleasure, now they had a right to theirs. It was also never any good."[29]

So it seems that Martha Gellhorn was a woman who maintained a certain emotional detachment in her personal life but who also wanted to engage the world of action, to be a part of great events, to write about them, to do the work she had committed herself to, even when, or especially when, those events were tragic and heartbreaking. She loved being with exciting men who were also at the center of things, whether they were writers or soldiers or artists. And in return for acceptance and amusement she went to bed with them; it was nothing really to her anyway, because it was "never any good." Physical intimacy was not especially important to her, and so giving herself was a small enough exchange for what did matter to her—access to exciting events and people, access that would lead to interesting work. And yet she also had a corresponding need for distance, so her life became a series of episodes in which exciting engagement in events alternated with periods of isolation and privacy, periods in which her emotional and physical resources could regain their strength. "I want a life with people that is almost explosive in its excitement, fierce and hard and laughing, and loud and gay as all hell let loose, and the rest of the time I want to be alone and do my work and my thinking by myself and let them kindly not come to call."[30] It was the perfect mind-set for a war correspondent. Work almost always involved lengthy trips to faraway and turbulent places and events. (She had to see events in order to write about them; she always said she could not rely on imagination—a statement that conflicts with her lynching story.)[31] These trips were then followed by isolation and privacy during which she could think and write about what she had experienced. It was a formula for happiness for Martha, but it was hardly a workable formula for a successful marriage—especially not with someone like Hemingway, who wanted a wife at home, in bed, and a woman who, at the very least, was able to give the impression of being happy to be there. And happy with the results.

But despite the complexities of her personality, her detachment, and her preference for an episodic structure to her life, there is one thing to remember about Martha Gellhorn—when it came to journalism and especially reporting in World War II, she was really good—far better than Hemingway during this period. Whether she knew it or not is a different question. So too whether he was really trying or just mailing it in.

Despite her misgivings, she agreed to marry Hemingway as soon as his divorce from Pauline could be arranged. Hemingway, too, must have had significant reservations, for in his 1938 play about the Spanish War, *The Fifth Column,* he described a thinly veiled version of Martha as "lazy and spoiled and rather stupid and enormously on the make . . . [a] bored Vassar bitch . . . [who has had] affairs, abortions, ambitions." (Martha had attended Bryn Mawr, and she was hardly stupid. But the last three words were accurate.) In reviewing the play critic Malcolm Cowley described the Martha-like character as "a Junior Leaguer pitching woo on the fringes of the radical movement."[32] Why on earth Hemingway ever wanted to marry her, if he really felt that way, even a little bit, and why she ever agreed to marry him are two questions that seem unanswerable. Maybe he thought she was not only beautiful but also complicated, and, since she was occasionally withdrawn and unattainable, she was vastly more interesting than the previous women in his life—women who were apparently eager to conform to his specifications. Getting through to Martha, on the other hand, was a challenge. And it would be naïve to overlook her physical attractions, attractions that were very different from first wife Hadley's matronly figure and the diminutive, slender, and delicate Pauline.[33] When his friend Scott Fitzgerald heard about the proposed marriage, he said it was "odd to think of Hemingway married to 'a really attractive woman,' [and that] 'I think the pattern will be somewhat different than with his Pygmalion-like creatures.'"[34] In an odd reversal of then current mores, Hemingway wanted to marry, whereas Martha would have been content merely to carry on an affair. "Living in sin" involved fewer obligations: ". . . I can do very well without marriage. I would rather sin respectably, any day of the week. E thinks of course that marriage saves you a lot of trouble, and he is all for it. . . . I like it better clean. I think sin is very clean. There are no strings attached to it."[35] Hemingway, it would seem, carried with him a streak of middle-class conventionality, one that survived wars and bohemian expatriate life, whereas Martha was the true rebel. Her contempt of Middle American life extended to Middle American morality. Her unconventionality was aided by her utter lack of personal interest in sex per se: "If I practiced sex out of moral conviction, that was one thing, but to enjoy it, probably, (in my subconscious) seemed a defeat. Anyway, I didn't, and envied those who did, realizing it made life so much easier."[36] It was easy to give something that didn't mean anything to her, and it was even easier because middle-class American morality meant nothing to her, either.

As for Martha's interest in Hemingway, in the early years of their relationship she was still somewhat impressed by Hemingway the artist, and the famous artist at that. And perhaps lurking in the back of her mind was the notion that being married to him would certainly open some doors for herself, professionally. Such thoughts are not incompatible with genuine affection—not necessarily, anyway. As it turned out, the publisher of her next book—a collection of short stories—would be Scribner's, and her editor would be Maxwell Perkins—Hemingway's publisher and editor.

During the buildup to the wider war, *Collier's* sent Martha on assignment to France and England to report on the mood of the people there and their opinion on the likelihood of war. She also traveled to

Czechoslovakia after the 1938 Munich Agreement to report on the German army marching into the Sudetenland. Back in Spain, she and Hemingway watched the ragged remnants of the Republican army trying to flee across the border to France (where they would be interned in wretched refugee camps and thousands would die). Later she would go to Finland to report on the war between the gallant but outnumbered Finns in the "Winter War" against the Soviet invaders.

Between assignments Martha and Hemingway lived in Cuba. Martha had found a dilapidated farmhouse on the outskirts of Havana, and they renovated what became their Finca Vigia ("Lookout Farm"—an accidental bit of irony). When Hemingway's divorce from Pauline came through, Ernest and Martha married in a civil court in Cheyenne, Wyoming, in 1940. They were in the West as guests of the Sun Valley (Idaho) resort. But Cuba would be their home. She would travel with Hemingway to China to assess and report on the situation there—she for *Collier's*, he for *PM Magazine*. She hated it, especially the smells; she was always fastidious about hygiene (unlike Hemingway who seemed to adapt to the appalling conditions without difficulty), but she made some more than intrepid trips with him to various locations in China, usually by harrowing airplane flights. The entire trip was partially in the service of the American government, which was trying to evaluate how China could survive against the Japanese invasion and, as importantly, how Chiang Kai-shek could survive against Mao and the communists. Martha's friendship with the Roosevelts opened the opportunity not only to report on the military and political situation but also to provide a strategic assessment for the policy makers back home. Those who think of Hemingway as a military poseur should remember that he was sent to China in part to assess the strategic situation, and that the US government was interested in Hemingway's opinion of the military and political situation, and debriefed him thoroughly when he and Martha returned.

It was a miserable trip; Martha came down with a skin disease caused by washing her hands in local water. After weeks of stench and poor food and real danger from disease, she was more than happy to return to Cuba. The contrast between Cuba and the stinking misery of China was too stark. In those early days she was happy there and happy to be back: "It is perhaps wrong to be so happy in this present world, but my God how I love this place and how happy I am."[37]

It wouldn't last.

CHAPTER TWO

"Be harsh."

—Admiral Karl Dönitz, Commander
of the German U-boats

F or the first few months of 1942 Hemingway spent his time editing a book that would be published as *Men at War*. It is a thousand-page anthology of writers as disparate as Julius Caesar and Stephen Crane, and as the name indicates, it is the work of writers who wrote about war. Never given to modesty, false or otherwise, he included three selections from his own novels. Hemingway also wrote the introduction. The introduction is a curious document in some ways, unsatisfying, and an indication to careful readers of Hemingway polishing the Hemingway image. The first line is: "This book will not tell you how to die." That is Hemingway being

Hemingway, but not the best of him. He goes back and forth between descriptions of the works included alongside conversations with his family and friends, and the result is somewhat discursive. And in what surely is an unintentional visitation of irony, he writes that Mussolini's bluster and military posing were designed to cover up the fact that he had been fearful, even terrified, during World War I. Surely Hemingway would be enraged to know today that that is almost exactly the criticism that was, and is, leveled at him, in some quarters. Worse, that same criticism is also used to question his sexual identity—does a hairy chest conceal some different needs? He would not have liked that, either. And in fairness, that sort of analysis—the defense mechanism argument—is facile and in some cases has a whiff of agenda-driven criticism. But if you, meaning Hemingway, are going to use it, you cannot be surprised when others do it to you.

Once Hemingway finished with *Men at War*, he had other things to think about, for the U-boats had come to the Gulf of Mexico.

In less than seven months in 1942 German submarines sank 360 vessels in the Gulf of Mexico, the Caribbean, and off the US eastern coast. It was what the U-boat commanders called "the happy time." Their losses were minimal by comparison—seven U-boats sunk. Their risks were also minimal, to the point that frequently they would attack on the surface, using their deck gun and thereby saving expensive torpedoes. In the first stages of the war some U-boat commanders would allow the crew of a target ship the chance to lower their lifeboats and pull away before the Germans opened fire. But the bombing campaign against German cities infuriated Admiral Dönitz and his order to "be harsh" meant that the crews of target ships would not be spared, and even in the case of a surface attack, crewmen trying to escape in their lifeboats were machine-gunned.

Swimming crewmen were left to drown. Or worse. Shark attacks were not unknown.

The primary targets for the U-boats were Allied tankers carrying oil from Texas or South American refineries up the eastern seaboard of the United States. Other vital targets were ships carrying bauxite (used to make aluminum) from South American mines. But the U-boats did not discriminate; they would attack any and all shipping even down to wooden fishing boats manned only by a handful of men. Often the U-boats would surface, relieve the fishermen of their catch or any fresh fruit or vegetables that might be on board, and then destroy the boat with gunfire. One U-boat (U-166) destroyed a wretched little onion carrier with a crew of three. As long as these little vessels were destroyed economically, i.e., with a minimum of ordnance expended, there was merit attached to the attack. Any success would look good on a captain's report, and any supplies denied to the enemy meant a step closer to victory. The British people were on short rations because of the U-boat depredations; the Americans, the Germans hoped, could soon experience shortages too.

In the early stages of the war, antisubmarine tactics were primitive. Merchant ships sailed alone, unguarded, and it would not be until later in the war that the complicated procedures involved in organizing and protecting convoys were developed. Further, there were not enough navy escort vessels available, even if the convoy system had been in place. To make matters worse, antisubmarine warfare (ASW) was almost entirely dependent on the human eye. (Sonar, or what the British called ASDIC, was available, but it was used primarily for identifying close-in contacts and then targeting after the "sighting." In that case the U-boat was like a fish on the line, but ASDIC did not have the range to be useful as a sweeping search method.) Indeed, a line in the U-boat commander's handbook reads: "He who sees first, wins." Radar was still in its infancy and could not be installed in aircraft because of the size of the equipment. It would be later in the war when microwave radar could be carried by aircraft, and that development was crucial in fighting and ultimately defeating the U-boats. But in 1942 there were not enough planes to cover the vast stretches of open water, and for those that were available, the pilot's and the crew's eyes were the only means of spotting U-boats. Obviously that was virtually impossible when the U-boat was submerged, but the submarines had to cruise for long periods on the surface to recharge their electric batteries that provided propulsion when submerged. Surface propulsion was by diesel engines that not only drove the boats but also recharged the batteries in essentially the same way that a car engine charges its battery. While on the surface German lookouts were of course always posted to watch for aircraft, and a nimble captain could submerge to escape an attack from the air. "He who sees first, wins." What's more, in the early stages of the war, a U-boat captain would surface at night to recharge; there was nothing to threaten him then. It would only be later in the war that aircraft would be able to see farther, using radar, and it was then, along with convoy tactics and an augmented US Navy and Army Air Corps, that the battle against U-boats would be won. And it would be won; in the end three-quarters of the U-boat fleet (770 U-boats) were sunk by a combination of Allied surface ships and airplanes, planes being the slightly more deadly in terms of numbers sunk.

But that was to come later in the war. It was small wonder that 1942 represented the happy time for the U-boats. The United States had not enough aircraft, no sophisticated electronic detection gear, and not enough surface ships to search the incredible expanse of the sea. The seven U-boats that were spotted and sunk were simply unlucky for one reason or another. And Admiral Dönitz was most likely more than willing to trade seven U-boats for 360 merchant ships. The grim equation one aspires to in war is something like what the Germans achieved at sea in 1942.

No one in the civilian United States knew what was happening. Censorship of the news drew a curtain over this increasingly difficult and dangerous period. But there is no doubting the seriousness of the situation. A memo from General George Marshall to Admiral Ernest King on June 19, 1942, states the bleak facts:

"The losses by submarines off our Atlantic seaboard and in the Caribbean now threaten our entire war effort. . . . We are all aware of the limited number of escort craft, but has every conceivable improvised means been brought to bear on this situation? I am fearful that another month or two of this will so cripple our means of transport that we will be unable to bring sufficient men and planes to bear against the enemy in critical theaters to exercise a determining influence on the war."[1]

If finding U-boats was a matter of human vision, as it was at this stage of the war, and if the Navy and Army Air Corps' assets were limited, as they were, and if finding a U-boat in the vastness of the sea was a matter of sheer luck, then the question became—what sort of improvised means could Admiral King devise to meet the conditions?

In the classic tradition, the answer was: volunteers. When the only source of intelligence about enemy movements was visual, the more eyes watching, the better. Hundreds of yachtsmen, fishermen, and civilian pilots stepped forward. (The *New York Times* reported that twelve hundred boats ultimately were deployed along the eastern seaboard and the Gulf of Mexico.)[2] Their job was not to engage the enemy but rather to patrol certain assigned sectors and radio the Navy or Air Corps if they spotted a surfaced U-boat or even a periscope. Although this was an improvisation, it was no amateurish lark. There was genuine risk to these volunteers, for as the *New York Times* reported: "Axis submarines ranging from the straits of Florida to the coast of Canada have taken to preying on small fry and have sunk two fishing boats costing the United Nations [i.e., allies] the loss of forty thousand pounds of onions and nineteen swordfish."[3] As mentioned, much the same thing was happening in the Gulf and Caribbean.

The idea of patrolling for U-boats appealed to Hemingway. And note, the idea did not originate with him, as some of his detractors assert. Nor was it a publicity stunt or a meaningless and useless exercise, or even, as Martha said, an excuse to go fishing and drinking with his friends. The idea for the volunteers came from Admiral King, a man with no patience for grandstanding. When he took the job of Commander Atlantic Fleet (CINCLANTFLT), he said: "When they get in trouble, they send for the sons of bitches."[4] The difference between Hemingway and the other volunteers was that he was living in Cuba, an ally but a foreign country that might have some objections to the idea. But he worked with the US ambassador there to get permission and also to make arrangements for the necessary radio and electronic equipment (for which he had to place over $30,000 in cash—a particularly healthy sum in 1942—as a bond for the safe return of the gear). He also arranged for weapons—Thompson submachine guns, grenades, and a bazooka.

There was one other difference between Hemingway and the others in the so called "Hooligan Navy." Hemingway intended to do more than just radio information about a sighted U-boat. He intended to attack it.

His plan was ideal for a man courting death, although it's not clear that he was at that point in his life actually seeking it. But had he been, his plan would have achieved it. He intended to sail his 38-foot wooden fishing boat, named *Pilar*, along the Cuban coast. (Part of his mission was to look for hidden fuel dumps manned by German sympathizers—Cuban and Spanish Falangists, of whom, according to Martha, there were about 700,000 in Cuba at the time.) He was posing as the owner of a harmless sport fishing boat, which of course is how the *Pilar* was rigged. He would hope that a U-boat commander would either spot him from the surface and come to investigate, or surface to relieve him of any useful items, including fresh food. Given *Pilar's* insignificant size Hemingway could be confident that a U-boat would not waste a torpedo on her. Hemingway planned to maneuver alongside the U-boat and toss grenades into the conning tower, followed by a satchel charge packed in a fire extinguisher. If all went according to plan—a rarity in combat—the grenades would first kill the officers on the tower and the fire extinguisher would then tumble down through the hatch and explode and damage important navigational gear below. At that point Hemingway intended to escape at top speed and call the Navy or Army Air Corps to come and finish off the crippled U-boat.

Hemingway had extensive experience of war, but he apparently knew little about war at sea. He included some accounts of sea battles in *Men at War*, but that would give him only theoretical knowledge of sea tactics. Of course he knew the waters of the Gulf of Mexico, but there is a difference between fishing for marlin and hunting for U-boats. The simple fact is, no captain of any warship would allow the scenario Hemingway envisioned. Even going back to World War I the Germans had learned to be wary of any vessel that appeared to be harmless, since then there were merchant ships tricked out as Q ships—vessels armed and waiting in ambush. Assuming the U-boats surfaced and wanted to loot an apparently harmless fishing boat, they would man the topside guns—cannon and machine guns—and then send a boarding party in an inflatable dinghy to examine the pickings. And if the fishing boat made a mad dash to attack, they would blow it out of the water with one shot from their 105mm deck gun while spraying the target with machine gun bullets. A wooden fishing boat, along with the crew, would simply disappear in a cloud of splinters. *Pilar's* top speed was something like twelve knots, so there was no hope of making a mad dash at the enemy.

Even supposing that his plan succeeded—a very long shot—and he tried to run away at top speed, the U-boat's deck gun had a range of something like fourteen miles, so *Pilar* would have been in range for over an hour—not that the U-boat crew would have waited very long, once they got over the shock and confusion of the explosions.

Even so, Hemingway believed his plan could work, and it seems fair to suggest that his willingness to patrol and his plan of action more than contradict the criticism that his bravado was faked. Anyone who has gone into harm's way understands that you cannot know what's coming, and that the plan will more than likely not work out as envisioned, and that simply going requires some degree of courage. That is something Hemingway knew, and if occasionally he made too much of it, well, that did not contradict that essential truth of war.

And it seems fair to say that Hemingway regarded this potential confrontation between a wooden fishing boat and a steel and iron U-boat as a metaphor. An unseen U-boat suddenly rises from below, a machine of modern warfare, pitiless and virtually invulnerable, only to be confronted by a wooden boat manned by civilian volunteers. It is a scene reminiscent of El Sordo's last moments on a mountaintop, a few vulnerable men confronting mechanized war in the form of fascist bombers. The symbolic associations would be obvious even to a lesser imagination than Hemingway's. As he stood on the flying bridge of *Pilar*, he knew what he was doing and what was happening. And he knew that what was happening had at least two levels of meaning.

Hemingway made periodic cruises from July 1942 until the following summer; one patrol to the eastern end of Cuba lasted two months. During all that time he never found enemy fuel dumps and never spotted a U-boat, although on one occasion he thought he did, and he and his crew of friends headed for the contact, intent on putting their plan into action. But the contact disappeared and the attack plan was never put to the test. But the experience was not wasted, for he would turn the hunt for a U-boat crew into the final third of what would ultimately become *Islands in the Stream*.

Between patrols he also managed a motley collection of shady characters who were his semiofficial intelligence gathering unit. He called this operation the Crook Factory. Their job was to keep an eye on the Falangists, and they would appear suddenly at all hours of the day, irritating Martha repeatedly, especially when the meetings turned into drinking parties. They never succeeded in developing any information of much value, and the local FBI agent dismissed the whole idea. But Hemingway reveled in the notion that he was a secret agent of sorts. His play, *The Fifth Column*, featured a Hemingway-like character who was doing clandestine work for the Republican side in the Spanish

Civil War. That was the same play that the Martha-like character appeared in not very flattering form. Hemingway later volunteered for the Office of Strategic Services (OSS), a newly formed US intelligence service that is usually described as the forerunner of the CIA. But he was not accepted. An internal memo stated that he was too much an individualist to operate in a military structure.[5] That assessment would be proved again and again when he finally got to the war in Europe, where he would go under the cover of a war correspondent, but where he would engage in action, not observation, proving that whoever wrote that OSS memo somehow knew what he was talking about.

No one would accuse Hemingway of being a model husband. Far from it. He was moody and occasionally violent, often hot tempered, demanding and, at other times, needy and overly sensitive and susceptible to bouts of depression and, when Martha was away on assignment, intense loneliness. And to speak plainly, he drank far too much, and it did not serve him well. He was the kind of alcoholic who should have done his drinking alone, perhaps sitting beside his swimming pool, gradually growing more mellow and letting his imagination wander, watching the sunset over the Gulf of Mexico—and then, after a while, padding foggily off to bed, looking forward to the next morning's work. But he was not good at being alone. Except when he was writing, he needed to be with people—friends, cronies, admirers—and the wife of the moment. Drinking with friends or acquaintances, he could be the center of attention, the life of the party. With people who interested him, he could be solicitous and attentive, even charming—but with others he could turn in a moment and become truculent and abusive. Often, his wife was the target. Hemingway was hardly unique in this sort of erratic and aggressive behavior, but unlike most garden variety alcoholics, he was famous, and people noticed what he said and did, and they remembered and talked about it. After a while it became difficult for many people to separate the man's behavior from his work, difficult to admire his writing while deploring his occasional lapses in good manners and taste. Critics asked themselves: can a genuine artist and a sometimes boorish blowhard really inhabit the same body, the same personality, the same intellect? As one critic observed: "Perhaps we really know too much about Hemingway, or at least his public poses, to judge his work impartially."[6] Fellow World War II correspondent, Andy Rooney, spoke for many who knew Hemingway: "He was not your ordinary run of the mill jerk. He was a Big Jerk and more often than not a poor writer."[7] Conflating the man and his writing became conventional wisdom in the postwar years; the quality of his work was judged in part by reaction to his lifestyle and behavior: "He was a jerk. What's more he liked to shoot birds and animals and to catch fish and drink and talk and now and then fight with rivals, and therefore his writing was bad." This was an easily accepted interpretation in the salons of New York. Even Martha ultimately was unable to make a distinction between the man and the work, especially as their marriage deteriorated into acrimony. And in fairness to the critics, much (though not all) of his World War II reporting and his postwar writing lacked what he had had before. Something was missing. On the other hand, critic Scott Donaldson writes: "There can be little doubt that [Hemingway] chose the image of a rugged warrior-sportsman as a shield against invasion of his extraordinarily complicated personality—in particular his emotional vulnerability—by outsiders. Once these stereotypes took hold, they proved hard to get rid of and undoubtedly damaged [his reputation] . . . before and beyond the grave."[8]

Martha was not right for Hemingway, and he was not right for her. (And as events proved, neither was really right for anyone.) Ideally, Hemingway wanted a wife who would cheerfully manage the Hemingway ménage and stay at home while he went wherever he wanted to go and with whomever he wanted to take along, knowing that the home fires would be burning, the legion of cats would be fed, and the martinis would be chilled and waiting when he walked through the door. And he wanted a wife who was enthusiastically responsive in the bedroom and who could also share his passions for fishing and hunting, when it suited him to have her come too. And it wouldn't hurt if she subordinated her own needs and ambitions to support his writing—whatever that required. (Although in fairness, Hemingway strongly encouraged Martha's writing, especially her fiction. That was work she could do at home, and did not require lengthy trips to some scene of troubles.) The desire for this sort of arrangement was not unique to Hemingway; others no doubt dreamed similar, improbable dreams. But the image of what he wanted in a wife, and the personality and character of his third wife were so dramatically different that the marriage was doomed from the start, even though Hemingway genuinely loved Martha, and she returned the affection—at least in the first years. But even in the early days of their affair, while he was trying to separate from his second wife, Pauline, so that he could marry Martha, Martha knew that life as "Martha Hemingway" would probably not go well. As she wrote to her friend Allen Grover: "In principle we are marrying this summer. In principle I have a quiet horror of marriage."[9] Whether Martha's "horror" of marriage was generic (marriage of any kind) or specific (marriage to Hemingway himself) would ultimately be academic. But it seems reasonable to suppose that, if Martha had been a compliant wife, Hemingway might never have gone to Europe in the spring of 1944. She was the one who was desperate not to miss out on world-shaking events; he had little if any interest in revisiting his role as a war correspondent. If she had been able to squeeze herself into the highly restrictive Hemingway wife-mold (to Martha a kind of psychological iron maiden), he might have been content to stay in Cuba, sailing *Pilar* in the Gulf, now and then looking for German submarines, but more often fishing for marlin. It's also possible that, had she adapted herself to Hemingway's criteria, he might have eventually lost interest in her, since the very things that attracted her to him were her verve and independence and talent.

In July 1942, just as Hemingway was starting his patrols, Martha left for a two-month assignment for *Collier's*. Ever intrepid, she hired a small potato boat with a five-man crew to tour the Caribbean to report on U-boat activity and shipping losses. During the excursion (during which she was marooned by her boat and had to scramble to continue), she found no evidence of shipping losses and did not see a U-boat or even any evidence of one. She therefore concluded that the danger was greatly overstated, and that Hemingway's patrols were nothing more than some of his typical self-promotion. It was not until after the war that she realized how thoroughly censorship had deceived her. She said: ". . . we didn't understand how bad it was; piecemeal and (now I see) wisely censored, the news gave us no whole view . . . I think my ignorance was typical. We did not realize that the fatal danger was on the sea."[10] This lack of information made her dismissive, to say the least, of Hemingway's contribution to the war effort, and she apparently overlooked the reports of the Hooligan Navy as printed in the *New York Times*, and, no doubt other papers. She was also feeling some sense of guilt, because she believed she was living safe and secure in a tropical paradise while the war was raging. She filled her time by writing a novel—a project Hemingway warmly supported. But then she could stand it no longer. In September 1943 she went to New York to meet with the publisher of her novel and to arrange a trip to London; in October she left for England on assignment from *Collier's*. She would not return to Cuba until the following March. During that time she wrote loving letters to Hemingway urging him to join her. Like perhaps some other couples, the two got along better and were more affectionate when they were not together. Or more accurately, Martha felt more affection for him when they were apart.

That all changed when she returned to Cuba in March '44. Hemingway had been simmering in anger ever since Martha left those months before. Now that she returned that anger boiled over and turned into a series of bitter arguments and wild accusations. The cause for this eruption is difficult to pinpoint. His patrols had been shut down, largely because the ASW techniques and detection equipment, along with the development of convoy procedures, had virtually eliminated U-boat activity in the Gulf of Mexico. The happy time for the Germans was over. While he was on patrols he could tell himself with some truth that he was a useful participant acting independently and in command not only of his boat but of his crew of four or five comrades. It was exhilarating and satisfying work, and the fact that he never had any real success does not diminish the effort or the willingness to go into harm's way. The vast majority of sailors and soldiers in the war never engaged an enemy even at a distance; most in fact never saw one.

Now the patrols were over. And there was Martha hectoring him about coming to England, where all the world knew that the invasion of France was coming and coming soon. Of course, few knew the exact date and place, but everyone knew it was coming, including the Germans. So naturally Martha was keen to be on the scene and she could not understand why her husband did not share her vital interest.

Another reason for his hostility was the fact that Martha had abandoned him to months of celibacy and loneliness, all because she apparently valued her career and her need for excitement more than her marriage. And there was a fair amount of truth in that. She did. Finally, it seems clear that Hemingway was beginning to exhibit the signs of manic depression that would ultimately overwhelm him. As Hemingway biographer Michael Reynolds writes: "His son Gregory firmly believed that his father changed during that 1943–1944 period into a different person."[11] The unanswerable questions, though, are when did this change occur and why? Was it his growing depression or was it related to what he saw in the war in Europe—because he would soon see some terrible fighting, fighting that was more than enough to unnerve even the bravest.

All of these factors combined to create a climate of acrimony and accusation. Hemingway decided that he had little choice but to go to the war in Europe. Whether he felt it was necessary to save his marriage, or if he just had no other ideas is hard to say. But he felt like a major league ballplayer who was being sent to the minors. He understood the game and disliked it. He felt that the journalists were bench players, not involved in the drama of combat or tactics or strategy. True, a few now and then were killed, but they were just unlucky. They were just observers, not participants. Besides, he was an internationally known, best-selling novelist; he would be associated with literally hundreds of print and radio reporters whose talent would never elevate them to his status. It was the major leagues of war, but journalism was the minor leagues of writing. Those who actually fought were where the major action lived. And died.

Even so, he contacted the editor at *Collier's* and arranged to be their frontline correspondent. *Collier's* was also Martha's freelance employer, and in fact she and Hemingway shared the same editor. While this may seem rather convenient, Martha resented the arrangement and asserted that Hemingway was essentially stealing her plum assignment. There was no truth in that, though, because the army did not allow women to be frontline correspondents. They could operate behind the scenes but not at the sharp end. Surely Martha knew that. Still, this arrangement did little to warm the chilly relationship that was about to reach the freezing point and shatter.

It's interesting to wonder—had he stayed in Cuba, happy with his home and his home life, might his later work have recaptured the quality of *For Whom the Bell Tolls?* Certainly, he would not have written the much-criticized *Across the River and into the Trees*, which was largely based on his experience in the horrific fighting in the Germany's Hürtgen Forest (the Hürtgenwald) in the fall and winter of 1944. But he did go, and when he got there he plunged, unsurprisingly, into the thick of the action.

Hemingway's first assignment would be with the RAF. Indeed, his assignment came as a result of the influence of Roald Dahl, who was an RAF officer stationed in Washington as assistant air attaché. Part of Dahl's job was promoting Britain's point of view about the war to the American public. He told Hemingway that if he would write an article on the RAF, Dahl would arrange passage to London for him on a military flight—something that would otherwise not be possible; only high priority passengers engaged in important war work were allowed. This fit nicely with Hemingway's idea for a novel of the air, sea, and land. He had the least experience with war in the air, and he was eager to gather as much as possible before having to head for mainland Europe in the wake of the invasion.

They both would leave for England from New York—Hemingway on a military aircraft, Martha on a slow ammunition-carrying vessel, where she would suffer from the ban on smoking (though it's hard to believe that she observed it in her cabin) and where she was at risk from enemy submarines for two very slow weeks. An ammunition ship that's hit by a torpedo does not simply sink; it disappears. During this long and tedious voyage she came to the conclusion, perhaps reluctantly, that her marriage was over. And perhaps good riddance. She didn't really want to be married in the first place, and now with this sudden, inexplicable, erratic, and abusive change in his behavior, the relationship was obviously untenable. He had gone to London at her urging. But it seemed unlikely that he had gone for her. And even if he had, she did not really care.

CHAPTER THREE

"*He was the only American war correspondent who made a large personal impress [sic] on the nation in the Second World War.*"

—A. J. Liebling

L iebling was not talking about Hemingway; he was talking about Ernie Pyle. Of the hundreds of Allied war correspondents (in London alone there were five hundred just prior to D-Day), Pyle was the most famous. He also was one of the fifty-one correspondents who were killed in action. They were not there to fight, but to watch and write or film what they saw. A Japanese machine gun bullet put an end to Ernie Pyle, just as the war in the Pacific was drawing to a close. It was a version of every veteran's nightmare—being the last man killed in the war. He wasn't the last literally, but he had survived many years of combat reporting, and he'd have been justified in thinking that he'd earned a break from the gods of war. He was killed on the tiny island of Ie Shima, which lies just off Okinawa. He was forty-four, but like the troops he covered, he looked older than his age. As he wrote: "They are young men, but the grime and whiskers and exhaustion make them look middle aged."[1] So too Ernie Pyle. At the end he was bald and thin and looked a feeble sixty.

Toward the end of the war, his columns were carried by seven hundred American newspapers, an astonishing number, especially from the perspective of the sorry state of today's newspaper business. And so it is not surprising that his death occasioned significant sadness among his readers who were, many of them, the fathers and mothers and other loved ones of the regular soldiers, sailors, and marines he wrote about—the people back home who were tortured by uncertainty and unrelenting worry, always in fear of the dreaded telegram. He was an avuncular figure in some ways, and reassuring. His was not a particularly technical description of the war. Grand strategy was not his beat. He did not seek to hobnob with generals, although his stature allowed him that, when and if he wanted it. He specialized in writing about the sailors and soldiers at the sharp end of the war, the draftees from Detroit or Brooklyn or Albuquerque or any of the myriad American towns and cities and villages—men who had been plucked from their ordinary lives and thrust into mortal danger and often hideous physical conditions. And he developed a style that always included mentioning the names and hometowns of these men, so that the people across the country could empathize and identify with the boys who were in harm's way, as well as those who were wounded and suffering. You had the sense that he felt it was the least he could do. He had a folksy style and perfected a stance of the Everyman, a classic Midwesterner, who was there by an accident of history, but willing to do what was necessary—just like the men he covered. As Liebling wrote: "To a list that includes the frontiersman, the Kentucky colonel, the cowboy, and Babe Ruth, [Pyle] added GI

Joe, the suffering but triumphant American infantryman. The portrait was sentimentalized, but the soldier was pleased to recognize himself in it, and millions of newspaper readers recognized their sons and lovers in Pyle's soldiers and got some glimmer of the fact that war is a nasty business for the pedestrian combatant."[2] I don't agree that it was sentimentalized; or perhaps it's more accurate to say that sometimes sentiment is appropriate. Some things deserve emotion, sentimental or otherwise. Even so, Pyle's was an approach and style that endeared him to much of America, and a style that sent much of America into mourning when he was killed, although, by then, America, and many ordinary families throughout the country, had more than enough reasons to mourn. He covered the war from North Africa into Sicily and Italy, and on to Normandy and, when that was won, he went to the Pacific and found his appointment in Samarra. Liebling says that Pyle was a hypochondriac who was constantly terrified in combat, and he says that not in a critical way, but in a way that suggests that Pyle suffered from many of the same terrors that afflicted the boys and men he wrote about. That's probably why he wrote about them the way he did—with such interest and understanding. He could picture them back home, on Main Street or in the local soda fountains. Or maybe in the local bar where everyone knew your name, as the theme song goes. He knew they were just younger versions of himself. Or he was an older version of them. His dedication to his book, *Brave Men*, which is a compilation of his articles about Sicily and Normandy, read: "In solemn salute to our comrades—great, brave men that they were—for whom there will be no homecoming, ever." It's impossible to believe, with the war still raging, that he did not think that line might soon apply to him. People who go into combat often have dire premonitions. Pyle's last one came true on Ie Shima. He knew, as others did, that the difference between a historian and a man who goes to war is that the historian knows what happened, whereas the warrior never knows what will happen, only what could happen.

Pyle is important because, as Liebling wrote, "Pyle set the style." His popularity was such that his rival journalists naturally adopted some of the same techniques. The style worked. Editors and readers expected it. Reporters routinely gave the names and hometowns of troops they featured, and most tried to give a sense of what life as a GI was like. And there was something else—Pyle regularly inserted himself into his stories. He used the first person and was not shy about describing harrowing situations he found himself covering. But he never did so to call attention to himself or to any phony heroics or posturing. It was a fine balance. The troops were the focus of his columns. He was there, but they were the ones who mattered. Other writers tried to do the same, and some managed it. Others did not.

In his article "Street Fighting," Pyle underscored the importance of what the correspondents were doing:

"Lack of recognition definitely affects morale. Every commanding general is aware that publicity for his unit is a factor in morale. Not publicity in the manufactured sense, but a public report to the folks back home on what the outfit endures and what it accomplishes. The average doughfoot will go through his share of hell a lot more willingly if he knows that he is getting some credit for it and that the folks back home know about it."[3]

And who exactly was this aforementioned A. J. Liebling? He was a correspondent for the *New Yorker* magazine. As such, he had license to write longer features; he was not there merely to report the facts. He could reflect on outcomes. And he was good. He once said he wrote faster than people who wrote better and better than the ones who wrote faster. He also said of an actress: "She was a butterscotch sundae of a woman, as beautiful as a tulip of beer with a high white collar."[4] Clearly, this is a mixed metaphor, but allowable for its richness. And who does not like the image of a tulip-shaped glass of beer? What's more he wrote a lot. His World War II writing amounts to nearly one thousand pages in a volume of his collected work. Like Pyle he traveled with the troops through North Africa, Sicily, and France, after D-Day.

A confirmed Francophile and fluent Francophone, he was in Paris mere days before the Germans came marching in, and he was there when they surrendered, four years later. A pudgy New Yorker from a wealthy family, Liebling became a gourmand and a food writer after the war. He also had an improbable passion for boxing and for the less respectable side of life in Manhattan. Like Damon Runyon before him, he liked colorful characters, sometimes being one himself. Both before and after the war he was a bon vivant in New York—the kind who considered Toots Shor's and like establishments as the natural haunts of all right thinking men. He was fond of quoting Canadian boxer Sam Langford: "You can sweat out the beer, and you can sweat out whisky. But you can't sweat out a woman."[5] It was a line that Hemingway would also use now and then. All three men knew what they were talking about.

Like Ernie Pyle, Liebling managed the nice balance between using the first person without overtly drawing credit to himself. Both he and Pyle apparently understood that simply being where they were, and doing what they were doing, earned them more than enough credit—if that's what they wanted, though nothing in their styles suggests that they cared more about being the story rather than reporting it, which is as it should have been.

Liebling was there on D-Day, in a landing craft that was hit by shell fire. They got their troops ashore under severe fire, and several sailors were wounded. Two others were killed, and in a representative incident that illustrates his measured style, he wrote about the sailors hoisting one of the wounded up the side of a hospital ship. Suddenly the wounded man hemorrhaged and drenched his handler in blood, so that the handler "didn't know what happened, seeing the world through a film of red, because he wore eyeglasses and blood had covered the lenses." In a footnote to a later publication of this story he identified the handler: "This was me. It seemed more reserved at the time to do it this way—a news story in which the writer says that *he* was bathed in blood would have made me distrust it, if I had been a reader."[6] This is an example of appropriate restraint. Liebling and Pyle shared many similar adventures and dangers, which given their mutual travels through the many theaters of war, is not surprising. But they also shared an understanding of what mattered in the story.

A. J. Liebling is not a household name these days, although he deserves to be better remembered. But there were plenty of reporters in Europe who are well remembered characters. Edward R. Murrow was a star, or at least would become one, of the same magnitude as Ernie Pyle. His radio reports from London during the Blitz established his enduring credentials throughout the admiring media world. Later in the fifties on the new medium of television he became a caricature of the sophisticated reporter, interviewing celebrities and chain-smoking cigarettes, like a journalistic version of Rick from *Casablanca*.

Walter Cronkite, a writer for the United Press, flew in multiple bombing missions over Germany and was frequently under fire. His preferred place in a B-17 was in the nose gunner position, a seat below and in front of the pilot—literally in the nose of the airplane. It was a good place to see and a good place to get killed. More than once he fired a machine gun against attacking Luftwaffe fighter planes. He claimed no hits but could be justified in assuming he had at least worried a German pilot or two. This sort of information is relevant to Hemingway's ultimate adventures, because Hemingway's use of weapons became a major story and a legal difficulty, whereas Cronkite's (and others') participation in combat aroused no significant comment. But no one saw them in action, except the airplane's crew. And they didn't say anything about it.

Another future television fixture was Andy Rooney. He was actually in the army, having been drafted and originally assigned to the artillery as an enlisted man. Eventually his talent for writing got him assigned to *Stars and Stripes*, which was an army publication designed in style and content to appeal to the average GI. His path would cross Hemingway's on at least two occasions. More than fifty years later Rooney would write of Hemingway: "It is with barely mustered resolve that I refrain from referring to him in the popular idiom identifying the posterior of a horse."[7]

Most of the other correspondents were civilians, of course. More accurately, they were civilian members of the military—an obvious contradiction in terms. They wore uniforms without rank insignias (they had no rank, but were given officers' privileges); instead there was a correspondent's patch on the jacket. If captured, they became prisoners of war. And, undeniably, they risked injury or death when they went to the scenes of combat, since the enemy could not distinguish between them, even if they cared to do so, which of course they did not. A target is a target. Besides, most of the casualties in the war came from a long range—artillery, bombing, naval gunfire, or torpedoes that sank ships. There was seldom an opportunity for individual combatants to select a target, consider it, and then either fire or pass up the shot. The range of a .30-caliber bullet was about a thousand yards. Riflemen would fire confidently at three hundred yards, far too distant to read a shoulder patch. Or to worry about what it said. Nor would they, on any side, realistically make a moral judgment about the fairness of the target. Navy hospital corpsmen (who were and are medics for the marines) and army medics were routinely targeted, despite Geneva Convention protections. But despite the dangers, correspondents were not permitted to carry weapons or engage in the fighting—unless they were actually in the army, like Andy Rooney. Cronkite, for example, was clearly violating those rules when he fired at marauding German fighters, and he was not the only correspondent to do so. But there is an obvious difference between firing a machine gun at fifteen thousand feet and walking around with a .45 pistol on the hip and a Thompson submachine gun slung over the shoulder. One seems understandable, the other like dramatic flouting of the rules. That there were such rules in the bestial savagery of World War II is perhaps an absurdity. No, not perhaps. Yet even so, Hemingway ran aground against them. When Hemingway ran afoul of the law (or, rather, conventions) while he was in France, it was because he had chosen to follow the infantry and the French Resistance—men who followed few, if any, rules. He was visible, and made himself so. More to the point, he was deeply unpopular with many of his colleagues, unlike someone like Cronkite, who was at that stage no one special and therefore no threat as a rival to anyone, except his competitors who were scrambling for the latest news.

Hemingway was a different story. Someone turned him in for carrying—and possibly using, if you believe Hemingway—weapons. He was certainly reported by one of his many rivals, or someone whom he'd insulted or offended. There were lots of those people around. More on this later. (In 1977 the conventions were changed to state that reporters who were not officially in the military were civilians only, so that they were due all the protections given to other civilians. They were not to be interned as POWs. The rule against carrying and using weapons remained. As an aside, the actions of combatants and especially the German, Japanese, and Russian troops, make a mockery of the rules regarding regular civilians. So, too, the bombing campaigns. Much, indeed most of the grotesque savagery of the war was visited upon civilians, Geneva Conventions notwithstanding.)

To say that there was competition among the war correspondents is a laughable understatement. Liebling reports an incident that occurred just after the town of Saint-Lô, France, had been taken by the Allies. "The press association boys competed among themselves on a strict time basis, like milers. [As a magazine feature writer, Liebling could afford to look down his nose at the scurrying news writers.] The day after the capture, a United Press man wandered through my tent carrying a copy of a cable he had received from his home office. 'Beat nearest competitor one minute forty five . . . kudos, kudos, kudos.'"[8]

The rivalries were multifaceted. On the one hand, there were the reporters for the large syndicates, like the Associated Press, United Press, as well as syndicates put together by major newspapers, such as the *Chicago Tribune* and the *New York Herald Tribune*. Naturally these organizations competed with each other not only for access to important events and people but also with individual reporters working for individual newspapers back home. It was the *Front Page* writ large. Then there were the magazine writers, like Liebling, and, eventually, Hemingway and Gellhorn, who were viewed to some extent as different, since they wrote for weekly publications and could hardly break any immediate news. Gellhorn was at a significant disadvantage, because, as mentioned, women reporters were not allowed at the front. Not surprisingly, she would find her own personal ways around this, eventually. But the magazine feature writers also had less pressure and could write longer pieces—advantages that caused some envy among their scurrying colleagues, who no doubt, most of them anyway, had larger literary dreams. Ernie Pyle seemed to escape this sort of rivalry. He was sui generis and, as Liebling wrote, he set the style. And he was a columnist, not a reporter. But there was plenty of jealousy and competition among writers who were theoretically on the same side of the war.

The army had *Stars and Stripes*. In addition to the work of young Andy Rooney, who with his colleagues tried to report the news, *Stars and Stripes* published Bill Mauldin's cartoons that featured two average GIs, Willie and Joe. The cartoons did nothing to burnish the image of the infantry or glamorize the war, since Willie and Joe were invariably portrayed as badly needing a shave, a change of uniform, some dry socks, or other basic creature comforts that much of the time the infantryman at the front could only dream about. In one cartoon Willie (or Joe) is washing his feet in his helmet. (There's also a genuine photo of Ernie Pyle doing the same thing.) In another, an equally disheveled sergeant says to his squad, including Joe and Willie: "I need a couple guys what don't owe me money fer a little routine patrol." It would be easy to assume that the editors of *Stars and Stripes* might be tempted to print propaganda and paper over the grim hardships of the war, but in fact Eisenhower wanted the style and content to reflect the realities of the war and also the tastes of his troops—men who appreciated the likes of Joe and Willie. Every dogface could identify with them, and Eisenhower understood the strength of the morale that emanated from the recognition and appreciation of the griping comradeship and the ironic and humorous endurance of the GI. It was better to have them laughing and nodding with Willie and Joe than trying to feed them half-truths or bombast. Ike had been a soldier all his adult life, and he knew his men. As historian Timothy Gay writes: "Ike and his staff wanted something that had the feel of a hometown newspaper, complete with reasonably honest coverage of war developments (the two censors in the *Stars and Stripes* newsroom rarely killed stories), local news, sports, and gossipy features about Hollywood and Broadway. Plus of course cheesecake photos of starlets. For every picture of Ike there were dozens of scantily attired pinup girls like Betty Grable and Rita Hayworth."[9]

Among Ike's greatest attributes were his understanding of nuance and subtlety, and his willingness to forego traditional military orthodoxy, posturing, and prejudices, both in his treatment of his troops and in his relationships with the often prickly British. Willie and Joe existed because Ike and Mauldin and the editors of *Stars and Stripes* understood that printing the truth did more for a GI's morale than any even marginal fabrication. The boys at the front would see through any window dressing. They were the ones washing their feet in helmets.

There were, however, plenty of Americans (and British) in uniform who were washing their feet at the Savoy, and such places. Chief among them were the public relations officers in London—as well as their confreres attached to some general's staff. General Mark Clark, for example, is said to have had fifty public relations officers working for him. Aside from being a commander about whom the verdict is mixed, at best, Clark was famous for wanting only the left side of his face photographed. An examination of his many photos reveals no reason for this. But he gave the attention to detail that one likes to see in a general—just not on that subject. Historians are divided on whether Clark was competent or a vainglorious bungler. Points can be made for each.

He was commander of the Fifth Army, which was slogging its way up the Italian boot after a mismanaged amphibious landing at Anzio. He was facing stiff resistance from the Germans but finally found himself in a position to cut them off in retreat and score a significant victory. Instead he approved the order to divert the army to Rome—a city that had little or no military value, having been evacuated by the Germans. The storm of well-founded criticism that this move aroused would later have an effect on Ike's and Bradley's thinking about whether or not to send troops to liberate Paris—another city that most US and British commanders regarded, largely accurately, as having obvious symbolic value, but little or no strategic value.

As for Clark, there can be little doubt that a general with his eyes squarely on the ball cannot possibly need fifty public relations flacks to burnish his image. And his subsequent performance in struggling up the Italian peninsula is hardly the stuff of legend. He marched into Rome, even while the German army escaped and headed north, where they would dig in again and again and make life difficult—and even impossible—for the likes of Willie and Joe. Perhaps lurking in the back of Clark's mind were images of his troops riding into Rome, the ancient and symbolic imperial city, while delirious crowds who were enthusiastic (and recent) converts to antifascism, cheered, and the cameras rolled. Surely these images would almost rival the expected images of the US-supplied French troops rolling into Paris. It would take a more focused general, and perhaps a more than extraordinary human than Clark, to ignore the chance. After all, if you care about which side of your profile is taken, would you rather be at the Coliseum waving to cheering crowds or in some muddy field or trench somewhere outside of Rome? Clark of course was not the only general who cared about his image. On either side. There was a lot of strutting going on. No doubt the positive press images were viewed as useful, even necessary factors in the competition for power—which is not to say that the strutting generals were incompetent, although there might very well be an inverse relationship between the two—historically. General George

S. Patton seemed to be able to combine the two and achieve success. Montgomery, on the other hand, was a frequent target of Patton's contempt. Hemingway's too. He named a martini after Montgomery. It was a 15 to 1 ratio of gin to vermouth, because as Hemingway said Montgomery required a 15 to 1 advantage before attacking.

On the other hand, it is easy to turn these men, egotistical as they no doubt were, into cartoon figures, and to forget the inhuman amount of work and stress and danger, as well as moral doubt they had to feel, for they were the ones who ordered Joe and Willie into misery and potential death. Even the enlisted men's scribe, Ernie Pyle, acknowledged that pride in the unit and its commanders was a major element in maintaining morale. They endured it all together, and the fact that, regardless of missteps they made along the way—missteps that are axiomatically inevitable in war—they actually won: they and Willie and Joe and "Tommy Atkins" (Britain's version of GI Joe) and the home fronts that supported and supplied them all. In the end, they killed the beast. Egotism in commanders is different from vanity in war. Egotism can be managed by intelligent commanders, like Ike. Vanity is more dangerous; it can make them cautious.

Of lesser military use, however, were the aforementioned public relations officers, especially those in London. Liebling describes the scene: "The Public Relations situation reached a high point in opera-buffa absurdity in the spring of a year ago [1944] before the invasion of France. There were at one time nine separate echelons of Public Relations in London at once: PRO SHAEF, [Public Relations Office, Supreme Headquarters, Allied Expeditionary Forces]; PRO Twenty First Army Group (Montgomery's command), PRO FUSAG (First Army Group which later became Twelfth Army Group); PRO First Army; PRO ETOUSA (European Theater of Operations, US Army) which handled the correspondents' mail, gave out ration cards, did publicity for Services of Supply, and tried to horn in on everything else; PRO Eighth Air Force; PRO Ninth Air Force; the PRO for General Spaatz's highest echelon of the Air Force's command; and the Navy PRO. The

Air Force's publicity people were unpretentious but aggressive; the navy was helpful; the . . . other echelons spent most of their time getting in each other's way. The PRO's, [Public Relations Officers] mostly Colonels and Lt. Colonels (a major in this branch of service, was considered a shameful object, to be exiled to an outer office) had for the most part been Hollywood press agents or Chicago re-write men in civilian life." [10] (A rewrite man works in an office and writes the stories phoned in by reporters in the field.) It is probably needless to say, but these characters seldom, if ever, heard a shot fired in anger. Of course they could tell themselves that London had been attacked from the air (and, little did they know, it would soon be attacked again by German V-1 flying bombs and V-2 rockets). They were therefore in harm's way, doing important work, but the contrast between these purveyors of information and Joe and Willie at the front could hardly be more distinct. As Liebling says of the PR men: "They looked as authentic in their uniforms as dress extras in a B picture." [11] Bureaucracy. Is it any wonder that Hemingway disdained the process?

It's hard to escape the conclusion that the job of the public relations staffs in the field was to manage the news, not so much the news of the larger war, but to present to the public the excellent work performed by the units of service they represented—their clients. Mark Clark's fifty or so PR men were there to extol his, and the Fifth Army's, abilities and achievements, and to explain away any unhappy events and outcomes, of which there were more than a few. But at least they were almost close to the fighting. The PR bureaucracy in London was a maze of politics and what the English mean by "interest." Not bothered by having to face the actual enemy, they could develop other enmities within their own ranks. Careers were there to be built, and if that required building them over the dead reputations of competitors, well, you can't make an omelet without breaking eggs. (That aphorism was originated by French royalist Francois de Charette, an officer who fought against the French Republic and was captured and executed.) There was, for example, a rivalry between Murrow's protégés, including

Charles Collingwood, and other radio reporters. CBS's Murrow was at the head of his elite group of courtiers, much resented by rival, hovering, would-be media stars.

Then there were the British who had essentially the same kind of PR organization and media, including most notably the BBC. The BBC was however vitally important to the morale of the occupied countries and, as important, as a means of sending intelligence. Code phrases that seemed nonsensical were in fact specific orders, the most important of which were the announcement of the D-Day event and instructions for the French Resistance. The BBC and other UK news outlets were carefully censored so that nothing was mentioned that might give useful information to the enemy. As an example, during the murderous V-1 and V-2 attacks on England in 1944, little specific information about the attacks was reported, and little or nothing about their effects in London, Hitler's main target. Instead there were reports of flying bombs hitting "southern England." Further, some reports were designed to mislead the German attacks by stating that the V-1s had overshot the capital, so that the Germans adjusted their range calculations. As a result, more missiles fell short of London.

How much of the reporting could be described as propaganda?

The indisputable fact that the Allied cause was the righteous one in this war makes drawing the line between news and propaganda a little more vague than is usually the case. Simply stating the Allied cause and drawing a clear line between the Allies and the enemy seems like a kind of oversimplification. But the facts say otherwise. The binary morality that is usually so lacking in nuance, and therefore often inaccurate, was not inaccurate in this case. The enemy people running the show were monsters. They were evil, and many of their subordinates, all the way down to the level of the foot soldiers, were equally monstrous. In today's age, in which strict moral judgments are regarded with suspicion, it's well to remember that the primary enemies in World War II—the German and Japanese leaders and many of their troops—were fanatical criminals, people for whom language has no adequate words. It's also well to remember that such clear-cut moral judgments (and therefore the resultant strategic judgments) are not only proper, but necessary. People so evil deserve to be killed for their actions, and so they must be. The difference between the barbaric societies and those that are civilized lies in the criteria about who is monstrous and who deserves death. This is in no way intended to dismiss the Allied bombing of enemy cities and civilians—a morally and militarily debatable strategy. The air chiefs believed that they could win the war by bombing. They were not exactly right, but they kept at it, killing indiscriminately—and in some cases, killing their own troops because of the inaccuracy of the technology. For the same reason, they killed the usual innocents. A bomb dropped from fifteen thousand feet has no notion of the specific target and can just as easily explode in a kindergarten as in a munitions or ball bearing factory.

The US Office of War Information, a creation of the Roosevelt administration, has been called a "propaganda machine."[12] Perhaps. Certainly OWI was a machine for producing information in every conceivable medium, including even exhibitions in museums. OWI also commissioned movie makers, such as the immigrant Italian and sentimental devotee of his adopted country, Frank Capra. Capra made a seven-part series documentary called *Why We Fight*. Once the project got started, Capra worked directly for the army chief of staff, General George C. Marshall, who understood the uses of film as a means of explaining the origins of the war and the war aims of the Allies. Capra received an Academy Award for his work and the rank of colonel in the army, and he was awarded the Distinguished Service Medal by General Marshall himself.

Other Hollywood directors got involved in making documentaries about the war. John Ford (future director of the memorable *The Searchers*, and others) was a naval reserve commander, and he was on the island of Midway during the Japanese air attack against the military installations there. He captured the attacking "Zeroes" on film and was wounded. The attack on the island was a sideshow compared to the epic battle at sea, a battle that surely was a turning point in the war against Japan. Though in the navy officially, Ford was recruited by "Wild Bill" Donovan who headed the Office of Strategic Services (OSS), and later in the war Ford transferred to the European theater as commander of the OSS Photographic Unit. He was there to film the D-Day invasion. It may be remembered that the OSS was the outfit that turned Hemingway down for being too individualistic to work well in a military structure. But Hemingway and the OSS would later cross paths in France.

George Stevens was another Hollywood director who filmed the war in Europe. Stevens and his crew were members of the army's Signal Corps and filmed action from the landings at D-Day, across France to the liberation of Paris, and in Dachau to capture the horror of that death camp. (Martha Gellhorn was there, too, and wrote about it.) Stevens's film was later used as evidence in the Nuremberg trials. After the war, he would go on to notable Hollywood triumphs, the greatest perhaps being *Shane*.

John Huston made *The Battle of San Pietro*, a documentary about the fighting near Naples that is gruesome in its realism. Shots of American soldiers being made ready for burial are hard to watch even today. The film was resented by many of the army brass; they worried it would damage morale. But none other than General George C. Marshall thought it would make a good training film, because seeing what might happen to the troops would make them pay closer attention to their training.

Of course, all sides in this war were well aware of the propaganda value of film. Perhaps the most stunning of all is the German Leni Riefenstahl's *Triumph of the Will*, about the 1934 Nazi Party congress in Nuremberg. Though that was shot well before the outbreak of hostilities, there can be no doubt about its militaristic intentions, nor about the stunning quality of the images.

It is no secret that Hitler's regime made use of sophisticated propaganda that was conveyed by all available media to the German people and to the conquered territories. Joseph Goebbels is generally regarded as the genius presiding over the program, but he was a tactician, whereas Hitler was the strategist. He had a keen understanding of the use of information. As he wrote in *Mein Kampf*: "The receptivity of the masses is very limited, their intelligence is small, but their power of forgetting is enormous; in consequence of these facts, all effective propaganda must be limited to a very few points and must harp on these in slogans until the last member of the public understands what you want him to understand by your slogan."[13] Our current culture is bombarded by advertising and political talking points that use much the same strategy, for many of the same reasons.

In short, the Allies used every medium in order to provide actual news, to inform their public on the larger strategic issues and events, and to rally the home front with messages that now and then walked the line between hard news and propaganda. Of course the Allies had a tradition of freedom of the press—as well as a swarming press corps eager to compete with their rivals—even though the reporters understood the necessity of some level of censorship. The enemy press and media were, like Goebbels, Riefenstahl, and a swarm of faceless correspondents, either true believers, or people who knew where their bread was buttered, or, more to the point, knew that the Gestapo could read. The Nazi news providers seldom, if ever, told the truth to their own citizens and certainly not to the suffering people of the countries they occupied. They also believed, with some justification, that propaganda could help to prop up the morale of their troops—or at least stiffen their resolve to fight. By describing the Allied soldiers as Chicago criminals who would not scruple to kill prisoners, the Nazi propagandists tried to discourage their troops from surrendering. Better to fight, and perhaps be able to run away, than to surrender and be shot out of hand. Propaganda also reported that the Germans were winning the war, so that the troops would not lose heart even after losses in battle.

(As an aside on the subject of propaganda, Bill Mauldin tells of the United States firing artillery shells filled with propaganda pamphlets instead of explosives, and watching the Germans across the way eagerly gathering them up—not to read necessarily, but to use in the latrines. Now and then the Germans would return the favor, firing back stories about smarmy American war profiteers back home seducing the wives and girlfriends of the troops. These were illustrated in comic book style and consequently were popular with the troops, who were chronically short of reading material and who no doubt missed the Sunday comics and the latest antics of Li'l Abner and Daisy Mae, not to mention Felix the Cat and Popeye.)

As Timothy Gay writes: "Allied correspondents had to wrestle with constantly changing censorship rules; inevitably, especially given the wickedness of the enemy and the rightness of the Allied cause, their reporting at times bordered on propaganda. Yet they weren't vacuous cheerleaders; their copy was surprisingly pointed, sometimes irreverent. They ticked off their share of Allied commanders."[14] The notoriously spit-and-polish General Patton called Bill Mauldin into his office and complained for forty-five minutes about the slovenly appearance of Joe and Willie, and about a particular cartoon that showed enlisted men pelting officers with tomatoes during a victorious parade through a captured city. (The officers thought the tomatoes, which landed on the back of their helmets, were part of the tribute of flowers and wine being showered on them by the villagers. The caption reads: "My sir, what an enthusiastic welcome!"[15]) But even though Mauldin was a relatively lowly sergeant, he refused to change his style. He was not insubordinate, and Patton's biographer Ladislas Farago writes that the meeting was not contentious, and that "the confrontation produced no fireworks. The general and the sergeant discussed the problem in civilized language, each defending his view and nether giving ground. When it was over, nothing changed. . . ."[16] This account may well be accurate, but it does not conform very well to the well-known personality of Patton, nor does it seem a credible description of a conversation between a three-star general and a sergeant.

When Mauldin was assigned by *Stars and Stripes* to cover Third Army, Patton wanted to ban *Stars and Stripes* from his entire army, or at the very least censor it rigorously. He thought Mauldin was subversive and a threat to discipline and morale. He wanted his Third Army wearing neckties and helmets at all times, whereas Willie and Joe looked like vagrants who had wandered into a war by accident. ". . . Patton's opposition to Mauldin and his stuff was implacable. He took up the matter with Colonel Egbert White, publisher of *Stars and Stripes*, suggesting that Mauldin either start shaving his characters or the paper stop featuring them, but White gave him no satisfaction. Patton then took his beef to Eisenhower. But the Supreme Commander dismissed the complaint with a hearty laugh and a spirited defense of Willie and Joe."[17]

At one point Patton wanted to "throw his ass [Mauldin] in jail,"[18] but Eisenhower overruled him. To Patton, Mauldin was little more than an anarchist and incipient mutineer, but to the troops he was an enlisted man who had been there and understood the war from a foot soldier's perspective. And they loved him. The military has forever been a class war operating as a team effort, and a team effort operating as a class war. Or at least, a class conflict within understood bounds. It's not true that the noncoms run the army and the navy; but they run a good part of it. And the part they run usually works. Mauldin had been there, and he knew how it was, and he also knew that the GIs he was writing for knew it too.

To Eisenhower's credit and Patton's disgust, the rules for the *Stars and Stripes* reporters were extremely lenient. There were only two censors for the paper, and they rarely killed a story or greatly altered its content. Of course, it was an army paper written and edited by soldiers who might be expected to understand what information was too sensitive to publish. Moreover, the paper had few if any real competitors (some divisions had their own paper but *Stars and Stripes* was aimed at the entire army); and so there was no real incentive to stretch a point or provide a competitive scoop.

Censors were often the bane of the civilian reporters. Walter Cronkite said: "We argued like fury with the censors. There were violent scenes going on all over. . . ."[19] The censors themselves could be anyone from a rear echelon public relations officer (PRO), or in the field a line officer, or even a noncom who did the job as a collateral duty. Naturally their standards varied widely, although the basic rule was not to allow anything that could in any way assist the enemy. That included stories that were overly critical of the commanders or the performance of the army. It was a delicate balance. Since the civilian reporters were working for civilian companies, and since their readership consisted almost entirely of people back home, the reporters and censors were mindful of the effect bad news—such as a series of disasters—would have on civilian morale. Homer Bigart, a correspondent for the *New York Herald Tribune*, wrote about censorship and the home front: "The quarrel is not over battlefield security. . . . [Some army commanders believe that people on the home front] do not yet realize that war involves risks, that breaks do not always go to the Allies. They are afraid that the public cannot stand the shock of bad news and that it must be broken to them gradually over long periods of time and preferably after a victory."[20] In retrospect this attitude is understandable, but shortsighted. The British public had been suffering attacks against their cities, had seen the disastrous retreat from Dunkirk, and many, many homes had received the dreaded telegram. And there would be more violence to come in the shape of flying bombs and rocket attacks. Yet they endured. The American public had felt the shock of Pearl Harbor, the loss of the Philippines, and assorted other early disasters, so it's fair to say their morale would hardly be dented by the news, for example, of Mark Clark's slow and nearly disastrous campaign in Italy, or other such blundering.

The same attitude applied to censoring the troops' letters back home. There was little chance of Willie's or Joe's letters back to their wives revealing anything of interest, even in the unlikely event that they were intercepted and read by the enemy. But there was a fear that any negativity, any suggestion of dwindling morale, would affect the home front and generate a climate of defeatism. In view of the *Stars and Stripes* cartoons, that worry was vastly overstated. And knowing that is the difference between Ike and Patton. Ike knew his people, both the troops and the folks back home. Willie and Joe may not have liked what they were doing, but they were doing it and doing it well.

Early in the war, when reporters were on the front lines, they would write their stories under the nose of the censor who would then edit out any questionable material. The story would then be sent back to local headquarters, which would send it back to Allied headquarters in London for transmission to the United States. This was a catch-as-catch-can system, and often the reporters would send other copies of their reports by any means available—airplanes returning to London being one favorite device. But by 1943 the army had moved beyond its rather ad hoc approach to reporting and had developed "a mobile field press camp that became the template for future press operations in the Mediterranean and European theaters. Besides facilitating the gathering of battlefield news, it fed and housed correspondents, transported them to the front lines, and relayed their dispatches via army tele-printers and air couriers."[21] The press center also improved the process and quality of censorship, since professional public relations officers replaced some sergeant in the field. Of course, these PROs had their own agendas, including protecting and promoting the images of their bosses. But at least the flow of information, however accurate or otherwise, was rationalized.

Is it any wonder that Ernest Hemingway, who had spent the last year commanding his own voluntary mission against the U-boats (there is nothing like the feel of commanding a ship in a war zone, however small the ship) would balk at becoming a part of this vast bureaucratic information machine when public relations officers of little or no experience could cut or change what he wrote? He was judged too independent to join the nascent OSS—a spy organization that by definition would involve clandestine and solitary missions. How could he attach himself to the growing, squabbling journalistic mechanism that was the foreign correspondent business? He knew how the business worked, and that was why he had stayed in Cuba for the first years of the war. After all, he was famous for talking about the need to write one true sentence and go on from there. It's hard to write one true sentence when you have a censor looking over your shoulder, someone who's an amateur but has the power to change what you've written. Or cut it out entirely. Editors are the (generally useful) banes of a writer's existence; censors are worse. True to his independent spirit Hemingway would spend most of the war in Europe off on his own, sometimes using a captured German car and motorcycle to go where he wanted to go. And he would gather around him a small group of followers, both US and French Resistance fighters. It was the patrols of *Pilar* all over again, with Hemingway in command, but this time there would be no shortage of contacts with the enemy.

Did Hemingway come to Europe for Martha? Probably not, though it's impossible to look into the mind of a romantic like Hemingway, or into anyone's, for that matter. Maybe he did. What he said and wrote about their relationship subsequently is only a part of the truth, since post-divorce retrospectives have been known to contain some venom. But certainly their marriage was not working out. And even if it had a chance in Hemingway's mind, Martha's letters written during her hazardous voyage to London more than suggest that she had had enough. Did he come because he needed material for the next big book? That seems more likely. War was a subject he knew, after all. And he had long been planning and occasionally working on a project about the war—a trilogy based on "sea, air and land." He had the material for the sea part as a result of his U-boat hunting. Now he could gather material for the rest, and because of his own experiences on the ground in World War I and Spain, he really only needed experience in the air. Further, there's no doubt he was bored living alone at the Finca Vigia, and perhaps he felt that Martha had some justification in hectoring him, however gently, about missing the great events of the world. Probably it was a combination of all those things, and perhaps he felt there was some possibility of setting things right with Martha. As difficult as she could be, or more accurately, as difficult as their relationship had become, she was still his wife and still a beautiful and accomplished woman. In any event, in May 1944, he came to London, a city he had never been to before and a city where he would meet his next wife, and from which he would begin this next phase of his war. The coming year would be eventful.

CHAPTER FOUR

"The politicians were right; something had to be done."

—Samuel Eliot Morison

D-Day was fast approaching, but the planning for it had begun almost as soon as the Americans had entered the war. It was not necessarily a foregone conclusion that the invasion of Europe should take place by means of an amphibious attack on Normandy. Other entry points, especially in the Mediterranean, were considered, but all were ruled out because they offered difficult terrain once the landing had been made. Only southern France, along the Riviera, offered a reasonable alternative and, as it turned out, a landing was subsequently made there to support Allied operations in Normandy. But the early discussions between the Americans and their British allies revealed a deep division in strategy. As John Keegan, a

British military historian, has written, war reflects culture. To that one might add, war reflects historical memory. And none more so than Winston Churchill's.

Churchill, it will be remembered, was himself a historian of genuine merit, but even if he had not been, he would have reflected the nation's memory of the agonies and disastrous casualties of World War I. And that memory affected his concept of strategy. He abhorred the idea of an early and massive assault on Germany's European positions, especially in France, because he feared the assault would break down into another stalemated trench war with appalling casualties. "While I was always willing to join with the United States in a direct assault across the Channel on the German seafront in France, I was not convinced that this was the only way of winning the war, and I knew that it would be a very heavy and hazardous adventure. The fearful price that we had to pay in human life and blood from the great offences of the First World War was graven in my mind. Men of the Somme and Passchendaele were not to be blotted out by time or reflection."[1] He might have added Gallipoli, an amphibious operation that ended in disaster for which Churchill was largely responsible.

Churchill was not alone in these views; many of his top advisors felt the same way. "In brief, [Churchill's strategy] consisted of 1) a tight naval blockade of the Axis countries; 2) an intensive aerial bombardment of Germany; 3) propaganda to break down German morale and arouse rebellion among conquered peoples; 4) a series of peripheral landings by small armored forces at points on the coast from Norway all around to the Aegean; and 5) a final assault on the German citadel."[2]

Almost everyone understood that France and then Germany would at some point need to be invaded, but Churchill wanted no cross-channel attack until the Germans were so battered that there would be no chance that the invasion could fail or even be strongly opposed. No doubt he hoped that if his encirclement strategy worked, D-Day might even become unnecessary. Sir Alan Brooke, chief of the Imperial Staff had similar ideas, although he did agree that an invasion would ultimately be necessary. He wanted to wait, however, because "no such operation could succeed until the German army had been worn down by the Russians, the Luftwaffe bled white by Allied airpower, the U-boats thwarted, and American war production expanded."[3] As it turned out, that is precisely how it happened.

All of this was frustrating to American strategists and planners. They wanted an early and specific date for the invasion so that they could implement plans for training and production. Without a firm date they felt they could not effectively mobilize and motivate the vast resources and capabilities of the US economy and expanding military. To state the obvious, the cross-channel invasion would, aside from the paratroopers and glider troops, come by sea, as would the supplies that had to be constantly streaming in to support the troops. That meant hundreds of assault vessels had to be built. (On being appraised of this obvious fact, a frustrated Churchill later remarked: "The destinies of two great empires . . . seem to be tied up in some God-damned things called LST's."[4] LST stands for Landing Ship, Tank, a flat-bottom ship that can carry massive amounts of weapons, vehicles, and material and land them on the beach.) And assault vessels were only part of the industrial challenge—tanks, supply ships, fighters, bombers, ordnance, to say nothing of the fuel for the vehicles and food for the troops. All the necessities of war had to be produced. The job would be huge, and US planners needed some specific date to shoot for. Moreover, since these discussions between the Allies were taking place early in 1942, the US strategists wanted to plan for the invasion to take place the following year, in the summer of 1943. That date seemed too ambitious and troubled the British. They wanted more time to let the bombing campaign soften up, if not utterly destroy, Germany's capacity to wage war. Moreover, the U-boats were still enjoying their "happy time," and were a menace to the ships that would be carrying troops, equipment, and supplies from the United States to the invasion ports of England—to say nothing of the food that England desperately needed. Fighting the U-boats was therefore a top British priority.

The British were also somewhat unnerved by the unsuccessful raid on the French port of Dieppe. In August 1942, six thousand troops—British and mostly Canadian—sprang a poorly planned amphibious assault on the beach at Dieppe, a beach that was enfiladed by machine gun and mortar emplacements and separated from the town by a high sea wall. (Enfilade fire comes from the sides of the targeted troops, shooting down the line.) The entire operation was a disaster: 3367 Canadians were killed, wounded, or captured, as well as 275 British commandos. The Royal Navy lost one destroyer and 33 landing craft to German artillery. Just as bad, the Luftwaffe and antiaircraft artillery shot down 106 RAF planes. There was nothing gained; in fact there was little or nothing really *to be* gained. The stated objectives of the raid were to hold the position through two tides and to gather intelligence. Odd as that first objective may seem, the raid failed even to achieve that. The raid was a textbook case study in how not to run an amphibious operation. Too few men, no initial bombing, not enough naval gunfire support—these were the lessons learned, but as many have pointed out, those lessons should have been understood before the raid, and had they been, there would have been no raid at all. Indeed, those points were obvious on their face.

No doubt the failure of this venture firmed Churchill and his advisors in their resolve to continue the bombing strategy and delay the bitter day when the Channel had to be crossed. And it also no doubt gave him reason to rethink his encirclement ideas. After all, this was precisely the sort of thing he advocated, and its abject failure and cruel losses must have given him pause. Churchill may have been an effective politician and brilliant rhetorician, but he was a military meddler who was constantly coming up with ideas that were impractical and potentially ruinous. Even his top military advisors despaired of having to spend time arguing against impulsive suggestions. Indeed, they sometimes enlisted the help of their American allies to dissuade Churchill from some unlikely inspiration. Like Mr. Toad in *The Wind in the Willows*, Churchill needed watching by his more reasonable friends. Unlike Roosevelt, who rarely intervened in strategic planning, Churchill had his fingerprints everywhere, much to the chagrin of his generals and the occasional frustration of his allies.

As ever in democracies, politics inserted its unwelcome nose into the discussion of strategy. In the United States, leftists and communist advocates echoed the cry of the Russians for a second front that could alleviate the pressure on Soviet Russia. Most of these advocates were the same people who championed the earlier Molotov-Ribbentrop nonaggression pact with Russia, but they were subsequently instructed in the error of their ways, and therefore did an about-face with no blushes after the Wehrmacht surged into Russia. Even so, given the doctrinaire response of these leftist commentators, to say nothing of the appeals from Russia, the embattled ally of the United States, Roosevelt felt the need to do something to engage US forces in the battle against the Germans. A massive invasion into France was all very well, and most likely in the cards eventually, but something needed to be done now—something dramatic and, with luck, militarily useful, or at least, sensible.

That something became the invasion of French North Africa, code-named Operation Torch. It was Roosevelt's decision to join the British in this hitherto unprecedentedly massive and long-distance amphibious attack against territory controlled by Vichy French politicians and troops.

The landings were made at Casablanca and other points along the western areas of North Africa. Whether the French would resist was unknown. They did initially, killing 526 and wounding 837 American troops before surrendering. Additionally, 41 Americans were listed as "missing." The invasion was resisted by Vichy loyalists who considered themselves bound by the armistice with Germany, but in the grand scheme of things their resistance was feeble and quickly collapsed.

This was of course cold comfort for the families of troops killed by those assumed to be allies.

While undoubtedly a military success, Torch also exposed some potential problems for those planning the ultimate cross-channel invasion of France. This report from the US Army Center of Military History highlights some of those problems:

Most of the Army's problems during TORCH occurred in the ship-to-shore phase of landings, when amphibious forces are most vulnerable. The whole idea of night landings had to be reexamined. While the transfer of troops and equipment from transports to landing boats could be accomplished with only moderate difficulty in darkness, the shuttling of boats between transports and beaches after their first trip ashore became a source of delays. Boats returning to transports had great difficulty avoiding subsequent boat waves and finding the right transport in the darkness.

A more serious problem concerned transport of vehicles to shore. Because vehicles required deeper-draft landing craft than troops, sandbars that light troop-carrying boats overrode became obstacles to heavier tank and truck lighters. Even on beaches without sandbars, lighters frequently bottomed some distance from the shoreline and had to discharge vehicles into several feet of water, disabling electrical systems. Problems such as these provoked a spiral of unloading delays and forced troops ashore into a tactical disadvantage during the crucial early hours of the landings. Reaching shore sooner than tanks and artillery, infantry units on [TORCH] D-day often found themselves attacking French coastal batteries and armored units with little more than rifles and hand grenades. Most other problems relating to navigation and handling of hazardous items such as gasoline could be corrected with training and experience. But one phenomenon affecting movement to shore remained beyond human reach: the weather.

Operational fires (large-caliber supporting fire) proved generally satisfactory to all landings. The assignment of an aircraft carrier to each landing site gave the task forces a great advantage: Allied aircraft could prevent reinforcement of enemy garrisons, but the French could not prevent Allied buildups ashore. Only at Safi and Algiers did lone sorties of French aircraft inflict damage, and both were quickly driven off.

Naval gunfire provided essential support in neutralizing coastal batteries. In coordinating with friendly troop movements ashore, however, problems arose. Most landings took place near urban areas, which placed troops in civil-military minefields. Since Allied leaders looked forward to eventual French cooperation against the Axis, gunnery officers aboard ships and field commanders ashore had to exercise great care to avoid civilian housing as well as port facilities and oil supplies they hoped to use. With surface units ten or more miles offshore, naval gunfire margins of error could not be ignored. Such considerations forced Army units to operate without some of the large-caliber support that could have shortened the duration—and reduced the casualty total—of some battles.

For advancing units ashore, a more immediate tactical problem with naval gunfire occasionally arose. In the Fedala area a conflict in calls for support almost caused the tragedy of American fire landing among American troops. As troops of the 7th Regimental Landing Group neared an objective they requested continuation of naval gunfire. At the same time, 30th Regimental Landing Group officers asked the ships to hold fire for the moment, since their troops were nearing the impact zone. Safety concerns dictated a halt of fire support missions but at the cost of delay in the advance ashore.

The story of the success and sometimes failure of the American and British armies in North Africa is a topic for another day. But the immediate effect of Operation Torch and the quick capitulation of the Vichy forces was to send Hitler into a rage and cause him to order the immediate occupation of the rest of France, i.e., that part of southern France controlled before by the Vichy government. In his letter announcing this move to Marshal Philippe Pétain, Hitler said: "Thus, after receipt of certain information, Germany and Italy are left in no doubt whatsoever that the next step of Britain and America is directed toward Corsica and the south of France. In consequence of this the foundations of the armistice have ceased to exist, as France is no longer able to acquit herself vis-à-vis Germany and Italy."[5]

The expansion of the occupation, combined with the Germans' apparently insatiable appetite for essentially slave labor plus the southerners' quite natural aversion to being occupied and under the ruthless eyes of the Gestapo, led many of the young men to take to the woods and form Resistance groups. These were called the Maquis, a Corsican word that essentially means "the bush." And whether they went there to escape deportation to German factories or because they wanted to be actively involved in underground fighting, it hardly mattered. The area around Toulouse especially became a hotbed of resistance. Worse, it also became a major Gestapo installation that was aided and abetted by the Nazi sympathizers among the French, some of whom joined a paramilitary police force known as the Milice. These people were especially dangerous to the Resistance because, as Frenchmen, they could easily infiltrate Resistance cells. As a result they were prime targets for Resistance attacks and assassinations. Oddly, the Germans, who were quick to arrest and murder whole villages of civilians in response to attacks against one or more of their own (whether the villagers were responsible or not), never seemed too concerned about reprisals against their French Nazi sympathizers and putative allies. The politics of these various Resistance groups are tangled and complicated. Hemingway's own story in Europe would become part of this story.

There were other results from Torch. For one, it moved the eventual invasion of France back a year. The Americans wanted to shoot for summer, 1943. The British however, including most significantly Churchill, wanted to delay in the hopes of softening up the German capacity to wage war even as the UK built up manpower. Torch also demonstrated that more training in amphibious landings, in combined naval and army operations and intelligence-gathering were necessary, for the German defense of the French coast was obviously going to be more spirited than the French African Vichy supporters. The other major result was that, once North Africa was cleared of Axis troops, a cross-Mediterranean attack became inevitable. And despite Hitler's entirely reasonable assumption that southern France would be the target, in fact it would be Sicily and then Italy. This was no doubt in line with Churchill's continuing search for the "soft underbelly" of Europe. In the event, the campaign found Italy anything but a soft underbelly. Although the campaign did eventually knock Italy out of the Axis alliance and remove Mussolini, the Germans put up a defense that was determined and costly to both sides. Ably led by Field Marshal Albert Kesselring, the Germans stymied Allied forces that were led by Lieutenant General Mark Clark—a contest that many would consider a leadership mismatch.

Hemingway got to London just in time. He arrived on board a military transport plane on May 17. The invasion of Europe was less than three weeks away. He checked into the Dorchester Hotel, an imposing and upscale hotel located on Park Lane, just across the street from Hyde Park. The city that Hemingway was visiting for the first time was showing the effects of five years of war. How could it be otherwise? The area around St Paul's, for example, used to be filled with shops and houses. Now it was an empty field with long grass and wild flowers growing. One US sailor likened the city to "a very respectable char

woman carrying on her onerous duties and waiting for better times."[6]
Nearly everything was rationed. In fact, one of Hemingway's fellow
passengers was the actress Gertrude Lawrence, who brought along a
dozen eggs as a present for friends. (They didn't survive the flight.)
Another passenger, Lieutenant William Van Dusen, was carrying a sack
of buckwheat flour. The city was swarming with men and women in
uniform. But the Dorchester managed to maintain some semblance
of luxury, and Hemingway's room soon became a gathering place of
old and new friends, including famed photographer Robert Capa and
Hemingway's younger brother, Leicester, who was in the Signal Corps
and attached to a film unit. Despite the rationing Hemingway always
seemed to be able to gather sufficient supplies for parties.

The luxury, such as it was in wartime London, was in sharp contrast to Martha's quarters. She was still somewhere in the middle of
the Atlantic on a merchant ship carrying the most dangerous cargo
imaginable. It was the earliest available transport she could arrange,
and always intrepid, she took it.

If Hemingway had second thoughts about coming to London in
May 1944, they appear to have disappeared quickly. Swept up in the
excitement of coming action and by the bonhomous and bibulous
atmosphere of the circle of friends and fellow correspondents that
quickly attached itself to him, Hemingway seemed to put aside all his
earlier reservations about the next phases of his career. And though
he did not say so publicly, he did not put aside his intentions to be
actively involved in the fighting, and he did say that he was only going
to write enough so that he wouldn't lose his *Collier's* assignment and
get sent home. Beyond that, he intended to be a free agent.

But there was more than a war beckoning. If Martha intended to
regard her marriage as an impediment to professional success and, most
likely, an exercise in abuse and conflict—all of which seemed likely,
in fact almost certain—there were other opportunities, other women.
London was full of men and women, many of whom were keenly aware
that life was uncertain and often short and that when the opportunity

for love or romance or simple sexual pleasure presented itself, it only made good sense to take it. One of these was Mary Welsh. She worked for Time Inc., was married to Australian war correspondent Noel Monks, and was the frequent companion of writer Irwin Shaw and correspondent Bill Walton, since her husband was often away on assignment.

Hemingway met her at the White House restaurant, a frequent hangout of reporters. Apparently, the often susceptible Hemingway was immediately smitten. An aggressive courtship ensued. Hemingway biographer Michael Reynolds writes: "Before Martha Gellhorn ever stepped ashore in England, Ernest was telling Mary Welsh: 'I don't know you, Mary. But I want to marry you. . . . I want to marry you now, and I hope to marry you sometime. Sometime you may want to marry me.'"[7] Here again Hemingway's emotions were in high gear and here again was his curious middle-American conventionality. Mary Welsh was more than likely an available conquest, but Hemingway was mentioning marriage apparently even before he had taken her to bed. She rather quickly came to his bed, but whether she wanted anything more than a liaison with an attractive and famous author is another question—one that she asked herself. Knowing him as she came to do would intensify rather than answer her questions. And, as Reynolds writes, she did not "imagine the emotional maelstrom into which she was being drawn."[8] She soon began to see disturbing signs, though: "When he is good he is more endearing, more stimulating . . . with gaiety and wisdom, than anyone . . . but when he is bad he is wildly, childishly, unpredictably bad."[9]

Carlos Baker echoes Mary's thoughts: "His odd combination of benignity, gaiety and boorishness did not make him universally popular during these early weeks in London. Some of his acquaintances believed that he was acting a part. Although he had immense charm when he chose to use it, and often when he did not, there were other occasions when he behaved childishly."[10]

Regardless of Mary's reservations, Hemingway, now going to war, had a new romantic focus for his imagination. Martha was useless in that role and beyond hope. Warriors going into harm's way need someone to remember as well as something to live for, and they also need an avatar of home: the girlfriend, the family, a current wife, a future wife. The ideal in this case is a warm and passionate woman waiting and worrying and rewarding the warrior when he returns intact, or, if not, someone to nurse the wounded soldier, the way Agnes von Kurowsky—the model for Catherine Barkley in *A Farewell to Arms*—nursed Ernest and, as importantly, entered and remained in his imagination. And it's fair to wonder whether Ernest was all his life looking for Agnes again, much like Yeats's "Wandering Aengus"—not the real Agnes, but the Agnes of memory. Perhaps losing her just after World War I motivated his strange addiction to marriage, as though that was the best way to hold on to the current woman forever. His own personal experience, of course, should have taught him that method did not work. Martha was exhibit one. Marriage made their relationship more difficult, not less. But the imagination of a romantic is immune to reason, or even to common sense. Or, perhaps it is more accurate to say, that it is indifferent to both.

Hemingway's addiction to the vision of his dream girl would arise again, after the war and after his marriage to Mary, and it would become an aspect of the emotional "maelstrom" that she would have to endure. It would be part of his novel *Across the River and into the Trees*—a novel that was based on his experience of the war in Europe and on his lifelong romantic imagination, two themes that were the basis of his earliest and best work. The dream girl would not be Mary, since wives generally cannot fill that role—at least not after the first flush of passion—but rather a teenaged Italian aristocrat named Adriana Ivancich. In the novel her name would be Renata, a word that suggests rebirth. And rebirth for a romantic could hardly come more appropriately in the form of a beautiful young woman who arrives in the life of a middle-aged man. This book, however, would not measure up to the earlier work. It was a marriage of ideas that could have worked, but somehow did not.

When Martha Gellhorn finally arrived in London she learned that her husband was in the hospital. Apparently always accident prone, Hemingway had been injured in a car crash after an all-night drinking party at Robert Capa's apartment in Belgravia. He was a passenger when the car smashed into a water tank in the dark of blacked-out London. He was thrown into the windshield and suffered a gash in his head that he said required some fifty stitches. The concussion would cause severe headaches for weeks to come. Both knees were severely bruised against the dashboard. The injuries would prevent him from flying missions with the RAF; those would have to wait for a few weeks.

When Martha went to visit his room at the hospital she found him entertaining the usual suspects of well-wishers, hangers-on, and cronies. There were bottles aplenty, and the atmosphere and the drinking did nothing to spur any sympathy for his injuries. Just the opposite. That is probably the moment when she made her decision to leave the marriage. She had written a letter about his voyage: "He is a rare and wonderful type; he is a mysterious type too and a wise one and all sorts of things. He is a good man, which is vitally important. He is however bad for me, sadly enough, or maybe wrong for me is the word; and I am wrong for him. . . . I am wondering now if it ever really worked. . . . I feel terribly strange, like a shadow, and full of dread. I dread the time ahead, the amputating time. . . . It is, note, my fault. I am the one who has changed. . . . And I am ashamed and guilty too, because I am breaking his heart. . . . We quarreled too much, I suppose. . . . It is all sickening and I am sad to death, and afraid. . . . I only want to be alone. I want to be myself and alone and free to breathe, live, look upon the world and find it however it is. . . . I want my own name back."[11] Writing that letter left open some sliver of doubt about the possibilities of the relationship's demise. But after her visit to the hospital, those doubts evaporated. It was more of the same, and she wanted out, not only because of his outsized behavior but also because of her own needs, the needs she tried to sublimate from the beginning of their relationship, but which were now more important than ever. As she wrote to one of her friends: "As far as I am concerned it is all over. There may be miracles but I doubt it. I have never believed in them." [12]

Aside from the understandable anger and bitterness Hemingway felt at Martha's apparent lack of concern for his injuries—a lack of concern that he no doubt interpreted as a symbol of their life together—Hemingway could recognize the arc and the end of a story as well as any. As in *A Farewell to Arms*, this story effectively ended in a hospital room—for different reasons, of course. But, still, there was a certain recognizable convergence there. Well, he knew some things are inevitable; inevitable loss had been one of his themes, so he understood it. Besides, he had already installed a new woman in his imagination: Mary, who had sympathetically visited him in the hospital and brought him flowers. So just then the future was not so grim after all. Perhaps he even believed it, just then. A romantic will always have an image in his thoughts, someone to dream of; and Mary at this time seemed to play that role. Whether she wanted the Dream Vision role and wanted to be there or not was a separate question. And whether she would retain her role as his Dream Vision was an equally different question entirely.

CHAPTER FIVE

"You will enter the continent of Europe and, in conjunction with the other Allied Nations, undertake operations aimed at the heart of Germany and the destruction of her Armed Forces."
　　　　　　　　　—Joint Chiefs of Staff directive
　　　　　　　　　　　to General Eisenhower

"O Lord give us faith . . . With thy blessing, we shall prevail over the unholy forces of our enemy. Help us to conquer the apostles of greed and racial arrogancies [sic]. Lead us to the saving of our country, and with our sister nations into a world unity that will spell a sure peace—a peace invulnerable to the schemings of unworthy men. And a peace that will let all of men live in freedom, reaping the just rewards of their honest toil. Thy will be done, Almighty God. Amen."
　　　　　　　　　—June 6, 1944, President Roosevelt's
　　　　　　　　　　　National Prayer

*"A landing on a foreign coast in the face of hostile troops
has always been one of the most difficult operations of war."*
—Captain Sir Basil H. Liddell Hart (1895–1970)

It would be impossible to exaggerate the complexity of the planning and the execution of what has become known as D-Day. (Other amphibious operations, such as Torch, also had their D-Days, but the June 6, 1944, invasion of Normandy is the one most people regard as *the* D-Day.) Similarly, the German strategy for countering what they knew was an inevitable invasion was equally complicated, though in different ways. The difference lay in the requirements of offensive versus defensive warfare.

In March 1944, about the same time that Martha returned to Cuba to face an unhappy and fractious Hemingway, Adolf Hitler convened a meeting with his three top commanders in Western Europe. He said, in part:

"It is evident that an Anglo American landing in the west will and must come. How and where it will come no one knows. . . . The enemy's landing operation must under no circumstances be allowed to last longer than a matter of hours or, at most, days, with the Dieppe attempt as a model. Once the landing has been defeated it will under no circumstances be repeated by the enemy. Quite apart from the heavy casualties he would suffer, months would be needed to prepare for a renewed attempt. Nor is this the only factor which would deter the Anglo Americans from trying again. There would also be the crushing blow to their morale which a miscarried invasion would give. It would for one thing prevent the reelection of Roosevelt in America and, with luck, he would finish up somewhere in jail. In England, too, war weariness would assert itself even more greatly than hitherto. . . . *The destruction of the enemy's landing attempt means more than a purely local decision on the Western front. It is the sole decisive factor in the whole conduct of the war and hence in its final result."* [1]

In other words, lose to the invasion forces on the Western front, and the war most likely would be lost. Win that battle, and the British and Americans might possibly discard their objective of Germany's "unconditional surrender" and maybe even agree to a separate peace with acceptable terms. That would allow Germany to turn her full attention to the Russian front, where things were going badly. At the very least victory over the invasion forces would buy Germany many months of time that would in turn allow her to concentrate on the Russian front.

So the object was clear. The question then became how to achieve it.

Certainly the defenses on the coast and especially along the English Channel would be key to repelling or at least stalling the initial attack. But the man in charge of those defenses, Field Marshal Erwin Rommel, did not believe those defenses alone could stop the invasion. The key to his strategy was the placement of mobile reserves and panzer divisions in close proximity to the shoreline, wherever the attack came—ideally only a few miles behind the line. In other words, the reserves had to be positioned to make a quick counterattack, and it would be the counterattack that sealed the victory. There were some obvious locations that were reasonably close to each other: Brittany, Normandy, the Pas-de-Calais, and the Low Countries. Hitler and most of his generals assumed that the Pas-de-Calais, which is closest to England, would be the logical target. In an April letter to Colonel General Alfred Jodl, Hitler's chief of operations staff, Rommel said, in part:

"If, in spite of the enemy's air superiority, we succeed in getting a large part of our mobile force into action in the threatened coast defense sectors in the first few hours, I am convinced that the enemy attack on the coast will collapse completely on the first day. . . . But without rapid assistance from the armored divisions and mobile units, our coast divisions will be hard put to counter attacks from the sea and from airborne troops inland. Their [the German coast defenders] land front is too thinly held for that. The dispositions of both combat and reserve forces should be such as to ensure that the minimum possible movement will be required to counter an attack at any of the most likely points . . . and to ensure that the greater part of the enemy troops, sea and airborne, will be destroyed by our fire during their approach."[2]

The paragraph touches on several key points. First, to state the obvious, the massive invasion force (ultimately 150,000 men) could not arrive all at once. The men would come in waves of landing craft and in subsequent days. (Hemingway came on the first day in the seventh wave, for example.) So Rommel figured that the beach defenders in their concrete pillboxes could hold off the initial waves, while the mobile reserve could reach the fighting and employ tanks and artillery to destroy subsequent waves, since the most dangerous aspect of an amphibious invasion is during the seaward approach—the landing craft are essentially defenseless targets. What's more, counterattacking German infantry, artillery, and tanks could, if Rommel's plan was approved, outnumber the first few waves who managed to make it ashore.

Second, Rommel was well aware that the Allies controlled the air. During his years with the Afrika Korps, he gained a sincere respect for airpower's ability to limit mobility. Even in the featureless desert where you might think mobility would be fairly easy, the Allies' airpower was able to interdict the movement of Rommel's tanks, mobile troops, and artillery. Further, the German mobile reserves in France would not be traveling over featureless desert but along roads and through villages and over rail lines—all of which could be bombed (or sabotaged) in advance of the invasion and rendered either unusable or so torn up as to cause massive delays. Rommel was certainly prescient enough to anticipate a massive attack against transportation infrastructure. Not only would that affect the movement of combat troops and vehicles toward the front, it would also slow the movement of supplies. Rommel was correct; the Allies fully intended to smash the transportation systems in France. Labeled the "transportation plan," the combined RAF and Army Air Corps bombers began strategic bombing of transportation facilities, with, to quote Admiral Samuel Morison, "immediate and spectacular results. Before long some 1600 trains, 600 carrying German army supplies were 'back tracked' in France and by 26 May all rail traffic over the Seine between Paris and the sea was stalled."[3] But this apparent success came at a terrible cost to the French and especially to the Parisians, since Paris was after all the hub of the French rail systems. As the eminent historian Michael Neiberg writes: "Allied bombardments killed 67,078 French citizens in all, 35,317 in 1944 alone. One raid, on May 30, killed 5,358 Frenchmen, wounded 7,075 more, and left thousands of men, women, and children homeless."[4] The Allies and Churchill in particular were deeply disturbed by these grim statistics but saw no alternative to the often inaccurate high-level bombing, although Churchill continued to protest. And although, as Morison said, the attacks did more or less hamper the Germans' ability to move troops to the invasion sites, they also destroyed France's ability to move food to Paris—which became one of the many factors that worried both the Allies and the Resistance forces inside Paris. More on this later.

All of these factors (and apprehensions) convinced Rommel that he needed to command the armor and mobile reserves (which he did not at the time) and that they should be placed as close as possible to all the most likely invasion sites. During the March conference with Hitler, Rommel believed he had convinced him of the wisdom of his proposals, but a day later Hitler changed his mind and adopted the opposing strategy put forward primarily by General Leo Geyr von Schweppenburg who commanded Panzer Group West and who feared an airborne attack on Paris and so demanded to keep his panzers there. He also had a legitimate fear of naval gunfire. He had been in Sicily when the Allies invaded and learned to his chagrin that his tanks were extremely vulnerable to naval gunnery, not only those along the invasion beaches but also tanks behind the line, tanks that tried to maneuver but fell victim to the accurate naval gunfire that was directed by spotters in the air and on the ground.[5] Nor did he agree with the strategy of "Festung Europa," or Fortress Europe. He said: "The Atlantic Wall was an outpost position. Therefore, the whole defense theory of Hitler, Jodl, and Rommel was unjustified. Since Hannibal, decisive battles had not been fought in outpost positions. With their theory, Hitler, ignorant of military matters, Rommel the pure tactician, and Jodl, who was untouched by the holy spark as far as strategy was concerned, stamped themselves as indistinguishable from the trench war soldiers of 1918."[6] As an aristocrat and professional soldier, Geyr von Schweppenburg expressed the contempt he and many of his peers felt for Hitler and his immediate circle. (That contempt was widely shared among the professionals/aristocrats and led in part to the July 20, 1944, attempt to assassinate Hitler in his Wolf's Lair in eastern Prussia.)

Rommel, on the other hand, finished his letter to Jodl with: "I have disagreed very violently with Geyr von Schweppenburg over this question, and will only be able to execute my ideas if he is put under Army Group [Rommel's] command early enough."[7] It didn't happen. As Rommel's friend and subordinate, Lieutenant General Fritz Bayerlein, wrote: "On the question of operational reserves, Hitler and his staff were more inclined to accept Geyr von Schweppenburg's proposals, as they too did not believe that the enemy air force could exercise so great an influence over the movement of troops."[8] These kinds of frustrating contretemps caused Rommel to say of Hitler: "The last out of his door is always right."[9]

It should be noted that Gerd von Rundstedt, who was the commander of the west and therefore both Rommel's and Geyr von Schweppenburg's superior, tended to agree with the latter. Both men were wedded to the concept of maneuverability in order to counterattack, ideally by encirclement—the very theory that Rommel feared was no longer viable because of Allied airpower. Counterattack, yes, but not from a distance. In a grim kind of irony, Rommel would be wounded when his car was strafed by an Allied fighter a few weeks after D-Day. (It was the end of the war for him. Moreover, Hitler suspected him of involvement in the assassination plot and soon arrested him and forced him to commit suicide; Rommel had no choice, since that was the only way to guarantee that his wife and son would be protected. Rommel's reputation and popularity with the German public would also be protected. His death would be explained as a result of his wounds.)

The generals close to Hitler had most of their experience on the Russian front, a war that Rommel described as mostly "two dimensional" involving "fanatical hordes [who were] driven forward in masses against our line with no regard for casualties and little recourse to tactical craft."[10] Having faced the British and Americans in North Africa, Rommel knew that the Allies approached war with precisely the opposite tactics from the Russian "hordes." "[The Anglo American enemy is one who applies] his intelligence to the use of his many technical resources, who spares no expenditure [of] material and whose every operation goes its course as though it had been the subject of repeated rehearsals."[11]

As Geyr von Schweppenburg feared, there was another factor that would come to overwhelm Rommel's coastal defenses, as well as restrict the mobility of his interior formations and movement: sea power. The accuracy and intensity of naval gunfire would be a vital determinant in the initial stages of the invasion and, more surprising to the Germans, a key factor in subsequent days' fighting. Even an aging battleship like the USS *Texas* could send fourteen-inch shells a distance of sixteen miles and drop them in a target the size of a football field. And when the shells landed, the football field disappeared along with any people or vehicles unlucky enough to be there. (A battleship's sixteen-inch gun range is twenty miles; the US battleships at Omaha Beach, however, were armed with fourteen-inch guns.) Even though those targets are out of sight, the fire can be directed and corrected from spotters on shore or by air-based spotters. (A spotter radios a target's map coordinates to the ship and then makes corrections by radio after the initial salvos.) The fact that the Allies commanded the air meant that the spotters were able to operate without too much difficulty and that naval gunfire support could therefore attack German formations that were well behind the line, destroying tanks and troop vehicles, to say nothing of the troops themselves, without ever seeing them, either visually or on radar. It's unlikely that Rommel's experience (unlike Geyr von Schweppenburg's) led him to anticipate or appreciate the effect, range, and accuracy of naval gunfire. The German navy was essentially bottled up and had almost no impact on the June 6 Allied attack, although they would make some troublesome attacks on subsequent days, as the buildup proceeded. But these attacks would have little if any impact on the outcome of the invasion, because they were limited to a handful of destroyers, torpedo boats, and U-boats. Just as the Allies controlled the air, they controlled the sea, and the control of both elements would be decisive. This would not be a "two dimensional" attack. What's more, control of the air meant that German warships, such as they were, were vulnerable to the constant air patrols of the Allies.

But Rommel believed there was a chance to stop the invasion on the beaches. And if he had a favorite defensive weapon, it would be the mine. He gained great appreciation for the minefield, when he was attacking the British at Tobruk. "In the fighting . . . we again and again found ourselves in the position of fighting against an enemy who had established himself with large numbers of antitank guns and, in some cases even tanks, deep in the mined zone. . . . It certainly taught me the value of the British large scale mining." [12] In describing his plans for defending the likely invasion locations, Rommel wrote: "Between and around the stationary tanks, strong point groups, and resistance nests, minefields of great depth will be laid. These minefields will contain mines of all kinds and are likely to be highly effective. If the enemy should ever set foot on land, an attack through the minefields against defensive works sited within them will present him with a task of immense difficulty. He will have to fight his way through the zone of death in the defensive fire of the whole of our artillery."[13] By May 20, 1944, 4,193,167 mines of all types were laid along the Channel coast in fields "of great depth."[14]

As an aside, his use of the term "zone of death," reminds us that the careful and scientific discussion of defenses and resources, is in fact a formula for killing. The science and the art of war are designed ultimately to result in body parts and mass graves. Only some casualties in Normandy have their own private resting places, in the cemeteries of France. Many more are listed as "missing."

All mines are insidious, but perhaps the one Allied troops feared most was the S-mine, also known to the ever grimly humorous GIs as the Bouncing Betty. When tripped, the mine sprang up to a height of three to five feet before detonating steel balls across three hundred and sixty degrees. It was certainly lethal to a range of twenty meters and capable of inflicting wounds at one hundred meters.

Then there were the underwater mines. Allied planners had to assume that the Channel was heavily mined. These mines could be sown either by U-boats or aircraft, and so they could be, and were, replaced even as Allied minesweepers located and destroyed the originals. More on this later.

Rear Admiral Samuel Eliot Morison describes Omaha beach, the beach that Hemingway would "assault": "Here is a brief description of the defenses. The first was the beach itself, which slopes at a low gradient of one foot in 190 for most of its width above low-water mark and increases to one in 47 as it nears high-water mark. The local range of tide, 22 feet in the morning and 23 feet in the afternoon of D-Day meant that a width of at least 150 yards was bared at low water. The inshore half of this entire area had, by June 1944, been planted thick with underwater obstacles of the most formidable kind, in three rows. First, the attack force would have to encounter a row of 'Element C,' or 'Belgian Barn Doors,' or 'gates'—steel frames 7 by 10 feet with waterproof teller mines lashed to the uprights. About twenty yards inshore of these were 8 to 10 foot deep *chevaux de frise* consisting of sharpened wood or concrete poles angled toward the sea, with about every third one mined. The inner row of obstacles consisted of 'hedgehogs' (also known as 'horned scullies'), each consisting of three six-foot steel bars welded together at right angles, like a giant jackstone. These were interspersed with curved steel rails and V-shaped wooden ramps, all mined. . . . Concrete tetrahedra had also been built, but few had been planted by D-Day. . . . The level shelf between the seawall and the bluffs was crossed by antitank ditches and heavily mined. Clustered around each beach exit were strong points, and along the edge of the bluff were trench systems, machine gun emplacements and mobile 88mm guns, together with many 75s. Most dangerous to the troops were gun emplacements so cunningly dug into the bluffs as to enfilade almost the entire length of beach and protected from offshore observations and gunfire by three foot concrete shields." [15] The seawall Morison mentions was a concrete wall that ran about half the length of the beach and was protected by coils of concertina barbed wire.

Regarding the offshore obstacles, Rommel's Army Group War Diary states: "Up to the 13th of May, 1944, a total of 517,000 foreshore obstacles were constructed along the [entire] Channel front, 31,000 of which were mined." [16] And the Germans had several more weeks to add to those totals.

The obstacles on, for example, Omaha Beach were no secret. Allied air reconnaissance gave the Allied planners a clear understanding of what lay in wait, although as Admiral Morison said, the intelligence did not reveal many of the concrete pillboxes hidden in the cliffs. But the beach obstacles were mostly obvious. That meant a greater proportion of army engineers would have to take part in the initial landings. Specialists in blowing up obstacles, bridging tank traps, destroying barbed wire and concrete pillboxes, the engineers numbered 10,000 men total and two battalions of them would land with the first waves.

Moreover, almost every infantryman destined for D-Day landings was sent through a vigorous three week course of training at the US Army Assault Training Center in Devon. As historian Joseph Balkoski writes: "There they learned landing craft drill, demolition techniques, mine clearing and assault tactics with special weapons. . . . [They also] learned how to use the complex array of weapons formerly associated only with sappers [combat engineers], such as bangalore torpedoes, flamethrowers, wire cutters and satchel charges."[17] The intense training boosted the confidence of the troops that they could get the job done.

There were six sectors of Omaha Beach. One of the more easterly beaches was labeled Fox Green. Leading out of the entire length of Omaha were five exits, or "draws." These were breaks in the cliffs, and capturing them was critical to the success of the invasion. Infantrymen could scale the cliffs, and some did at the cost of many casualties from mines. But tanks and other vehicles could not. Those five draws therefore had to be captured. And of course the Germans understood that too, and so these five were protected by concrete pillboxes on both sides of the draw as well as in the case of the Fox Green sector a massive concrete wall blocking the entire width of the draw. (The wall protecting the westernmost exit was 125 feet long, nine feet high, and six feet deep. It's reasonable to assume that the wall protecting the exit by Fox Green was of similar proportions.) These walls could only be destroyed by TNT. In Hemingway's *Collier's* story "Voyage to Victory," he would describe the assault craft he was riding in and its attempt to land troops on Fox Green. In the bow of the landing craft were crates of TNT.

Rommel also knew that the Allies would drop paratroops behind the German front lines in an effort to secure the draws. This was one more good reason to position reserves close to the front lines. Rommel also flooded the low-lying fields, and that water would see the end of many a paratrooper.

H-Hour—when the air assault would begin—was planned for 6:30 A.M. because that would be just after low tide, and the waterside obstacles would be revealed, obstacles that would be submerged and a hazard to landing craft soon after the tide began to rise. It would require the services of navy and army UDT (underwater demolitions teams) to destroy these obstacles. Morison writes: "Before the rushing flood, rising twelve inches every eight minutes, forced them to vacate, these brave men had blown five big channels and three partial ones through the hideous array of murderous obstacles. Unfortunately there was too little time to mark the gaps before the tide covered them. Coxswains of landing craft could not see where the gaps were until the obstacles were exposed by the afternoon ebb."[18] There were sixteen UDT teams consisting of seven sailors and five army engineers each.

Even so, in the face of the German defenses, it beggars belief that an invasion could succeed. Of course, historians know what happened. But the officers planning the attack may be forgiven for moments of doubt. They had seen the intelligence reports. They thought they knew what was waiting, although in the event it was worse than they realized. The attack at Omaha Beach, especially, would be, as Wellington said of Waterloo, "the nearest run thing."

❖

While Rommel's troops were busily laying minefields, Hemingway was in London pursuing Mary Welsh. Martha Gellhorn was also staying at the Dorchester, although in a room a floor above Hemingway's. Their infrequent meetings were anything but affectionate. Hemingway still resented Martha's lack of sympathy for his injuries. And even if he had not been nursing his resentments, he had other plans for his romantic future. And Martha had other plans, period.

It's not exactly clear when his affair with Mary began. Most likely it was shortly after he arrived, because he wrote "First Poem to Mary in London" and dated it "May, 1944." (Carlos Baker says that he wrote it in June.) It is a poem because Hemingway called it a poem. Otherwise, it bears little resemblance to poetry as most people think of it, even given the rather elastic standards of the modernist period. It's the kind of poetry that caused Robert Frost to say that "writing free verse is like playing tennis with the net down." Hemingway wrote poetry occasionally throughout his career. None of it is really worth reading except to people who are interested in Hemingway the man and writer of fiction. If that seems harsh, it is only said with knowledge of his best fiction, such as the opening paragraph of *A Farewell to Arms*. There his prose is far more lyrical than anything he ever wrote and labeled "poetry."

"First Poem to Mary in London" is a strange piece. Mostly, it has Hemingway sadly reminiscing about his U-boat patrols and missing his friends and his boat. Now caught in the massive machine of wartime journalism, he no doubt reflected sadly on the freedom of his patrols aboard *Pilar*. The patrols of *Pilar* were a metaphor for both individuality and creative writing just as London was a metaphor for bureaucratic journalism. If the poem was designed to arouse Mary's sympathy, maybe it worked, or if it was designed to magnify the extent of his anti-U-boat adventures, maybe that worked too. But the only specific reference to Mary in a rather long piece describes Hemingway in his room waiting for Mary to come "small voiced and lovely" to heal his loneliness and his sad nostalgia for his boat and crew. It's not hard to believe that that may have appealed to Mary's emotions, whether she thought of it as poetry or not. And it does not seem that Mary's resistance to Hemingway's impetuous and aggressive seduction tactics was all that stout. Sexually, she was no *Festung Europa*. And by today's standards (or indeed in the context of wartime London), it's hardly surprising.

❖

The ship that Hemingway boarded to cross to Normandy on D-Day—a troop carrier—was called the USS *Dorothea L. Dix*. It seems quite possible that Hemingway knew that the woman the ship was named for was a nineteenth-century activist who lobbied ceaselessly to establish asylums for the insane. Whether that caused an ironic smile or two is not known. But it sounds plausible.

The *Dix* was part of Assault Force O—the ships that would take the troops to Omaha Beach and then provide gunfire support. She was one of some seven hundred ships heading for Omaha. On board the attack transports and assault craft were 35,000 troops who would make the landing. They would be taken ashore in a variety of landing craft, many of which were also carried on board the transports. Other larger landing craft were making the cross-channel trip on their own steam (or more accurately, diesel). Once Force O arranged itself in a single file in order to move through the German underwater minefields, the column would stretch out to twenty miles.[19] Other task forces were heading for Utah Beach and for the three beaches to be assaulted by the British and Canadians—Juno, Gold, and Sword. This naval phase of the attack was code-named Neptune. And, as is commonly known, the attack against the beaches themselves was code-named Overlord.

It was assumed that there would be a dense German minefield that was approximately thirty miles off the invasion beaches and perhaps as much as ten miles across. There were three types of German mines: contact, acoustic, and magnetic. Contact mines detonated when a vessel brushed against its "horns." These necessarily floated at or near the surface. Acoustic mines detonated when their listening device (hydrophone) detected sounds of a ship's propeller. They could lie on the ocean bottom or be tethered. Magnetic mines detonated when they detected the magnetic field of a passing ship (which is the reason minesweeper hulls were wooden). The Germans had also developed a pressure mine that exploded when it detected the change in water pressure made by a ship passing overhead. Few of these were laid off Normandy, however, because Hitler, ever fascinated with wonder weapons, was afraid the Allies might capture one and learn its secrets.[20]

Leading all these convoys as they approached the German minefield were the minesweepers—255 all told, divided into flotillas that operated abreast to sweep channels. To everyone's surprise and delight, the German minefield in the Channel was not nearly as infested as was feared. Only twenty-nine mines were detected and destroyed as the enormous armada sailed on to Normandy.[21] Even so, as commander of the entire naval operation, Rear Admiral Alan Kirk said: "It can be said without fear of contradiction that minesweeping was the keystone of arch of this operation . . . The performance of the [mostly British and Canadian] minesweepers can only be described as magnificent."[22]

A minesweeper's primary technique is to drag a paravane off both sides of the ship at roughly 45 degrees at a distance of a hundred yards or so. The paravane is a torpedo-shaped device that is armed with saw teeth that slice through a mine's anchoring cable, so that the mine floats to the surface where it is destroyed by gunfire.

Usually the mines had to be tethered to the bottom of the sea, because otherwise they would merely drift with the current. Minesweeping was a hazardous business under any circumstances but the sweepers leading the way, in the dark, toward Omaha Beach had to clear not only channels for the attack transports but also zones for the gunfire support ships that would not anchor for fear of providing too good a target for enemy artillery. The channels were then marked with lighted "dan buoys." Interestingly, once the ships were through the offshore minefields and once they began sweeping lanes for the assault craft and zones for the gunfire support ships, they found no mines at all. This may seem odd given Rommel's dedication to land mines. But as the assault craft would soon discover, there were plenty of waterproofed land mines attached to the underwater obstructions, explosives that also included artillery shells with contact fuses.

The troop transports congregated eleven miles offshore. (The troops would therefore have a long and miserable ride into the beach—miserable because the flat-bottom assault boats wallowed heavily in the relatively rough sea. A great many men were violently seasick.) The gunfire support lanes approached as close as three miles, and once it was seen that destroyer gunfire was needed, some came as close as a thousand yards. Destroyers have a shallower draft than battleships and cruisers. A thousand yards is virtually point-blank for a naval gun. But the problem again was, many of the German artillery emplacements were so cunningly camouflaged and protected that finding them and silencing them was a continuing problem during the initial days of the invasion.

If a destroyer did spot a target, or if the naval gunfire support on the beach spotted them, the gunfire could be and was deadly. The way naval gunfire is managed with a visible (by eye or radar) target is as follows: at a high point in the ship there is something called a director, which is a steel enclosure that can accommodate one man. It resembles a gun turret, minus the gun. Atop the director is a radar dish. Inside there is an officer who focuses the radar on a visible target, on the sea, the land, or in the air. Once the radar locks on to the target, it sends a signal to the guns by means of an analog computer, and the guns turn to match the range and angle of the target. This of course is different from the gunfire support that is aimed at a spot on a grid map and corrected by spotters on shore or in the air. That is a more complicated problem, because the director's radar is not useable. What's more, the range is greater and the ship is moving, subject to currents and wave action. Further, when the target is well beyond visual range or hidden behind bluffs or in forests, there is the problem of potential casualties through friendly fire. As Admiral Harold Stark wrote in his report of naval gunfire operations: "Every firing ship was provided with an Army artillery officer, charged with maintaining up-to-date information about the position of Allied troops and with determining the desirability of firing at any given target. The organization worked as follows: a) The Shore Fire Control Party made contact with his firing ship by radio link and designated a target by reference to a grid. b) The Army liaison officer decided whether it was safe to fire at that target. c) The ship itself controlled the fire. d) The Shore Fire Control Party observed the fall of shot and corrected fire by means of a clock code."[23]

This is a sensible process, but it didn't always work as planned. In the case of one village, Colleville-sur-Mer, which was at the end of the draw at Fox Green Beach, the navy destroyed the town, not knowing that units of the US Army were fighting there. As one US company commander wrote afterward: "At 4:00 we were devastated with an artillery barrage from the navy. It leveled the town, absolutely leveled it, and in so doing we suffered the worst casualties we had the whole day—not from the enemy but from our own navy."[24] The Navy Shore Fire Control Party had been killed and their radio destroyed; the navy had fired on the Colleville-sur-Mer church steeple thinking it was an enemy observation post.

The key to success in the Normandy invasion was surprise. That such a massive effort involving so many people could remain a secret is nothing short of astonishing. But it did. Maintaining surprise, however, meant that the early morning naval bombardment of the German positions was necessarily short, perhaps thirty minutes. It was feared that a prolonged bombardment would give the Germans time to rush reinforcements before the Allied assault groups could reach the beach in sufficient numbers to overwhelm the defenders. That was certainly a potential danger. There was also the question of the tide. H-Hour was at 6:30 A.M., just after low water, so that the obstacles would be exposed. Finally, the troops would need as much daylight as possible to achieve their objectives: breaking through the German beach defenses and surging into the countryside beyond.

Along with the naval bombardment there was to be a massive aerial bombardment from the Air Corps' fleet of B-24s—450 of them in all. The B-24, also known as the Liberator, was an American four-engine heavy bomber armed with ten fifty-caliber machine guns mounted in turrets and in the waist, and capable of carrying five thousand pounds of bombs. The Germans would thereby be hit with devastating blows from the sea and the air. Unfortunately, early cloud cover meant that the huge air force bombing campaign that was to precede the invasion by the narrowest of margins was ineffective, because bombardiers were reluctant to release their bombs for fear of hitting the assault craft that were streaming toward the shore. As a result the bombs landed well beyond the German lines. Neither the naval guns nor the air corps bombers had the hoped-for effect of softening up the Germans. To make matters worse, the German artillery, undamaged by the naval and aerial bombardment, came alive and proved the axiom that the most dangerous part of an amphibious invasion is during the approach from the sea.

It would be up to the army, infantry, and engineers primarily to fight their way through Hitler's western wall. And they would have to do so without much in the way of support from armor or artillery. The tanks that were scheduled to come ashore were so called DD tanks, standing for "duplex drive." They were specially fitted with normal drive trains as well as two propellers that would move the tank through water. Flotation was provided by a strange canvas bathtub-like structure that was raised just before the tank was launched from a landing craft. This odd device meant that the freeboard (the distance between the water and deck) was only a few feet, which further meant that these things were not in the least seaworthy in anything other than an almost flat calm. These were to precede the infantry assault boats and would be launched from assault craft some two miles from the beach. The chop was too heavy for most of the tanks and many promptly sank when they drove off the lowered ramps of the assault boats. In the tank battalion assigned to the western edge of the beach, twenty-seven of the thirty-two tanks that were launched from the sea (at a range of six thousand yards) sank. The enterprising officers of the battalion landing on the eastern edge of the beach decided not to launch at sea and carried their tanks directly to the beach. But not nearly enough tanks made it to the beach, and the infantry that was depending on the tanks to support their landing suffered from the fact that many units had only small arms—rifles and grenades—to attack entrenched and hardly visible German defenders, who were firing down at them with machine guns, mortars, and the terrifyingly accurate 88mm cannons. Further, the artillery that was being delivered primarily by DUKWs, an amphibious truck, was also mostly lost, either in the heavy seas or to German artillery.

As mentioned, Hemingway was initially on the *Dorothea L. Dix*. Her captain, W. I. Leahy, wrote this after action report on the *Dix's* assault boats:

FROM: COMMANDING OFFICER USS DOROTHEA L. DIX
(OMAHA BEACH), BOAT GROUP COMMANDER

Summary of Landing Reports of Boat Officers and Boat Crews Attached to this vessel

The wave of six boats shoved off at 0542 to Fox Green Beach and landed at 0725 on a rising tide. All boats landed together in the midst of many obstructions. Heavy surf running almost parallel to beach caused boat to swamp when ramp was lowered. All troops got ashore through water approximately waist deep. Troops showed no hesitation in leaving boats, as machine gunfire and larger explosions (believed to be mines and 88's) made them run for cover. Boat #12 was believed to have hit an obstruction causing a hole in the stern, as that part sank first even though the ramp was down. Crew abandoned boat as it could not be taken off the beach. No salvage boats were seen.

A control boat (a PC, but not flying a Zero Flag) was contacted on the way in, but it was marked only by flags from the yardarm and was hard to identify. No marked channels were seen, and at time of landing no beach obstructions had been removed. All of the designated types were plainly visible on the beach and down into the water. Many carried mines.

The crew moved up the beach to the left, where they joined the crew of #10 boat under a sand dune at a point where cliffs begin to raise from the beach. From there they observed that the beach was closed as only one wave of 2 MCAs came in about 0830. Both of these were blown up in the water either by mines or 88's, but it was believed that most of the troops got ashore. Finally a demolition unit, (time of arrival 1500) arrived and began removing obstacles and mines. By evening a channel 100 yards wide had been cleared. There were no beach markers or ranges to come in on. Destroyers continually fired on gun emplacements and machine gun nests on the hill behind the beach.

There were many casualties, boat crews carried stretchers and administered what first aid they could during the afternoon. There was a noticeable lack of medical aid.

Approximately 15 tanks were knocked out on the beach, about 5 LCVPs broached to, as well as one unidentified LCI(L) and an LCT, which had apparently been hit.

Boat #3: Experienced difficulty alongside *Empire Anvil* because of hooks on davit falls and poor lines. Took aboard approximately 36 men, 2 mortars and a radio with other small gear. A First and Second Lieutenant were aboard.

The entire wave of six boats landed on the left flank of Fox Green Beach at approximately 0725. Troops left craft quickly and in good order, leaving some small gear in the boat.

Many obstructions were seen, but none were hit and boat retracted without difficulty although surrounded by machine gun fire. They observed all the obstructions upon which they had been briefed as well as a gate type affair which appeared to be a steel girder mounted athwart two triangular shaped uprights. On the center of this bar was a white disc believed to be a mine.

No control boat was recognized and there were no marked channels or beach markers. Demolition and salvage units were not present.

They observed boats #7, 10, 12 sunk on the beach but because of heavy machine gun fire were unable to give assistance. Only the crew of #12 was still in the boat. It appeared that LCVP#7 hit a mine.[25]

The details of Hemingway's trip to Fox Green are a little sketchy. Of course, there is his own report written for *Collier's*—more on this later. But at some point on the journey across the Channel he was transferred to the *Empire Anvil*—another troop carrier. In the morning of D-Day he clambered down the rope nets, despite a throbbing head and knees still stiff and sore from the accident, and dropped into a thirty-six-foot LCVP—landing craft, vehicle, personnel. It's not entirely clear whether this boat was from the *Empire Anvil* or from the *Dix*. (Leahy's report mentions a *Dix* boat loading men from the *Empire Anvil*.) The *Anvil*, as a British ship, employed LCAs, landing craft assault, which were not the same thing as LCVPs. And the crews of these units would most likely be British sailors, not Americans, even though on Omaha Beach the troops going ashore would all be American. In Hemingway's *Collier's* story, the CO of his three-boat unit was "Andy" Anderson, an American American Lieutenant Junior Grade. (The navy equivalent of an army First Lieutenant.) So there is a bit of a mystery there, and Hemingway detractors, of whom there were many, would have been quick to wonder aloud about these apparent questions in his story, if they noticed them.

In any event, Hemingway was on his way for an eleven-mile run through choppy water in a craft that is almost flat-bottomed and shallow-drafted, for obvious reasons, and therefore not easy to handle, especially in choppy water and windy conditions. It was also light, since the bulk of the boat was made of plywood. The bow landing ramp was steel. Further, there was the notorious east current in the Bay of the Seine, usually running at four knots, a current that easily pushed landing craft to the side even though the compass course seemed to be steady. The crew consisted of enlisted men: a coxswain, an engineer, a signalman, and a gunner (although Hemingway says his boat had no guns). But there was a naval officer aboard in charge of the flotilla, however large or otherwise. His job was to ensure that the boats under his command hit the right beach at the right time and landed together. Of course, this was an almost impossible job, in the face of wind, waves, current, and surf, and the more important facts that the Germans were firing artillery and mortar shells, and that the shore was a maze of mined obstacles. What's more, the beach objectives were obscured by the naval bombardment. The gunfire set the sea grass on fire so that, looking at the dense smoke, the officers commanding the waves of assault boats were unsure and confused about where they were supposed to land.

In Hemingway's *Collier's* story, he makes the point that Anderson was an experienced officer who had made amphibious landings in North Africa, Sicily, and Salerno. He goes on to say that the men had confidence in him.

"Voyage to Victory" is an important story, for a number of reasons. Indeed, none other than Admiral Samuel Eliot Morison called it "the best account yet written by a passenger in a LCVP."[26] Morison, it should be noted, was, after the war, a professor and historian at Harvard and the author of a number of highly readable histories, including his massive multivolume history of the US Navy in World War II.

The story accurately reflects the confusion of the voyage to the beach. Once in artillery and machine gun range the little boat comes under enemy fire and also observes other landing craft that were hit and sinking. Casualties from mines as well as artillery are strewn all along the waterside; the obstacles are thick, and many are tipped with mines and shells armed with contact fuses. Several times Andy stops to ask other boats for directions to Fox Green. No one is sure. No one except Hemingway, that is. He had studied the beach maps and was sure they were opposite Fox Green. Many accounts of Hemingway in a war zone mention his talent for reading and judging terrain, so this rings true. But there are some regrettable false notes. Anderson asks Hemingway to use his (Hemingway's) binoculars to check the color of a flag, presumably on one of the guide boats. Hemingway pulls out his pocket-sized Zeiss glasses and reports the color is green.

I think it is fair to say that no naval officer in command of any vessel would think of getting underway without wearing powerful binoculars strapped around his neck. Yes, the spray might make it difficult to keep them clean, but that would not change matters. The whole problem of attacking Fox Green or any D-Day beach was recognizing the right beach and working your way through gaps in the obstacles. That was Anderson's job and responsibility. An experienced officer like Anderson would hardly rely on an inexperienced Hemingway with his miniature glasses to assist him. (This was Hemingway's first amphibious action.) Nor would he have to borrow Hemingway's glasses to survey the beach. It's hard to avoid the conclusion that this was a device to give Hemingway a larger role, not as a journalist and observer but rather as a leading character in this drama.

Further, Anderson asks his coxswain the course he's steering. "Two Twenty, sir" is the answer, to which the somewhat edgy Anderson retorts, "Then steer two twenty, damn it. Don't steer all over the whole damn ocean." That is not how an officer gives course orders to a coxswain or helmsman. The correct method is to say "Two Two Zero." The navy is very precise about this, and even the greenest ensign knows that. A civilian fishing boat operator like Hemingway, however, might very well think in terms of "two twenty" terminology. What's more, Anderson's snappish order may have been designed to suggest that he was nervous, perhaps in contrast to his notable passenger. Hemingway cannot resist making suggestions. While they were milling around offshore asking other boats where they were, Hemingway tells Anderson that he should take Hemingway's glasses and check the beach but not tell the soldiers what he sees. Anderson does, and apparently disturbed at what he sees, he shakes his head and hands the glasses back to Hemingway. Hemingway then suggests that they turn to the right a little and check that area for a possible landing site. He says he's pretty sure they can get in there. The army officer is unsure of whether to go in or not. Hemingway then says to Anderson to talk to the army officer and "get it straight."

No officer in command of a vessel would take orders from a civilian, regardless of how famous. He might ask someone's opinion but would resent and ignore anything approaching, "Talk to him and get it straight."

There's quite a lot of this—Hemingway thrusting himself into the action, at least in the retelling. It's fair to wonder whether it really happened this way. Maybe it did. But despite Admiral Morison's remark, these scenes seem to strike quite a few false notes that undermine the otherwise useful depiction of the dangers and confusion of that day. (Morison was the navy's official historian, but his comments suggest that he had limited, if any, experience as an officer involved in an amphibious attack.)

Finally they got to Fox Green and unloaded their troops. Anderson and the crew of the LCVP then took Hemingway back to the *Dorothea L. Dix*. The *Dix* returned to London that night to collect another shipment of supplies and troops for a return to Normandy; Hemingway returned to the Dorchester and Mary Welsh. He had not set foot on Fox Green, but he had been under fire. And he had seen plenty of dead men floating or stretched out on the beach as well as burning tanks and sinking assault craft. He heard and saw the massive naval gunfire from the USS *Texas*, the USS *Arkansas*, and others. He had watched destroyers coming within a half mile of the beach and blasting German machine gun nests. The actual story was dramatic enough. But by making himself a primary character, Hemingway got in the way of the important things. Unlike Liebling, who also hit the beach aboard an amphibious vessel on D-Day, Hemingway could not resist becoming part of the story. Indeed, he ended the *Collier's* article with: ". . . if you want to know how it was in an LCVP on D-Day when we took Fox Green beach and Easy Red beach on the Sixth of June, 1944, then this is as near as I can come to it." In fairness the "we" could refer to the US troops; but Hemingway also knew it could do double duty.

In the end, "Voyage to Victory" is an important story not only because of his description of the action and the confusion of war, but also because it reflects some of the negative opinions about Hemingway's personality and its effect on his writing. These seemed to be only two camps: those who liked and often loved him, and those, like Andy Rooney and more than a few others, who detested his way of pushing himself forward, always wanting to be in charge or to be the center of attention. No one, it seems, was ambivalent about him. Jealousy and competitive spirit certainly informed these attitudes. But some sincerely disliked him and his style, not only him personally but also his writing. And during the next months of war, this pattern of behavior would be repeated again and again. And it would show in the articles he wrote for *Collier's*.

Several days later Hemingway was working on his story when he was visited by Roald Dahl, who had finished his assignment in the United States. Dahl found Hemingway alone in his room working on his invasion story. Dahl wanted to see it and was embarrassed by his own reaction; he thought it was poor. In order to hide his true opinion he asked Hemingway why he had left out a story he had told Dahl about the expression on the face of a soldier trying to get out of a burning tank. Hemingway responded in effect that the scene was too good to waste on *Collier's*, implying that it was reserved for future fiction. Here again he had the distinction between creative work and mere journalism firmly in mind.[27]

In his *Paris Review* interview with George Plimpton, Plimpton said: "You once wrote in the *Transatlantic Review* that the only reason for writing journalism was to be well paid. You said 'And when you destroy the valuable things you have by writing about them, you want to get big money for them.' Do you think of writing as a type of self-destruction?"

And Hemingway responded: "I do not remember ever writing that. But it sounds silly and violent enough for me to have said it to avoid having to bite on the nail and make a sensible statement. I certainly do not think of writing as a type of self-destruction, though journalism, after a point has been reached, can be a daily self-destruction for a serious creative writer."[28]

It's reasonable to assume that Hemingway was not only gathering experience for future fiction but that he had already begun shaping it. Simply reporting what he saw on D-Day apparently was not enough. That would have been mere journalism. Or as fellow correspondent Bill Walton said, "He was one of my closest friends, but you should never believe everything he said is true. He made his life out of writing fiction. He had a very hard time deciding where it ended and where the truth began."[29] It might be argued that Walton had that backward—that Hemingway had a hard time deciding where the truth ended and the fiction began. In his short story "Soldier's Home," he describes the main character, a returning veteran: "His lies were quite unimportant lies and consisted of attributing to himself things other men had seen, done or heard of, and stating as facts certain apocryphal incidents familiar to all soldiers."[30] Martha later dreamed up a word— *apocryphiar*—to describe someone who concocts or alters a story to display himself as the hero. She thought it applied to Hemingway perfectly. Deep down, Hemingway apparently agreed. After a while the difference between reality and its emergence through imagination would seem a little more difficult to determine.

Later in the Plimpton interview Hemingway also said:

"The most essential gift for a good writer is a built-in, shockproof, shit detector. This is the writer's radar and all great writers have had it."[31]

Did his detector fail him the day he wrote that story? More than a little, it must be said. Eminent critic Edmund Wilson said: "Something dreadful seems to happen to Hemingway as soon as he begins to write in the first person. Among his creations, he is certainly his own worst-drawn character, and he is his own worst commentator. His very prose style goes to pot."

Or this from James Salter, again quoting Wilson: "For reasons which I cannot attempt to explain, something frightful seems to happen to Hemingway as soon as he begins to write in the first person. In his fiction, the conflicting elements of his personality, the emotional situations which obsess him, are externalized and objectified; and the result is an art which is severe, intense and deeply serious. But as soon as he talks in his own person, he seems to lose all his capacity for self-criticism and is likely to become fatuous or maudlin. . . . In his own character of Ernest Hemingway, the Old Master of Key West, he has a way of sounding silly. Perhaps he is beginning to be imposed on by the American publicity legend which has been created about him."[32]

Wilson apparently forgot that *The Sun Also Rises* and *A Farewell to Arms* were written in the first person, but he was referring to Hemingway's later nonfiction efforts, such as *The Green Hills of Africa*, in which Hemingway himself is the main character. Reading Hemingway's World War II reporting for *Collier's*, Wilson would most likely have reiterated his earlier assessment. On the other hand, Wilson must have read *A Moveable Feast*, a collection of some of Hemingway's best writing. Writing in the first person, Hemingway quite naturally is the central character in his memoirs of early days in Paris. And while many have pointed out the level of maliciousness in his portraits of his friends and acquaintances (most notably Scott Fitzgerald), few if any are critical of his writing style.

To Hemingway's disgust, Martha Gellhorn had actually landed on Omaha Beach. Ever intrepid, she talked her way on to a civilian hospital ship in London, and locked herself in a bathroom until the ship got underway. She would witness the landings from the ship— or at least the departure of the assault boats leaving from the other transports. Soon the wounded were being brought back to the ship, and Martha pitched in to help, interpreting for the German prisoners, bringing water to the thirsty, making corned beef sandwiches. That night she went in with the ambulance teams and waded ashore. The fighting was still going on beyond the beach, and the noise was terrific. Her notes read: "Village really smashed—church like a collapsed paper bag."[33] To get to the village she had to pick her way along a narrow path that had been cleared of mines. Hemingway could never forgive her for beating him to Normandy.[34]

On returning to London she was arrested by the military police for crossing to Normandy without permission. She was more or less imprisoned in a US nurses' enclosure and told she could not go to France until the nurses were sent. She escaped by crawling under the fence that encircled the enclosure. Subsequently, she lost her reporters' credentials. Biographer Caroline Moorehead writes:

"Having lost any form of military accreditation, as well as travel papers and ration entitlements, because of the illicit crossing to France, she would spend the remaining year of the war in Europe, sometimes in uniform, sometimes out of it, ducking and dodging from front to front, using her energy and charm to win over officers into allowing her to travel with their regiments, scrounging lifts and filing stories whenever she could cajole wireless operators into giving her a line. Her looks, her obvious courage, and her utter disregard for authority came in very handy. Far fewer doors, she later admitted would have been opened for a man."[35]

Just after D-Day she saw Hemingway briefly in London and then went off to cover the fighting in Italy. That was pretty much the end of things between them. They would meet a couple of more times, the last being to discuss the details of the divorce. None of those meetings was without rancor and bitterness. That is hardly surprising. And their subsequent written comments are often venomous. As an example, Hemingway wrote: "Good night Marty. Sleep well my beloved phony and pretentious bitch."[36] She was more restrained in her memories of the relationship, but she did not sugarcoat her opinion of Hemingway, the man: "I hated his toughness for I know it for what it is: the brave do not have to be cruel; the brave can be gentle. The toughness is a pose to get away with being nasty and ungenerous . . . In Spain he was not tough; he was kind. He was never kind to me, even there, because I was the woman he wanted, which means the woman he intended absolutely to own, crush, eat alive."[37]

Coming back from Italy and joining the war in France, she had an affair with Major General James Gavin, the commander of the 82nd

Airborne. He wanted to divorce his wife and marry Martha, but she refused. She would be useless and unhappy as an army wife, and she told him so in a tearful letter.[38] She would go on to other affairs and even, oddly, another marriage. But "it was never any good." She was a lovely, talented, and fiercely ambitious loner, a combination that made it difficult for those who ever loved her.

CHAPTER SIX

"I was already in a state familiar with those who tangled with Ernest—I was acting against my better judgment."
—Group Captain Peter Wykeham-Barnes, RAF

"I've had it, chaps. You go on."
—Squadron Leader Joseph Berry, RAF

The Treaty of Versailles that ended World War I placed austere limits on Germany's armed forces and weaponry. The army was limited to 100,000 men, U-boats were prohibited, along with warplanes, and the navy was severely reduced. Not surprisingly, Germany chafed under these restrictions, and even before Hitler came to power German scientists began working on weapons the detested Treaty did not mention: guided missiles. Obviously a guided missile is primarily an offensive weapon, certainly at that early stage of development. And Hitler, ever wanting to be on the offensive, endorsed the development programs even as he began the process of ignoring the Treaty and rearming Germany. Ultimately, there would be two such weapons: a pilotless jet aircraft, also known as a flying bomb, and an actual rocket. The two weapons became known as V-1 (the flying bomb) and V-2 (the rocket). The *V* in both cases stood for *Vergeltungswaffen*—Vengeance Weapon. The vengeance was for the bombing attacks by Allied aircraft on German cities. The story of the appalling firestorm attack on Dresden is well-known, thanks in part to Kurt Vonnegut, but the July 1943 attack on Hamburg resulted in similar firestorms and the deaths of 50,000 civilians. Berlin was also hit, and the attacks against major German cities seemed almost constant, with the Americans coming in daylight and the British at night. These attacks involved sometimes over a thousand Allied bombers. Ostensibly the attacks were aimed at German manufacturing plants and were designed to destroy Germany's capacity to wage war by crippling her industry and transportation systems. And to some extent that was working. But a World War II high-altitude bomber was anything but precise in its targeting. Even the Allies found that out when their planes accidentally bombed their own troops. The technology simply did not allow for precision targeting and strikes. Then, too, there is the inescapable conclusion that the Allied attacks were also designed to destroy civilian morale, by destroying large swaths of civilians, as well as their homes and domestic infrastructure. A starving, homeless people, it was felt, could hardly continue to support a disastrous government policy that was destroying the country.

Having lost the Battle of Britain and now suffering devastating attacks, the Germans switched aircraft production priorities to fighter planes in order to defend their home skies. There were not enough bombers left to make massive retaliatory strikes on British targets, although London was now and then still subject to German night attacks. But the once vaunted Luftwaffe was a shell of its former self. During the Battle of Britain RAF Spitfires and Hurricanes alone shot down 1,185 German bombers and fighters.[1] Even so, Hitler wanted to hit back at the Allies, and the new V weapons were going to be the primary means to that end.

The V-1 was a small airplane with a jet engine mounted on its back and extending over the tail. The plane was 25 feet long and had a wingspan of 17½ feet. It used standard gasoline as fuel and had a top speed of 400 miles per hour. Range figures vary from 130 miles to 200 miles. In the nose it carried one ton of explosives. It was easy to build and inexpensive. German engineers had been working on a jet-propelled fighter plane (and ultimately produced a few), and no doubt much of their experience was useful in the design of the V-1. Unlike the rocket program that had been underway since the early 1930s, the V-1 program was completed in under nine months, by the end of 1942. Still to come, however, was further testing, the training of firing crews, and the location and development of launch sites. Furthermore, design flaws kept popping up. Most serious of course was failure to launch. The V-1 rumbled up its ramp and then immediately crashed, causing damage to the site and the personnel operating it. It would take another year or so to iron out these flaws so that the planes could be mass produced. As a result the actual launching of the first flying bombs toward London would not occur until little more than a week after D-Day in Normandy.

The V-1 was launched by a catapult, in much the same way as modern aircraft are launched from an aircraft carrier. The difference however is that instead of a flat deck, the V-1 was fired up along a rail on a sloping 120-foot ramp. The engine was started, the catapult fired, and the plane flew off, up, and on its way to London. Inside the plane was a simple gyroscope that kept the aircraft trimmed and an autopilot that kept the plane on a preset course. But the V-1 was not a sophisticated guided missile. It was simply aimed in the direction of London and sent on its way. It could not maneuver or change course, nor could anyone know where one might come down. Precise targeting was not possible. The launching sites for the first phases of the attack on London and southern England were in the Pas-de-Calais—the place most German strategists believed would be the site of the Allied invasion.

Historian David Johnson describes the V-1's propulsion system:

"At the front of the engine housing was a system of intake flaps. These flaps opened at the beginning of the engine's cycle, drawing air into the combustion chamber and mixing the air with 80 octane fuel. In the second stage the flaps closed and the fuel oxygen mixture was ignited. A burst of hot exhaust shot out from the rear of the engine with a tremendous flash, pushing the machine forward. Immediately after ignition, the flaps opened again, forcing air into the combustion chamber and repeating the cycle. All this sounds long and drawn out, but this simple jet could complete up to 500 cycles every minute, giving the Flying Bomb speeds well over 300 miles an hour. [Actually, almost 400 miles per hour.] The engine's open-close, open-close system also gave the Flying Bomb its distinctive *duv-duv-duv* sound that Londoners would soon come to recognize."[2]

That sound would abruptly cease when the bomb reached a random location somewhere in the hundred-square-mile expanse of Greater London. In the nose of the plane was a small propeller-like device. After so many revolutions, calculated and set by the crew firing the plane, the propeller tripped the plane's autopilot and sent the nose into a steep dive. At that point the engine cut out, and what had been the sound of a strange motorcycle suddenly disappeared, and there came the sounds of silence to be followed quickly by an explosion occurring somewhere in the city.

If that explosion hit a military target, it was quite by accident. More likely it was in a row of houses. Hitler did not care one way or the other. The bombs the British and Americans were dropping on Germany were hardly more discriminating.

The ever thoughtful George Orwell described living in London during the V-1 attacks: ". . . unlike most other projectiles, it gives you time to think. What is your first reaction when you hear that droning, zooming noise? Inevitably, it is a hope that the noise *won't stop*. You want to hear the bomb pass safely overhead and die away into the distance before the engine cuts out. In other words, you are hoping that it will fall on somebody else. So also when you dodge a shell or an ordinary bomb—but in that case you have only about five seconds to take cover and no time to speculate on the bottomless selfishness of the human being."[3]

David Johnson writes that this cutting out of the engine was a design flaw, because as soon as the plane started down to earth the fuel sloshed back toward the stern and away from the combustion chamber. Maybe. But it's hard to believe that the German engineers would have overlooked that problem. It seems so elementary. Maybe they did, but it seems more reasonable to believe that the engine cutoff was part of the design. After all, they tested the weapon for more than a year before deploying it. Surely they would have noticed the problem, if it was a problem, during that time. Certainly, as a psychological weapon, the sudden silence was a terror bonus to the Germans—as well as a reliable method of causing the weapon to crash. After all, they were not and could not be shooting at specific targets—the weapon was not controllable beyond a few calculations of course and range. Destruction anyplace in greater London would suit Hitler's purposes. Whether the engineers intended the engine cutoff or not is open to question. But surely the randomness of the devastating explosions was equally disheartening to the Londoners. From Hitler's point of view, that was sufficient. Of course he would prefer if the flying bomb hit a military target, but that was simply a matter of luck. The *V* in the V-1 stood for vengeance, and that was the primary object. Let English wives and children and greengrocers and accountants and bankers and all the rest of the working people of England have another dose of a new Blitz. Let them fear the terrifying silence when the engines cut off.

At the Volkswagen plant outside of Hamburg, the engineers had finally resolved the nagging problems, and the V-1s were ready for mass production, to put it mildly. Between April 1944 and the first of July, five thousand flying bombs were produced. Meanwhile, in the Pas-de-Calais, 140 steel and concrete launching ramps, all pointing toward London, were ready to receive the bombs. (The exact number of ramps is in dispute. Some reports, such as Andrew Roberts's, list only 92.)[4] These sites were visible from the air, so they were surrounded by a formidable array of antiaircraft artillery. To meet Hitler's increasingly hysterical demands for action, the opening launch site fired off the ten V-1s they had on hand. Four crashed after takeoff, two others crashed in the Channel, and the remaining four sped on their way to England, where one hit London at Bethnal Green, killing three people and destroying a railroad bridge. The others fell in the countryside and did little damage.[5]

On June 16, 1944, Hitler got his long-awaited spectacular attack. Two hundred forty-four V-1's were launched against London. Forty-five of them crashed at some point before reaching land, but the rest made the flight successfully. Flying at 2,500 feet the planes were easily visible to England's radar defenses on the coast, and so the alert could be sounded in London. And since the firing went on through the day, the tired Londoners realized that they were entering a new phase of the war. It seemed there was never an "All Clear"; they were under seemingly constant alert. At first they didn't understand what was happening, but they soon figured out that these flying bombs or "doodlebugs," as they came to be called, were a frightening new weapon. Londoners could see them flying at low altitudes, often coming straight up the Thames.

Carrying a ton of high explosives, the V-1 exploded on impact, and the explosion sent blast waves out in concentric circles. These blast waves were themselves deadly, so great was the speed and force of the air, perhaps analogous to a deadly tornado. The waves were literally supersonic. It is probably obvious that the blast phenomenon was not unique to the V-1. Any weapon delivering high explosives created the same kind of blast. The extent and the range of the blast depended on the amount and type of high explosives. At some point in the campaign the Germans replaced the Amatol (a mixture of TNT and ammonium nitrate) with Trialen, a mixture of TNT, powdered aluminum, and RDX, or cyclonite, that had two times the blast effect of the earlier warhead.[6] Ernie Pyle wrote that soldiers in the front lines, who were subject to high-explosive artillery, did not buckle their chin straps because the blast effect could rip their helmets off and break their necks. And of course those same waves would fling debris at incredible speeds, killing or maiming anyone in their path and weakening or collapsing buildings or rows of houses. A common story was of a Londoner, the front of whose house was shattered so that all the rooms were exposed. Flying glass was a major cause of injuries and deaths. The blast had a radius of some four hundred to six hundred yards. Of course, the farther out from the epicenter, the lesser the damage from blast waves and debris. But many victims who were at the epicenter were never found. Others were killed or wounded by collapsing buildings, victims of what had been their own homes or offices. The waves of blast also created a vacuum behind them, which was equally dangerous, so that some of the same debris that had been thrown outward initially came speeding back toward the epicenter. Several British WAAFs (Women's Auxiliary Air Force) were standing by a window when a V-1 hit nearby. The vacuum following the blast sucked them out the window and threw them to their deaths on the street below.[7] Fires were another source of injury and destruction, as the intense heat from the explosion met flammable materials or hit gas mains. And although the V-1 carried no shrapnel per se, the metal fuselage, engine, and wings served as a substitute.

"Damage to targets of military importance—factories, railways, communications centers—[was] . . . nothing to be shrugged off. [On one day] . . . no fewer than eleven factories were hit by buzz bombs. The essential war services were also thrown into a turmoil. Four telephone exchanges had been destroyed or badly damaged; gas supplies, water supplies, and electricity were cut off to various sections of

London, and several hospitals had been hit and evacuated. On top of this seven railway stations, including Victoria, London Bridge, and Charing Cross had been closed because of bomb damage."[8]

And it was not just the physical destruction. There was so much damage to repair that it sapped some of the manpower, energy, and much of the morale of the city—morale that had been high because of the D-Day landings. Plus it was hard to get any work done in war industries, because of the seemingly constant alerts. Further, simply getting the necessary materials to make repairs was increasingly difficult. Glass for windows, for example, was scarce.

The V-1 attacks started mid-June and lasted until early September 1944. During that time more than 2,400 flying bombs hit London.[9] Civilian casualties amounted to over 6,000 dead and 18,000 wounded. War production including both actual damage to facilities and lost time from alerts cost the British roughly $2,0270,000,000 (in 2015 dollars). And many Londoners were left homeless with little hope of a quick restoration. Not surprisingly, people began to evacuate the city, just as they had done during the Blitz. Approximately one million Londoners ultimately left the city, and of those who remained many criticized Churchill's government for a lack of effective response.

But there was an evolving strategy to deal with the V-1s. It involved a three-layer defense of the homeland coupled with bombing attacks on the launching, production, and storage sites, and also attacking the transportation system, mostly rail, between the storage sites and the Pas-de-Calais. Trains heading west were strafed by fighter-bombers; this was all part of the D-Day operation designed to prevent the Germans from resupplying their troops, including the troops at the launching sites. And in a story that Hollywood would appreciate, the French Resistance around Paris discovered that the Germans were storing V-1s in a cave north of Paris. The cave was impervious to traditional bombing. The RAF called on their elite Dam Buster unit, Number 617 Squadron. Composed of personnel not only from Great Britain but also Canada, Australia, and New Zealand, the group had originally been formed to attack German dams that supplied power to the factories in the Ruhr valley, using the celebrated "bouncing bomb." (That attack was successful, but costly. Eight of the sixteen bombers that went in were shot down. Coming in low and straight they were easy targets.) The Dam Busters were experts at low-altitude bombing, and on the Fourth of July seventeen Lancaster bombers hit the caves with devastating effect. They dropped massive six-ton "Tall Boy" bombs with delayed fuses that let the bombs penetrate the earth before exploding. Three days later they attacked again, collapsing the caves and burying hundreds of V-1s and not a few workers. That attack was the most effective bombing raid against the V-1s. It significantly reduced the number of attacks on London, but unfortunately the lull caused by a lack of supply lasted only a week. Other attacks against the launching sites were often ineffective and expensive in terms of planes and crews lost. The ramps that were destroyed were easily replaced.

While the bombing campaign may be considered offensive, the fight and eventual victory over the V-1s was largely defensive. (The D-Day invasion was also a massive element in the victory, because the Allies eventually overran the launching sites. But the Allied defensive measures greatly helped reduce the V-1 menace.) This defensive strategy involved three military elements: fighter planes, antiaircraft artillery, and barrage balloons. Augmenting these elements were strict censorship and disinformation.

The first line of defense was the fighter plane. By July there were sixteen fighter squadrons assigned to combat the V-1s. (A squadron generally had sixteen aircraft.) The justly famous Spitfire as well as the newer Tempest were the most used. Fighters were in the air round the clock, and although neither the Spitfire nor the Tempest could quite match the speed of the V-1s, they could intercept them by diving down and firing either their .303-caliber machine guns or their 20mm cannons. The machine guns fired a solid bullet while the cannons fired an explosive shell. The range of the cannon, however, was much less than the machine gun bullets, but the bullets sometimes ricocheted off the V-1's surface without doing much damage. Pilots preferred therefore to close in on the flying bombs and destroy them with cannons. That required them to get at least within three hundred yards. The great danger of this tactic, however, was hitting the warhead, in which case the V-1 and the fighter plane would both be destroyed. At least five fighter pilots lost their lives that way.[10] In the event that the pilots encountered a V-1 traveling less than 400 miles per hour, they would fly alongside and place one wingtip under the bomb's wing and then execute a turn so that the wingtip flipped the V-1 over. This maneuver upset the delicate gyroscope and the V-1 then tumbled out of control and crashed. This maneuver became common practice among pilots, although now and then there was damage to the plane's wing.

The greatest anti-V-1 pilot was Squadron Leader Joseph Berry. He accounted for sixty-one, which was more than twice the next-highest score. He was shot down during a raid against a rail yard. His last words to his wingmen were: "I've had it chaps. You go on."[11] He was twenty-four years old.

The best place to cause one of these flying bombs to crash, by whatever means, was obviously over the Channel. The patrols that were constantly in the air were therefore generally above the Channel. Behind the screen of fighters were the antiaircraft guns, the second line of defense. By July 19 there were 2,500 antiaircraft guns lining the Channel coast. Calibers ranged from 3.7-inch all the way down to 20-millimeter. There were over four hundred of the bigger guns, and their effectiveness was greatly increased by two new technologies. Whereas in the past the guns were aimed manually, a process that the fast-flying V-1s made nearly impossible, the new guns were aimed by radar in almost exactly the same way that naval guns were aimed by their directors. The radar locked on the target and communicated the course, range, and altitude of the target to the gun. The radar stayed locked on as the guns fired and adjusted. Aside from the radar operator, the gun crew's only job was loading.

The other development was the arrival of the American variable-timed fuse. Previous antiaircraft shells used a fuse that exploded the shell after a preset amount of time, which meant that a great number of shells would have to be fired at incoming aircraft. When used against fleets of bombers this technique could be effective because the time fuse exploded the shell creating clouds of flak through which the bombers in formation had to fly. Some of them inevitably flew into the flak. (At the risk of being pedantic, *flak* is a German term for antiaircraft artillery, not the explosion of the shell. But it has come to be used that way.) Unlike the time-fused shell, however, the VT Frag (Variable Timed Fragmentation) fuse emitted a radio beam that bounced off the target and returned. The shell exploded only when it reached the target's vicinity, sending a cloud shrapnel in front of, or just below, the target. Not every gun on the Channel coast was outfitted with VT Frag, but the new fuse added significantly to the score against the V-1s, which, as a target, had the extremely attractive virtue of flying in a straight line at a constant altitude.

Behind the lines of antiaircraft artillery was another group of fighters. They were there to pick up any V1s that made it through the artillery barrage.

The last line of defense was the barrage balloon. These were small blimps (about sixty-two feet long and twenty-five feet in diameter) that were tethered to the ground—or in some cases to barges in the Thames estuary—by steel cables. They were manned by a team of eight enlisted men and a sergeant. The balloon itself was not the primary defender against low-level aircraft. Rather it was the cable which was sturdy enough to cripple an aircraft. The balloon could be raised or lowered by means of a winch. During the height of V-1 attacks, there were 1,750 of these balloons arranged around London.[12] Since the V-1s generally flew at 2,500 to 3,000 feet, the balloons would not have been extended much above that altitude. Earlier in the war their objective was to discourage low-level air attacks, dive bombers, as well as to discourage night attacks. They were also tethered to barges in the

Thames estuary as an antidote to mine-laying aircraft which, by the nature of their task, had to fly very low.

Of the three elements of the defense against the V-1, the barrage balloons had the lowest number of "kills" by war's end: 231. Antiaircraft artillery accounted for 1,878, and fighters knocked down 1,846.[13] Even so, the flying bombs kept getting through. The two-thousandth V-1 hit London on August 7.[14] The best hope for an end to this carnage was the Allies' movement toward the Pas-de-Calais. Once they pushed the Germans out, the Londoners hoped that the Germans would be out of range.[15] Though that helped, unfortunately the Germans began launching V-1s from bombers, a risky operation involving flying just over the water to evade Allied radar until reaching the launch point at which the pilot would climb quickly, launch the missile, and then hit the deck again for the trip home. Over a thousand missiles were launched this way after the Allies had captured the launching sites in France and Holland.

Because of the severity of the bombing attack against Germany in which German fighters had to remain at home to combat the Allied bombers, and because of the superiority of the Allied air forces, the Germans had very little knowledge of the impact of the V-1 attacks. They could not do photo reconnaissance, and censorship of the British media was strict. British intelligence services used double agents to send false information about the effects of the attacks. Telling the Germans that they were overshooting caused them to adjust their range calculations and settings, so that the bombs began falling on the south side of the Thames, and away from central London. Still, the bombs kept hitting dense population centers in the suburbs. The people in central London were somewhat relieved; the people in places like Brixton were not. But this development was in the context of the random nature of V-1 attacks. The worrying thing about them is that no one, including their authors, knew where they would fall—a housing development, a school, a greenhouse, a factory, Westminster Abbey. It was a terror weapon, as well as a military weapon. Target-less and unpredictable, it understandably made Londoners nervous and fearful.

❖

Ten days after his return to London Hemingway finally began his research on the RAF. He visited a squadron of Typhoon fighter pilots operating from an airstrip near Stonehenge. Carlos Baker points out that Hemingway mistakenly called the fighter planes "Tempests," but this is not much of an error since the Typhoons were essentially a Tempest, redesigned to provide better performance in terms of maneuverability and speed. Both fighters were single-engine, single-seat planes (which meant that Hemingway could not go up in one), and both were used against the V-1s. Baker goes on to say that Hemingway admired these brave pilots immensely and wanted very much to be accepted by them.[16] Indeed it would be difficult not to admire these men, all young, all apparently modest, one in particular whose face had been badly burned and poorly repaired so that this skin had a purple tone. In his *Collier's* article "London Fights the Robots," Hemingway described him as "a fine, shy man who lived behind a destroyed face." It was he who responded to Ernest when asked what it was like to shoot down a V-1. The young man said he couldn't say there was one way of doing it. Whether the pilots actually described the tactics of shooting down V-1s or not, Hemingway could not put that information in his article, because of censorship and, no doubt, a sense of solidarity with these young men he so admired.

Next Hemingway went to the headquarters of the 98th Squadron in Surrey. This was a British outfit flying American B-25s, also known as the "Mitchell" (after the celebrated Billy Mitchell, the early advocate for US airpower). It was a twin engine medium bomber usually armed with six fifty-caliber machine guns in its nose and capable of carrying three thousand pounds of bombs. The B-25 was also the plane used in then–Lieutenant Colonel Jimmy Doolittle's raid on Tokyo and other

Japanese cities, early in the war, April 18, 1942. Launched from aircraft carrier USS *Hornet*, the medium-sized bombers lumbered down the flight deck and just barely got airborne.

The Mitchell could reach speeds of 328 miles per hour, and, capable of flying at treetop levels, it was a devastating weapon against vehicles and troops—part of Allied airpower that Rommel correctly worried could interdict supplies and reinforcements.

There were twenty-five of these aircraft in the 98th, and one of their primary missions was to attack the V-1 launch sites in the Pas-de-Calais. As mentioned, these sites were heavily guarded by German antiaircraft batteries, and to date they had shot down forty-one bombers and damaged another four hundred. The RAF had flown 4,710 sorties against the V-1 sites.[17]

As an accredited correspondent, Hemingway enjoyed an officer's privileges. He was in the 98th officers' mess on June 15 when he heard an incoming V-1. The bomb exploded close by, and he and the other correspondents ran to the site. They collected fragments of the bomb, an act that was strictly illegal, though Hemingway may not have known that. (While this may seem trivial, British scientists were no doubt trying to reverse engineer the V-1 fragments to see if they could learn something useful.) Hemingway returned to the bar at the officers' mess, and very soon thereafter was confronted by police who unceremoniously relieved him of his bomb souvenirs, and did so in an abrupt manner that left Hemingway feeling sheepish. Ever since he had gotten into trouble as a boy for shooting a protected blue heron, Hemingway had been wary of officialdom and law enforcement. Indeed, toward the end of his life he was certain that the FBI was shadowing him. (There was some justification for this, for the FBI did have a dossier on him. He was not the only writer to attract official attention; writers who had participated in some way in the Spanish Civil War, on the Republican side, were of particular interest.) And as mentioned, Hemingway would have another worrisome brush with the authorities, this time the Army Inspector General's Office, after being accused (or more like it, denounced) by fellow correspondents for carrying and using weapons. That event cast a shadow over his activities with his favorite outfit, the 22nd Regiment of the 4th Division.

On Sunday, June 18, Hemingway was back at the Dorchester hosting a pancake and bourbon breakfast with Rear Admiral Leland Lovette, who was head of the navy's public relations program. Lovette supplied the bourbon. Also there were Lovette's aide, Lieutenant William Van Dusen, as well as two navy junior officers, Henry North and Michael Burke. These two were assigned to the OSS and were training to parachute into France. All four and Hemingway had traveled to England on the same plane, and they had agreed they would reassemble at some point and convert the buckwheat flour Van Dusen had brought with him into pancakes. There was a fair amount of V-1 activity that morning and, as Carlos Baker reports, Hemingway was unconcerned, stating his pet theory that no one was in real danger unless the enemy was targeting you personally. This theory was borderline ridiculous given the totally random nature of the V-1, which could not target anything but which was costing London thousands of casualties, and—given the long-range weapons both sides were using—artillery and aerial bombs. Perhaps he believed it, or perhaps it was just a way of saying you cannot do anything about the randomness of most weapons, so there was no sense worrying about it. Critics would no doubt say that it was all part of the role he was playing. And surely he recognized that the Austrian trench mortar that wounded him in World War I was not aimed at him personally.

Just after eleven, while the pancake breakfast was underway, divine services were also underway in the famous old Guards Chapel on Birdcage Walk, near Buckingham Palace, Westminster Abbey, and the various seats of government and military planning. Henry North watched from the hotel window as a V-1 crossed over the Thames, plummeted down, and exploded on the roof of the Guards Chapel, collapsing it and killing or injuring the entire congregation. Reports of the numbers killed or injured vary, for some reason, but the most common listing is 124 dead and 141 wounded. The chapel was destroyed.

North and Burke ran out of the hotel, down Park Lane, across Green Park and St James's Park to the site of the disaster, no more than a mile from the hotel. Hemingway and the others stayed in Hemingway's room, sipping bourbon. Perhaps the memory of his recent brush with the police at a V-1 site gave Hemingway pause. Or perhaps the explosion of V-1s was now so commonplace in London as to excite little curiosity.

Hemingway's adventures in Europe during the war were treated exclusively in Charles Whiting's *Hemingway Goes to War*. The book can be considered a hatchet job. Whiting was an Englishman who shared some of his countrymen's resentment and dislike of most things American. And who was apparently more quintessentially American than Hemingway? Boisterous, obtrusive, noisy, egomaniacal, insensitive—these were the usual suspects of the American character, from Whiting's point of view. Incensed by Hemingway's apparent lack of interest in the Guards Chapel explosion, Whiting writes: "This apparent indifference to the suffering of the British civilians all around him was typical of Hemingway during his seven weeks' stay in the country. Naturally, he shared some of the arrogance of American soldiers who had believed they had crossed the Atlantic to 'American occupied England' to bail 'Ol' Jolly' out of the mess it had got itself into." There is a great deal of this sort of thing throughout the book. Whiting was also apparently obsessed with Hemingway's alleged continuing sexual impotence, though he gives no source for his claim that Hemingway was unable to consummate his affair with Mary. (But what better way to attack Hemingway's he-man image?) Indeed, the book has no references of any kind, simply a series of unsubstantiated claims and accusations. Further, it is full of factual mistakes. Whiting for example claims that the ancestors of the 22nd US Army regiment fought at the Little Bighorn. Custer would have been surprised at that. (The 22nd comes up because it became Hemingway's favorite regiment.) Whiting also says that it was "Jack" Kennedy who was shot down and killed in the war. These are such glaring errors that they call into question many of Whiting's unreferenced and unsupported statements and judgments. Of course, mistakes sometimes happen, but Whiting's book is replete with accusations and opinions that he does not bother to authenticate.

Later in June Hemingway returned to the headquarters of the 98th squadron and requested permission to go on a bombing raid. The target would be the launching sites for the V-1s. Carlos Baker says there were two "boxes" of six Mitchell bombers each. Hemingway says there were eight boxes of six each. In any event, Hemingway, who would refer to himself in his *Collier's* article as the "pilotless-aircraft editor" climbed into the copilot's seat alongside Wing Commander Alan Lynn. In a matter of minutes they were over the Channel and heading for the Pas-de-Calais. Soon they were over the target that Hemingway said was easy to recognize by the large number of Mitchell bombers that had been shot down and lay strewn around the sites. Then, too, black clouds of deadly flak began to appear as the bombers made their run. In his article Hemingway says these clouds were not as lonely as in the poem "I Wandered Lonely as a Cloud," and while that seems a rather lame witticism, he may deserve credit for assuming the reader would know the poem and draw the ironic parallel between the poem (which is Wordsworth at his joyfully bucolic sappiest) and the deadly nature of the bursting flak.

Each plane dropped eight bombs on the target and then turned for home. It was all over too quickly for Hemingway's taste, and he wanted to make another run to assess the damage. But Lynn said it would be too dangerous in the heavy flak, and in fact one of the planes in the second box was shot down during the raid.

Hemingway returned to London where he said he was grounded by the RAF flight surgeon because of his concussion and continuing headaches. According to Carlos Baker, it was during this ten-day period that he wrote his poem to Mary. And it may very well have been the occasion of their consummating their developing love affair. Certainly the passage about Mary coming "to cure all loneliness" suggests something more than just a friendly visit.

Toward the end of June Hemingway visited a squadron of Mosquito fighter-bombers. Despite its name, the Mosquito was one of the best performing aircraft in the war. Made mostly of plywood, the "Mossy" was a lightweight, twin-engine two-seater capable of speeds up to 415 miles per hour—more than enough to escape enemy fighters. Originally designed as strictly a bomber that would rely on speed for defense, the plane could carry bomb loads weighing four thousand pounds. A paragraph from the RAF official website extols the Mosquitos' bombing accuracy: "An example of the tremendous accuracy achieved by Mosquitos can be shown by comparing figures for the attacks on the V-weapons sites. The average tonnage of bombs required to destroy one of these sites by B-17 Flying Fortresses was 165; for B-26 Marauders it was 182 tons, and for B-25 Mitchells 219 tons. The average for the Mosquito was just under 40 tons!" The reason for this accuracy is that unlike the Mitchells and the B-17s that tended to release their bombs from altitude, the Mosquito's specialty was low-level bombing—very low level. Sometimes as low as fifty feet. Its bombs were therefore usually fused for delayed action, since at low levels a contact fuse explosion would most likely damage, or worse, the plane dropping it.

Later modifications added armament, usually four 20mm cannon and four .303-caliber machine guns. Its range fully loaded was fifteen hundred miles. When configured as a fighter-bomber, the Mosquito was a deadly weapon against vehicles and infantry, both bombing and strafing. What's more, by war's end the "Wooden Wonder" had accounted for more than six hundred downed enemy aircraft.[18] Its versatility was truly amazing.

Hemingway was particularly interested in some daring Mosquito attacks against Gestapo headquarters. The first of these occurred in Oslo, on September 25, 1942, and although the results were less than stellar, and involved the deaths of eighty Norwegian civilians, the RAF considered it time to reveal the hitherto secret Mosquito to the British public by publicizing the raid. Then came Operation Jericho, an attack on the German prison at Amiens, France, February 18, 1944. The object there—in addition to killing German guards and Gestapo agents—was to free political prisoners and French Resistance fighters. There were seven hundred prisoners in the facility, which was surrounded by a high stone wall. A squadron of Mosquitos was given two assignments: first to blow a hole in the prison walls and second to destroy the barracks and offices of the German captors. Protected by a squadron of Typhoons, the first Mosquitos went at fifty feet and dropped their bombs while their colleagues circled at five hundred feet to avoid the delayed explosions. The first attack did the job; the wall was breached, and 258 prisoners escaped, although many were recaptured (some reports say as many as two thirds). Unfortunately, 102 prisoners were killed in the bombing and 74 were wounded. Group Captain Charles Pickard, who was in command of the flight, was set upon by a German fighter and shot down; he and his navigator were killed. One other Mosquito was lost.

In some of these attacks against the Gestapo there have been suggestions that the targets were also prisoners who were being tortured and who would ultimately give out damaging information. While this has a certain Hollywood-esque flavor (e.g., James Cagney in *13 Rue Madeleine*), it's unlikely in this case, because if that had been the object the RAF would have done a better job on the main prison building. In fact the reserve Mosquitos did not even attack, because the prison was wreathed in smoke and prisoners were seen running away. There is some continuing controversy over the need for the attack as well as the mystery over who actually ordered it. But that does not detract from the astonishing skills of the RAF airmen or from the performance of their aircraft.

As another example, on April 11, 1944, Mosquitos attacked Gestapo headquarters in The Hague, and Wing Commander Robert "Pinpoint"

Bateson dropped his bomb "bang through the front door."[19] There would be other attacks against Gestapo headquarters, once again at Oslo in October and December 1944, and in Copenhagen March 1945. At the moment, though, the Mosquito squadrons along with other elements of the RAF and US Army Air Corps were busily turning Rommel's worst nightmares about supplies and reinforcements into a reality by bombing and strafing his lines of communication in support of the Normandy invasion.

These were heroics that naturally appealed to Hemingway and that, coupled with his admiration for these men, stimulated his interest in going up in a Mosquito and, perhaps, seeing a little action. In the afternoon of June 29, Hemingway got his wish.

Hemingway's contact was Group Captain (later Air Marshal) Peter Wykeham-Barnes. Wykeham-Barnes had won fame and promotion during the African campaign, having shot down seventeen enemy planes (three shared), and having been shot down himself. Crash landing in the desert, he walked back to his headquarters. When he arrived he was barefoot, wearing his boots slung around his neck, because he had just paid "a packet" to have them custom made and he didn't want to ruin them. His first words on arriving were, "For God's sake, give me a drink." Now commanding the Mosquito Attack Wing 140, he would lead the most successful of the low-altitude Mosquito attacks against Gestapo headquarters, this time in Arhus, Denmark. There the Gestapo had taken over buildings of Arhus University. Working closely with information provided by Danish Resistance teams, Wykeham-Barnes planned an attack with twenty-five Mosquitos. The object was to destroy Gestapo records, as well as to kill Gestapo personnel. To this end the attack would have two phases. The first would drop five-hundred-pound bombs (with the usual delayed fuses) in order to crack open the roofs and walls of the offices. The second phase would attack with firebombs to destroy records. In the end the attack killed thirty-nine Gestapo agents, including the head of security police in Denmark, and wounded another twenty-one. The attack occurred on October 31, 1944.

In short, Hemingway would be dealing with a man of considerable courage and professionalism and no little style—just the sort he admired and got along with.

In a long letter to Carlos Baker, Wykeham-Barnes described his experience with Hemingway. They took off on the afternoon of June 29, with the larger Wykeham-Barnes wedged uncomfortably side by side with the almost equally bulky Hemingway, who remarked that it resembled a grizzly bear trying to enter an Austin.[20]

Once airborne, "Hemingway urged me to roll the Mosquito and throw it around quite considerably."[21]

They went up again at midnight that same date.

The night was black with no moon. Wykeham-Barnes had been ordered not to take Hemingway over enemy territory, and since Wykeham-Barnes had no navigator, he was careful not to go too far afield and at too low an elevation. Soon enough, though, they found themselves in a "stream" of V-1s headed for Portsmouth. They dived on one and intended to fire at it, but they were suddenly in the range of the Portsmouth antiaircraft units. Wykeham-Barnes fired one burst of his machine guns but soon realized that they were in danger not only from the antiaircraft artillery but also from the cables of the barrage balloons. Hemingway was not particularly helpful because he was urging Wykeham-Barnes to continue the attack. They pulled out from the danger area and soon encountered another V-1 incoming. Though his orders were to keep Hemingway out of trouble, though there were RAF night fighters in the air that were better equipped to attack the V-1s, and though Wykeham-Barnes's personal Mossy was slower than the V-1s, Hemingway urged another try. Against his better judgment Wykeham-Barnes dived his Mossy and fired a few bursts without noticeable effect. Once again they found themselves in the Portsmouth barrage complete with searchlights and heavy flak, and Wykeham-Barnes prudently pulled away. Shortly thereafter there was a huge explosion that tossed the Mossy around like "a leaf in a whirlwind." One of the night fighters had apparently hit the V-1 warhead.

Both planes were lucky to escape the blast. They continued to patrol around amidst incoming V-1s and answering artillery barrages, but they were eventually able to return without damage to the plane or operators. Wykeham-Barnes later said, "Ernest seemed to have loved every moment."[22] Knowing that the Mosquitos' mission was not chasing V-1s, Wykeham-Barnes was simply happy to make it back to base.

The Portsmouth AA guns must not have been using VT Frag shells. Had they been, Hemingway's story would most likely have ended that night.

The next day Wykeham-Barnes ran into Hemingway and noticed that "he looked terrible"; he had been up all night writing. His story "London Fights the Robots" is limited because of censorship and says almost nothing about his flight in the Mosquito, since any information about the plane and the tactics was confidential. He does discuss the bombing raid against V-1 sites, since obviously the German targets of these raids were keenly aware of what that was about. But the general tone of the article is jocular, perhaps because there was little if anything he could say and perhaps because it blended with the casual style of the RAF pilots. Hemingway had a good sense of humor, although it doesn't always come through successfully in his writing.[23] The estimable Hemingway scholar Scott Donaldson writes "during nearly two years as a roving European correspondent based in Paris, Hemingway derided the empty life of do-nothing ex-patriots and refused to be impressed by the supposedly great men he encountered at conferences in Lausanne and Genoa. The watchword was 'irreverence,' the target—all received wisdom. The attitude most commonly struck was that of the 'wise guy,' and as Delmore Schwartz pointed out, it was in this role that Hemingway first made an impression. 'To be a wise guy,' Schwartz wrote, 'is to present an impudent, aggressive, knowing and self-possessed front to the world. The most obvious mark of the wise guy is his sense of humor which expresses his scorn and his sense of independence; he exercises it as one of the best ways of controlling the situation and demonstrating his superiority to all situations.'"[24]

It was this aspect of Hemingway's personality and behavior that so irritated many of his contemporaries. But with people he respected he could be polite, charming, and a good listener who was genuinely interested in what they had to say. Military men who knew their business, serious artists, and competent sportsmen were at the top of his list; politicians and most other writers near the bottom. They were the ones who saw only the wise guy mask.

In his introduction to *By-Line: Ernest Hemingway*, editor William White says: ". . . his second *Collier's* article, 'London Fights the Robots,' was chosen in 1962 as one of 'the masterpieces of war reporting' by Professor Louis L. Snyder." Snyder was an American expert on the rise of Hitler and Nazism. His assessment balances the acidic critique by Charles Whiting: "If someone other than Hemingway had written such garrulous, inaccurate, egocentric stuff, it would surely never have been published."[25] Most readers, I think, would say the truth about the article's quality lies somewhere in between these two extremes. But it is obvious that Hemingway had the distinction between creative art and journalism clearly in his mind. He knew he was writing only enough to avoid being sent back home, and to make a little money. And that applies to quality and effort as well as volume of output. Wanting to "get it down fresh," he stayed up all night writing.[26] It shows.

It was the 8th of September when the first V-2 rocket exploded in London. Since it was supersonic, it gave no warning. There was simply a devastating sudden blast. "Where once six suburban houses had stood, there was now only an immense crater."[27] For the next five months the Germans would fire 1,359 rockets against London. They would kill 2,754 people and wound another 6,523.[28] And there was no defense against them. They were launched from movable sites, so there was no way to bomb them. The only defense would be to push the Germans back beyond the rockets' range of 220 miles. That would take time.

Meanwhile London would continue to suffer attacks from Hitler's wonder weapons. Once the Allies captured the port of Antwerp, that city also became a target.

Hemingway would not see anything of the V-2's devastation, however. By the time of the V-2 attacks, he was with the US Army's 22nd regiment near the Belgian border, having joined them after witnessing and, in his way, participating in the liberation of the city he loved more than any other in the world, Paris.

CHAPTER SEVEN

"The Germans are staying in there just by the guts of their soldiers. We outnumber them 10 to 1 in infantry, 50 to 1 in artillery and an infinite number in the air."
—Major General Raymond O. Barton, US Army,
4th Division commander

"Although our troop morale is good, we cannot meet the enemy material with courage alone."
—German officer (anon.)

I ndustrial war is a matter of supplies and manpower, a process of management as much as a matter of military brilliance or heroics. Or at least in concert with occasional military brilliance and occasional heroics. Of course this has always been to some extent true;

an army always marches on its stomach—and in close proximity to its ammunition trains. Troops without food or ammunition cannot hope to prevail, or even survive. A tactical genius like Rommel could do little against the Allied flood of men and weapons coming ashore at Normandy. The German commanders in the West understood that once the Allies established a secure foothold in France, with secure supply lines, the war was most likely lost. They were doomed, and the only question was how many people they would sacrifice before they acknowledged the truth. German industry, under the constant bombardment of Allied planes, could not hope to match the industrial output of the United States. Nor could the badly depleted Luftwaffe do much of anything about the Allies' domination of the air and their ability to interrupt and interdict the Germans' attempts to resupply their beleaguered troops.

But outnumbered and outgunned, the Germans did have one advantage in Normandy. They had been in France for four years and understood the terrain, especially the *bocage* (rural terrain). They could make their eventual defeat very expensive, to the Allies and to themselves. Some professional Wehrmacht officers wondered why they should expend these lives in an outdated strategy; Hitler did not.

This may be a good point to explain the difference between the regular army and the Waffen-SS. Before the war, the SS were originally formed as a kind of Praetorian Guard for Hitler. They were political troops who took an oath of loyalty to Hitler, personally. They were therefore drawn from the ranks of the most fanatical Nazis. The term *Waffen* means "armed." Gradually during Hitler's rule they grew into separate units, a kind of parallel military. They were generally (but not exclusively) the chief perpetrators of the atrocities visited upon the civilian populations of the occupied countries. It is hardly surprising that aristocrats and professional army officers like Geyr regarded them and Hitler himself with profound contempt. But the SS arm of the army was the most fanatical and therefore the most difficult for the Allies to dislodge. So it proved in the bocage. Invariably, the truer the believer in Nazism, the more difficult it was to defeat him. One incident is illustrative: a German junior officer, wounded and captured, was on the operating table, and receiving a transfusion. He asked if the blood was English, and when the surgeon answered yes, the German pulled the needle from his arm and said he would rather die for Hitler. Which he did.

To an English speaker the term *hedgerow* suggests some suburban plantings, maybe of boxwood shrubbery—something that could stop neither a man nor a bullet. The hedgerows in the bocage of Normandy were something quite different. Historian Martin Blumenson explains: "In contrast to the Caen-Falaise plain [facing the British and Canadians], the Americans faced a sprawling mass of broken ground—low ridges and narrow valleys, a marshy depression of sluggish streams and drainage ditches, a cluster of hills. The natural features were discouraging enough for an offensive. But a manmade obstacle made things worse. Found everywhere in the Cotentin [peninsula in Normandy], this was the hedgerow. The hedgerow is a fence, half earth, half hedge, anywhere from three to fifteen feet. Growing out of a wall of dirt several feet thick is a wall of brambles, hawthorn, vines, and trees. . . . Surrounding each field, they break the terrain into a multitude of tiny walled enclosures. Since the fields are irregular in shape, the hedgerows follow no regular pattern. Wagon trails winding among the hedgerows are sunken lanes, damp and gloomy."[1] There were some ten thousand of these miniature fortresses in Normandy.[2] The Norman farmers used these centuries-old little fields—often no more than fifty yards by a hundred—either as corrals for their livestock or as arable land or as orchards for their much loved apples, the source for Calvados and cider. From the air these hedgerows looked like a checkerboard, although the varying size of the fields made the checkerboard appear like something Salvador Dalí would paint. And it has long been a point of discussion as to why Allied invasion planners did not account for the almost impenetrable nature of these hedgerows and for the fact that mobility of large units and multiple tanks was virtually impossible. Certainly the planners knew of the bocage from aerial photos, but that kind of reconnaissance could not convey the exact nature of these fields. Further, the French Resistance was not especially useful in Normandy where the locals seemed to cope with being occupied more easily than other parts of France. That was partially because they were mostly farmers and did not suffer so acutely from rationing—not as severely as their countrymen. Colonel David Bruce of the OSS described the typical Norman peasant family as "somewhat dour, substantial, conservative, apparently unemotional, well-fed, healthy looking individuals, devoted to the practical and little given to the aesthetics."[3]

Interspersed among the hedgerows were bogs that were barriers to any vehicle and a hazard for infantry as well—men who had to slog through these spongy flats while exposed to fire from snipers hidden in adjacent hedgerow foliage. And not just snipers, for the Germans in some instances had dug out a space for tanks and anti-tank artillery, and then camouflaged them to make them invisible to the air and nearly so to the foot soldier. Then, too, the Germans had the superb Maschinengewehr 42, a machine gun that could fire twelve hundred rounds a minute[4] and that could therefore quickly annihilate a small squad of infantry. It was a far better weapon than anything that the Allies had. And the fighting in the bocage country was one of small groups on both sides where the advantage lay with the hidden German defenders. It was not ground suitable for maneuver or mass formations. General Collins told General Bradley that the bocage was every bit as bad as the jungles of Guadalcanal.[5] And that was very bad, indeed.

Ernie Pyle described the difficulty the US troops faced in this terrain: "The fields were surrounded on all sides by the immense hedgerows—ancient earthen banks, waist high [and higher] all matted with roots, and out of which grew weeds, bushes and trees up to twenty feet high. The Germans used these barriers well. They put snipers in the trees. They dug deep trenches behind the hedgerows and covered them with timber, so that it was almost impossible for artillery to get at them. Sometimes they propped up machine guns with strings attached so that they could fire over the hedge without getting out of their holes. They even cut out a section of the hedgerow and hid a big gun or a tank in it, covering it with brush. Also they tunneled under the hedgerows from the back and made the opening on the forward side just large enough to stick a machine gun through. But mostly the hedgerow pattern was this: a heavy machine gun hidden at each end of the field and infantry hidden all along the hedgerow with rifles and machine pistols."[6]

The tactics for taking these positions called for bulldozing a gap in the hedgerow. There was, of course, an entrance usually by means of a stile, but just as obviously this was of no use to a tank. Nor did individual infantrymen want to enter the fields one by one by the stile, for they knew the hidden Germans would have that opening covered. Unfortunately, a bulldozer was not always available, and the army soon arrived at an ingenious device known as the Rhino tank. Welded to the front of the tank were steel teeth made initially out of the beach barriers. The Rhino tank could smash through the hedgerows in a matter of minutes. Following the tank a platoon or even a squad of infantry came through the gap and spread out, all firing at likely enemy positions as they moved forward. The doctrine for this kind of action was to keep moving forward even when fired upon. Either the enemy would panic and run, or you would overrun his position, which was less dangerous than going cautiously or going to ground. The worst maneuver would be to hit the dirt because you were now a stationary target, and if the entire squad hit the dirt more or less together, it became a target for mortar fire. Historian Antony Beevor writes of the fighting in the bocage: "Three times as many wounds and deaths were caused by mortars as by rifle or machine gun fire."[7] Beevor also says that the Germans had few snipers with proper equipment and training, and that the average German soldier in this theater was a surprisingly poor shot, due to lack of practice. While that may have been true, it did not reassure the US troops who had an inordinate fear of snipers. And when they captured one, they killed him. (Or her. There were stories circulating among the GIs of French women acting as snipers—women who, if they survived, would be later denounced for *collaboration horizontale*. No doubt there were far more stories than actual women snipers. But that is common in the rumor mill that is war, and the stories did nothing to dispel the nervousness of GIs entering a bocage field or an adjacent village, with stone houses and a church with a steeple that was perfect for sniper fire. Besides, you do not have to be a very good shot to kill someone advancing slowly at fifty yards.) The Germans also mined the lanes between the hedgerows and the fields within, often with the much feared Bouncing Betty anti-personnel mine. And when they did retreat from a position they left behind ingenious booby traps, such as mines in the bottom of their foxholes and shell holes knowing that the first instinct of a soldier under fire is to jump into the closest hole. Knowing also that the GIs were souvenir hunters they would attach a grenade to some tempting bit of equipment. And they would place grenades under the bodies of dead GIs, and on occasion under the body of a severely wounded but still alive GI. OSS Colonel David Bruce writes in his diary: "The Germans are using booby traps freely. An American soldier yesterday went into a house just abandoned by the enemy. Hearing a cat meowing from the locked closet of a bedroom, he opened the door. The cat sprang out. There was a cord around her neck. The charge exploded. The soldier was killed."[8]

General Barton's 4th Division had landed on Utah Beach and had been in the thick of the fighting ever since. In forty days of combat the division had suffered 7,876 casualties since D-Day. These losses were especially damaging because these were largely men who had undergone extensive training in the United States and England prior to D-Day. They were replaced under emergency measures by troops who had not been trained in some cases, or in others by men who

LEFT: Hemingway at the helm of *Pilar* during his hunt for U-boats. *Courtesy of The Hemingway Collection, JFK Library.*

RIGHT: Hemingway in Cuba with three of his favorite things—a loving dog, some books, and a bottle of something. *Courtesy of The Hemingway Collection, JFK Library.*

ABOVE: Hemingway and Martha Gellhorn in New York during a happy period. *Courtesy of The Hemingway Collection, JFK Library.* BELOW: Hemingway in Spain during the Civil War. *Courtesy of The Hemingway Collection, JFK Library.*

Martha in a pensive mood. *Courtesy of The Hemingway Collection, JFK Library.*

ABOVE: A Normandy beach at low tide. When the tide came in these obstacles would have been submerged but still able to tear the bottom of landing craft. Many of these obstacles were tipped with mines. The ship closest to the beach is an LST. *Courtesy of National World War 2 Museum.* BELOW: A Signal Corps photo showing US troops moving through a devastated Normandy village. It's worth remembering that Allied bombing, artillery, and naval gunfire caused most if not all of this damage. *Courtesy of National World War 2 Museum.*

ABOVE: Another Signal Corps photo. The caption says: "An American convoy passes thru the streets of Carentan, first city to fall to the invaders." *Courtesy of National World War 2 Museum.* BELOW: Despite the devastation of their villages, most French civilians were happy to greet the US troops who were advancing on Cherbourg. *Courtesy of National World War 2 Museum.*

ABOVE: Hemingway and an American sergeant along with a line of German prisoners. When Hemingway was operating with the French Resistance one of his particular skills was interrogating prisoners. *Courtesy of The Hemingway Collection, JFK Museum.* BELOW: Hemingway was a very good judge of terrain and was comfortable with military maps. Beneath his knee is an M1 carbine. *Courtesy of The Hemingway Collection, JFK Museum.*

ABOVE: Paris street scene during the liberation, complete with civilians, Allied troops and artillery, and a dead body, presumably German. *Courtesy of The Hemingway Collection, JFK Museum.* BELOW: Hemingway and Buck Lanham outside a captured German bunker in the Siegfried Line. Surrounded by trees and camouflaged with sod on the roof, this bunker, like most in the line, was almost impossible to see from the air and had to be taken by infantry action. *Courtesy of The Hemingway Collection, JFK Museum.*

ABOVE: Hemingway and Buck Lanham beside the remains of a German artillery piece. *Courtesy of The Hemingway Collection, JFK Museum.* BELOW: Hemingway admiring his muse, Adriana Ivancich, the model for Renata in *Across the River and into the Trees.* Silver-haired Mary Hemingway appears unconcerned—or she is putting the best possible face on the situation. *Courtesy of The Hemingway Collection, JFK Museum.*

had been trained for other duties: cooks and clerks who were hardly ready for combat and who, in fact, had never heard a shot fired in anger much less the explosion of an artillery shell. Beevor explains: "Replacements joined their platoon usually at night. The old hands shunned them, partly because their arrival came just after they [the old hands] had lost buddies and they would not open up to newcomers. Also everyone knew that they [the replacements] would be the first to be killed and doomed men were seen as somehow contagious. It became a self-fulfilling prophecy, because replacements were often given the most dangerous tasks. A platoon did not want to waste experienced men."[9]

One of the "most dangerous tasks" was patrolling, especially at night. Usually the object of a patrol was to capture prisoners for interrogation or simply to locate the enemy.

Colonel Charles "Buck" Lanham was commander the of the 4th Division's 22nd Regiment. Before the war he wrote a book called *Infantry in Battle*: "Successful patrolling requires the highest of soldierly virtues. Therefore, the selection of personnel for an important patrol must not be a perfunctory affair. The men should be carefully selected and only the intelligent, physically fit and the stout of heart should be considered. One careless or stupid individual may bring about the death or capture of the entire patrol or cause it to fail in its mission. The moron, the weakling and the timid have no place in this hazardous and exacting duty."[10] Lanham had been assigned to write this book by General George Marshall, and it received his official seal of approval. In short, the book was official army doctrine for small-unit infantry action. But as everyone knows, doctrine can run up against uncomfortable realities, and the use of replacement troops without proper training in these kinds of hazardous missions may be, if not forgivable, at least understandable. But it ran precisely counter to the way Lanham said it should be done. Few decisions are more difficult than those of a junior officer or even noncom when trying to decide who should go out into the night.

Later in the campaign Lanham would become Hemingway's favorite soldier and close friend. They would stay in touch long after the war, and regularly get together. In a letter to Lanham about *Across the River and into the Trees* Hemingway told him that the hero of the book was a combination of Hemingway himself, Charles Sweeney (a professional soldier of fortune), and Lanham.

Lanham took command of the 22nd Regiment on July 19. By that time the regiment, as part of the 4th Division, along with the 79th and 9th, had fought its way up Normandy's Cotentin Peninsula and captured Cherbourg, a vital port that would supplement the Allies' D-Day beaches as a supply center. Hitler had ordered Cherbourg defenders to fight to the last man; he had established sixteen such "fortresses" along the Normandy and Brittany coasts, and each was ordered to fight to the death. Geyr von Schweppenburg regarded all this as wasteful and suicidal, because it locked up two hundred thousand troops and equipment in static positions that could either be taken under siege or simply bypassed.[11] As a tank commander Geyr believed in mobility, not World War I trench warfare tactics. Cherbourg was a case in point. After a series of bitter house to house battles and attacks against the concrete fortresses and pillboxes scattered around the area, the Germans gradually surrendered, one fortified position or pillbox at a time. Even the green replacements soon learned that attacking a pillbox straight on was a formula for casualties, but if they surrounded one and blasted it with bazookas from the rear, the defenders could be persuaded to surrender, if they survived. This was a tactic that Hemingway would write about later, although in the case of his story, the pillboxes on the Siegfried Line would be blasted with heavier antitank artillery.

In the battle for Cherbourg, the navy was called in to provide gunfire support, and the Allied fighters bombed and strafed German positions and columns. It was modern three-dimensional warfare. Before surrendering on June 26 the Germans virtually destroyed the harbor facilities and mined the port. Thirty-nine thousand Germans went into captivity. Another six thousand had escaped toward Cape de la Hague, but by July 1, they too had been killed or captured.[12] But the victory was expensive for Hemingway's soon to be adopted 4th Division:

"After their successful D-day landing, the men of the Ivy division [IV, i.e., 4th] fought through the hedgerows of the Cotentin Peninsula en route to taking the critically important port of Cherbourg on June 25, 1944. The division was in continuous action during the period of June 6 to June 28 when the last resistance around Cherbourg was eliminated. During this period, the 4th Infantry Division sustained over 5,450 casualties and had over 800 men killed."[13] As the war wore on, it would get worse for the 4th, the outfit that Hemingway would ultimately follow. By the end of the war the 4th would have suffered a total of 35,545 casualties—4,488 killed, 16,985 wounded, 860 missing, and 13,091 "non-battlefield casualties." The non-battlefield category included accidents and illness but also and primarily "battle fatigue," or what had been called "shell shock." This sort of traumatic stress hit the replacements the hardest, simply because they had not been trained and did not know what to expect from combat. Take a man trained as a cook or truck driver, issue him an M1 rifle, and send him into combat, and the odds are he will not last very long. He will most likely either get shot, blown up, or he will break down. Such an assignment inflicts a strange and difficult realization that some stranger is trying to kill you, and that you must try to kill him instead, if you can find him. Surely this was existentially disorienting as well as frightening—what's it all about, why am I here? There were many different psychological responses to this nightmarish scenario, although to call it a scenario undervalues the terror involved. Self-inflicted wounds were not unheard of. These were usually in the foot or left hand, and although the trick worked in the sense that it got the soldier off the front line, it also cost him six months in the stockade once his wound healed. (The Germans wasted no time with stockades; they executed any soldier found guilty of a self-inflicted wound.)

Not surprisingly, Hemingway (like Patton, famously) had little tolerance for the whole concept of battle fatigue. In discussing the matter with an army psychologist, who dismissed the idea of courage and told Hemingway that every man had a breaking point, even Hemingway—Hemingway lost his temper. Bill Walton described what happened: "Hemingway exploded. He flushed deep red and pounded on the table so hard the wine bottles jumped around. . . . The [psychologist] was an ignoramus, an uneducated fool, a pervert, an enemy spy, and anything else unpleasant he could think of. . . . Something that was very deep in him had been touched. He couldn't forget it."[14]

Hemingway had had a similar discussion with Group Captain Wykeham-Barnes, albeit without the rancor. Wykeham-Barnes wrote: "He had a great deal to say on mental stress and strain, on courage and fear [and] he tended to take a tougher and brawnier line than was acceptable to us worn out old veterans (4 and ½ years non-stop). . . . [But] it was all very good humored."[15] Hemingway had genuine respect for Wykeham-Barnes and men like him, and so would not lose his temper as he would with a staff specialist and noncombatant—a character he would call a "ballroom banana."

As mentioned, battle fatigue affected the replacement troops at a far greater rate than the veterans. Aside from lack of training for combat, the replacements had no time to develop relationships with the "old timers" or with fellow replacements who came from different units. There was little or no small-unit cohesion, no sense of a comradeship, no fear of letting the others down—a key factor in morale and in maintaining the fortitude needed to withstand the stress of combat. The replacements were disoriented strangers in a strange land: "This is not to say, of course, that the carnage and death of battle are not horrible and that the fear of violent death and injury are not traumatic. These factors by themselves, however, are not . . . sufficient to cause the massive numbers of psychiatric casualties found on the modern battlefield. Similarly, army psychologist Lt. Col. Dave Grossman has argued that, 'Countless sociological studies, the personal narratives of numerous veterans, and the interviews I have conducted clearly indicate the strength of the soldier's concern for failing his buddies. The guilt and trauma associated with failing to fully support men who are bonded with friendship and camaraderie on this magnitude is [sic] profoundly intense.'" [16] The men of the 4th Division, for example, had trained together for almost a year before D-Day. They bonded, not necessarily with the Division so much (although there was pride in the Division) as with the others in their platoons. Small units. (It's worth remembering that on D-Day many of the LCVP amphibious attack boats carried only thirty men and one junior officer.) But not only did most of the replacements have no combat training, they had no friendships to fall back upon, nor any unit allegiance to support them in times of battle stress. If they found themselves in a desperate situation, they could not fall back on the knowledge that someone, a buddy, would do his very best to come to their aid. Not only did they have no friends, they were often, as mentioned, avoided by the veterans. And that increased their sense of isolation and fear. They were therefore prime candidates to become casualties, either physically or psychologically. It is hardly surprising.

That is not to say the veterans were immune to psychological breakdowns. Those who saw their buddies die, often in hideous fashion, blown apart by mines or artillery, were also prime candidates for battle fatigue. The noise and shock of an artillery attack, the deafening explosions and near misses, the actual concussion that shook the earth, were enough to unnerve even the old hands. Worse, there were too many casualties from friendly fire, both in artillery and bombing. And there is no discounting the impact of simple physical fatigue. Soldiers who had been operating for weeks under the most grueling and dangerous conditions ultimately broke down simply for the lack of rest. But the worst cases of battle fatigue found that even if they were sent to the rear for rest, they could not sleep. Nightmares were a common symptom, and small wonder.

One commonly used method of treatment was called narcotherapy which involved using sodium amytal to put a man to sleep for three days, keeping him hydrated with an intravenous saline solution. Then came hot food and showers and meetings with psychiatrists which often had a minimal effect. As historian Robert Rush writes: ". . . a neuropsychiatric casualty sometimes made an almost continual circuit between the exhaustion center and the front lines until he was either killed or the war was over."[17]

Hemingway could well understand the value of comradeship in combat, but he could not or would not admit the reality of battle fatigue. To some, his reaction to the army psychologist might fall under the "Methinks he doth protest too much" category. There are perhaps several explanations for his attitude, none of which can be proved with any degree of certainty. Supporters and detractors will no doubt choose sides. But he famously said that cowardice was simply the inability to suspend the workings of the imagination. Certainly there is much truth in that, but it is a far more complicated question than something that can be answered in one of his typical, simple, declarative sentences. He of all people should have known that. And at some level, it's hard to believe he did not. Readers of Hemingway's stories will recognize the symptoms—ones that would occur again during this war and its aftermath. The light Nick Adams needed in the night was a symbol of soul-defiling stress. To all those who had never experienced the trauma of combat, it was "a way you'll never be." Small wonder that Hemingway himself needed a woman's company in the night, and that loneliness was intolerable. His need for someone went beyond sexual desire. Her being there also allowed him to feel safe, and it's reasonable to think it was not just because of wartime nightmares but also because of some profound psychological condition that would gradually worsen. But who can say when those complications started? In a trench along the Piave? Or later? Certainly his abusive and erratic behavior in Cuba when Martha returned are warning signs of emotional trouble. And it is surely safe to say that it was small wonder that he needed a woman, that he hated Martha's desertion. Small wonder also that he enthusiastically pursued and welcomed Mary's arrival in his life, to the point of almost overwhelming her personality, her sense of self. She famously said he "was too big."

He was too big in many ways. His nightmares among them. The daytime was one thing; the nighttime alone was something else, entirely. The lonely nights in Cuba were purgatorial. Most combat veterans would understand.

Hemingway biographer Michael Reynolds makes the point that after Hemingway's experiences in World War II (which would grow progressively more dangerous and violent), he was never completely comfortable again with anyone who had not had the experience of combat. "Displaced and out of step with the home front, he was discovering the chasm separating combat vets from stateside civilians: they no longer spoke the same language. Those who had not been there did not understand. . . . When not with others like himself, he felt strange and vulnerable."[18] It was that alienation that he was in part trying to reproduce when he wrote *Across the River*. The main character, an embittered Colonel Cantwell, personifies that alienation, that sense of knowing how things were and knowing things that few others did. That few critics really liked or understood the novel would, to Hemingway, underscore the difference between men who had been there and those who had not, those who knew how it was and those who did not, between those who stayed at home and wrote articles for the *New York Review of Books* and those who waded ashore on D-Day. The very fact that the critics could not understand and appreciate the novel surely was, to Hemingway, prima facie proof of the novel's truth. He thought it was his best work. Most readers, including Martha and Mary, disagree. But knowing that, it would only strengthen his belief in the book. In Hemingway's cosmology there was always the "they," the malevolent "other." In this case, the "they" would be the critics who were no different metaphorically from the sharks that attacked Santiago's great fish. (Ironically, Buck Lanham, who did know what combat was and what it did to men who experienced it, did not like the book. But he never told his friend that.)

But all of that was in the future. For now, there was a war to be fought and, later, a book to be written about it.

❖

A week after Cherbourg was secured Hemingway arrived in Normandy. He rendezvoused with his new friend, correspondent Bill Walton, who had parachuted in with the 82nd airborne on D-Day. Walton was living in a chateau along with CBS correspondent Charles Collingwood, who was also friendly with Hemingway. He had hit Utah Beach in the second wave along with a UDT crew. Hemingway joined them at the chateau and the three men spent the next week covering the fighting to the south where the US troops were attempting to break out of the narrow beachhead they had won on D-Day. It would be more hedgerow fighting and the actual breakout would not come for several weeks. Hemingway took notes about the fighting, but he never wrote anything about what he saw.

Hemingway and the two correspondents also visited towns the Allies had taken and spent their evenings at the chateau drinking "compass fluid," which they got from the navy. (Compass fluid is used to float the circular compass card.) At least that is the story. Since compass fluid is isopropyl alcohol, which is toxic and can be fatal, it seems possible that the story is apocryphal. Collingwood wrote that they also found some rather cheap wine or Calvados, and perhaps they dubbed it compass fluid. On the other hand, maybe it's true. Perhaps they mixed it with water, or something else. Their evenings were bibulous and entertaining especially because of the presence of some Irish demolition divers who were involved in repairing the port and removing the mines and booby traps the

Germans left behind. Perhaps, stereotypically, the Irish spent the evenings in song and drink—activities that the happy correspondents joined in, and in the morning the divers, apparently no worse for wear, went about their extraordinarily dangerous business below the surface of the port.

After a week of this Hemingway flew back to London and Mary.

CHAPTER EIGHT

"How can anyone govern a nation which has 246 different kinds of cheese?"

—Charles de Gaulle

The "armistice" signed by the French allowed for the German army to occupy the northern half of the country and all of the Atlantic coastline. On the coast they would establish five U-boat bases from which they could send their submarines into the Atlantic, the Gulf of Mexico, and the Caribbean where, for a while, they would devastate Allied shipping, despite the best efforts of Hemingway and the other volunteers of the "Hooligan Navy." The bases were Lorient, Brest, Saint-Nazaire, La Pallice, and Bordeaux.

The new French government would be headed by octogenarian Marshal Pétain, who, ironically, coined the term *collaborate*, after he signed the terms of the armistice with Germany. Optimistically, he assumed that the word meant the French and Germans would be joint partners in the government of the whole of France. The Germans were quite happy with this arrangement because they could rely on the French institutions (such as the police and Milice) and the Nazi sympathizers among the politicians and bureaucrats to do their jobs and thus relieve the occupying Germans of the need to administer the country—though the Wehrmacht, the SS, and the Gestapo would keep a careful eye on their "partners." Initially (until Torch) the southern half of the country (minus the Atlantic seaboard) was unoccupied, and the French politicians operated from their new headquarters in Vichy. The armistice also allowed amnesty for the French troops who escaped from Dunkirk. Most of them returned to France and civilian life. The treaty allowed Vichy to maintain a standing army of one hundred thousand men. It would seem that these men would be a solid base from which to build a Resistance army, but these troops were professionals. They were also loyal to Pétain, who was, after all, a national hero, in part because of his defense of Verdun in World War I. Moreover, the remaining professionals had little use for irregulars like the maquis, irregulars that had no recognizable military structure, no cohesion, little if any discipline, and not much in the way of weaponry. To professional soldiers, the maquis in the countryside were little more than a disorganized rabble, hardly more than bandits. The communists in Paris were better organized but chronically short of weapons, and besides, many were plotting to overthrow the legitimate government—something few professional soldiers would endorse.

De Gaulle's rather dubious position throughout the Occupation was that the real government of France was in London, not Vichy, and that he was its head. He called it the Provisional Government of France. In other words, Vichy was illegitimate, a position many agreed with but also one that many considered an unfortunate fait accompli that was not easily reversed. Worse, Allied governments had initially recognized Vichy—a situation that made de Gaulle's claims even less compelling.

That recognition ended when the Germans occupied the rest of France after Torch. De Gaulle's position in London was also complicated by the French outrage over the June 25, 1940, British attack against the French naval base at Mers-el-Kébir (in French Algeria) in which 1,297 French sailors and marines were killed. The British were afraid the French warships would fall into the hands of the Germans, and after several tries to persuade the French to turn the ships over to the British, or at least to send them to one of their distant colonies, such as Martinique, the British felt they had little choice but to attack. Highly incensed, the Vichy government broke off relations with the British. In the early years of the war de Gaulle could no doubt understand why he was known as *de Gaulle le seul*—de Gaulle alone.

❖

To Hemingway, Paris was a city of memory and nostalgia, the place where he had served his apprenticeship as a writer, the place where he and his first wife, Hadley, and their son, Jack, nicknamed Bumby, had lived poor but happy, the place where cafés were indulgent to writers and let them sit with their pencils and notebooks for hours while nursing a café crème or a demi of beer. Of course, one's memories are not always attentive to the truth, and the Hemingways were not so poor as he later described them in *A Moveable Feast*. After all, Hadley had a small but useful—actually essential—trust fund, and Ernest was for a time doing freelance work for the *Toronto Star*, until he quit that work to write fiction exclusively. Still, Hemingway's version of his memories makes for better reading than a more unadulterated depiction, a less romanticized truth. What writer does not imagine himself or herself in Paris in the twenties? Oh, to be poor(ish) but young and hopeful on the Left Bank, knowing that the cafés were welcoming and cheap, so too the wine and baguettes, and that the exchange rate was favorable and that poverty was only a temporary condition that would soon be eradicated by a successful novel or book of stories. As much as anyone, Hemingway is responsible for a writer's wistful daydreams of that other time, for in his case, those dreams came true.

And there is something else—there is congruence between his memories of Paris and his memories of Hadley, a woman he continued to love and correspond with all his life. Part of him, perhaps a very large part of him, regretted that he left her. ("I wished I had died before I ever loved anyone but her."[1]) He wrote her affectionate letters long after they had divorced and she had remarried, long after he left Pauline for Martha, long after Martha left him for her career, long after Mary arrived to stay, albeit with some ambivalence. In some ways, Paris was Hadley, Hadley was Paris. She was always there with his memories—Hadley and the cafés, the chestnut trees, and the race courses at Auteuil and Enghien-Soisy, the food and wine, and the apartment above a sawmill—all memories mixed together and over time becoming his myth. And from a purely human point of view, his sentimental nostalgia surely can be forgiven. Who does not remember with affection the years of early struggles, especially (or probably entirely) if the struggles were rewarded with success? (No doubt few look back on early struggles with much affection or nostalgia, if they ended in failure.)

And so the liberation of Paris was important to Hemingway, both actually and symbolically. Paris was his past, most likely his most treasured past. A part of him perhaps was going back to recapture something, at least in his imagination. It was criminal that the detested Nazis should have infested and infected his city for four long years. He wanted to be there when Paris was liberated. And, as it happened, he was.

Others were not so sure the liberation of Paris mattered at all. Militarily it was largely irrelevant. Few, if any, of the Anglo-American senior officers had any sentimental memories of early days in Paris—certainly nothing that would affect their strategic ideas. The German forces in the city were weak—mostly a collection of clerks and administrators (excluding the Gestapo and some elements of the

SS). That small force of some thirty thousand troops—many of whom were Poles and Alsatians whose willingness to fight was questionable—could easily be bypassed and left isolated and bewildered by the Allied surge. Then there was the problem of logistics. The Allies were still in the process of repairing the port facilities at Cherbourg, still largely dependent on the facilities at the invasion beaches, one of which at Omaha had been damaged by the sudden terrible storm that had its violent and very unwelcome arrival mere days after D-Day. It was hard enough to supply the massive needs of the Allied armies, not only with food, ammunition, and medicines but also gasoline, which was obviously the vital ingredient in their armor and mobilized divisions. Paris was a city of two and a half million people, a city that had been on strict rationing for four years, always teetering on the edge of famine. It was also the hub of the transportation system that was steadily being degraded by Allied bombardment, and if that meant that the Germans could not use it effectively to supply their western front troops or V-1 sites, it also meant that Parisians could not use it to import food from the farmlands in the west. If the Allies took Paris they would then add the Parisians to their list of supply responsibilities. For the American and British high command, Paris not only had no military value; it was a logistical nightmare in waiting.

What's more, far from being a bohemian artist's carefree paradise of pleasant memory, Paris was a cauldron of competing moral and political factions—and had been throughout the thirties. (And, in truth, had been periodically throughout its history.) There were at least sixteen different Resistance groups in the city alone.[2] From his headquarters in London, de Gaulle had only limited contacts with some of these groups. He viewed the liberation of Paris as vital to the future of France and indeed Western Europe, because he understood that the communists who made up the majority of the Resistance in Paris were planning an insurrection as they watched the Allies growing ever closer. As historian Michael Neiberg writes: "De Gaulle [was] afraid of what the Germans might do to Parisians who took up arms but [he was] equally afraid of what might happen if the [Resistance] actually gained control of the city. If they did, it would undermine de Gaulle's claims to speak for France and possibly even resist the Provisional Government to assume power once the Germans left. As one of de Gaulle's advisors warned him 'at the very minute the Germans leave the communists will go back to their old tricks; they will try to take the levers of power for themselves.' De Gaulle wrote '[If the communists] establish a base of power in Paris, they will have an easy time establishing a government . . . They can present themselves as the leaders of an insurrection and [form] a kind of commune. That such an insurrection in the capital would, for certain, lead to a power dominated by the Third International I have known for a long time.' Once again the deadly specter of a civil war—like the one in 1871— raised its ugly head. The only way to prevent it, de Gaulle believed was to get regular military forces into the city as soon as possible."[3] (The Third International was an organization of worldwide communist parties dominated, of course, by Moscow.) From de Gaulle's perspective the ideal scenario would have the Germans leaving just as the Allies arrived—and without too much damage to the city.

By 1944 and D-Day, de Gaulle's objectives were therefore largely political and only secondarily military. He also worried that the retreating Germans would devastate Paris, as they had done in Warsaw. (The Germans had massacred two hundred thousand Poles in Warsaw in retaliation for a partisan uprising, and they leveled a quarter of the city. The Soviets were at the gates of Warsaw but did nothing because the Polish Resistance was largely anticommunist. As is often the case, ideology trumped not only humanity but strategy.)[4] Fearing the destruction of Paris was a perfectly legitimate worry for de Gaulle, since Hitler had given specific orders to do just that: Paris must be destroyed, ideally as a result of his troops fighting to the death. De Gaulle also knew that if the communist-led Paris Resistance gained control of the city, they would be difficult to dislodge, and they would also begin a massive set of reprisals not only against Vichy officials, collaborators, and black marketers who thrived during the occupation but also against their political rivals—socialists and republicans. That would be little short of civil war, and the innocent as well as the guilty would suffer, as they always do in civil conflict, for the communists were fighting not only a guerilla war but also a class war. Not surprisingly, most of them were from the working-class districts of Paris. The middle- and upper-class Parisians had good reason to be afraid—afraid of what the Germans might do, and afraid of their own Resistance. And who really could define collaborators? Of course the obvious Vichy officials, profiteers, and right-wing politicians were not difficult to spot. But what of the ordinary Parisian who was just trying to get by during the Occupation? What of the young women who actually fell in love with German soldiers, not all of whom were monsters? Where was the line? And was it safe to leave the drawing of that line to orthodox communists? And in fact there would be an *épuration*, a "purification" in which French men and women throughout France would take their revenge on their own countrymen and kill them in numbers that eerily matched the numbers of French civilians killed by the occupying Germans throughout the four years—roughly thirty thousand.[5]

What's more, unlike other Resistance groups that leaned toward de Gaulle and who just wanted the Germans expelled and the return of representative democracy, the communists were looking beyond the liberation of the city and the country. They were bent on gaining the "levers of power" in order to establish a communist government in France once the war was over. Or, at the very least, they wanted a major role in the postwar government, knowing that that participation could well be the camel's nose under the tent. To them, the liberation of Paris was only the first step in their desired direction. As Albert Camus wrote in the clandestine and left-wing newspaper, *Combat*: "Having begun with resistance, we want to end with Revolution."[6] Camus and his political coreligionists would find that establishing communism in France was a political boulder of Sisyphean dimensions. And the boulder was de Gaulle. Little known before the war, he had escaped to England and refused to agree to the terms of the deal between the Germans and Pétain. He gradually became known to the French people through a series of BBC speeches in which he encouraged the French people to hold out. The battle for France may have been temporarily lost, he said, but the war was ongoing and ultimately the Allies, including elements of the French army, would prevail. De Gaulle also gathered around himself a collection of like-minded exiles who agreed that he should head the Provisional Government of France. He sent some of these colleagues as agents into France to counteract the influence of the communists and also to counsel all *Résistants* to wait until the Allies were in Paris before engaging in open warfare. With luck there would be no need for an insurrection once the Allies arrived. No insurrection, no prestige for the communists.

The Allied armies cared very little about French politics and understood even less. They wanted to continue the momentum gained when they finally broke off the narrow beachhead and routed the Germans who then began to flee to the east. Taking the time to attack the thirty thousand enemy troops within Paris would be a distraction and also present tactical difficulties of street by street fighting. Although the German troops were generally of poor quality, they were still there and would offer some time- and resource-devouring resistance. Not only that, there were elements of the SS, who if so ordered, would likely fight until destroyed. Moreover, the Allied commanders were aware of the recent lessons of Rome—a militarily meaningless public relations triumph that allowed the retreating Germans to escape and then establish a series of strong defensive positions that would endure until the end of the war—and cost the Allies tens of thousands of casualties.

The newly assigned German commander in Paris, General Dietrich von Choltitz, had been summoned to a meeting with Hitler, who made it perfectly clear that he wanted Paris defended and then destroyed, perhaps as a result of the defense or, perhaps, as a deliberate act resulting from a failed defense. "Paris will be transformed into a heap of rubble. The general commanding in chief will defend the city to the last man, and, if necessary be buried beneath it."[7] Here again Hitler revealed his outmoded belief in static defenses, fortresses, and fighting to the death, as well as his maniacal hatred of his enemies and their institutions—indeed of their civilization. Still shaken by the attempted assassination, Hitler appeared to von Choltitz as "an old, stooped and swollen man . . . a trembling being [who was] physically broken."[8] Giving vent to his hatred of the aristocratic officer corps from whom the plotters had drawn their support, Hitler raged and ranted and demonstrated very clearly to von Choltitz that Hitler had finally lost his mind. But von Choltitz was not particularly disturbed by his new assignment, or Hitler's state of mind. He was in fact relieved not to be implicated in the assassination plot and also relieved not to be blamed for his role in the collapse of the German defenses in Normandy. His assignment was to reorganize the city defenses and treat Paris as a fortress city. And if the worse came to the worst he was to destroy the city's infrastructure—bridges, power stations, communications centers—and as much of its treasured architecture as possible. The object was "rubble." Even though he believed that Hitler was a madman, von Choltitz was prepared to carry out these orders. After all, his nickname was "the smasher of cities," based on his utterly ruthless destruction of Rotterdam and Sevastopol.[9] And although the "von" in his name indicated that he was from the same Prussian aristocracy that spawned the bomb plotters (and who now, as Hitler said, were "bouncing at the end of a rope"[10]), the Gestapo could find no mention of his name in their investigations. (There were almost five thousand officers and civilian political opponents implicated and ultimately executed, rightly or wrongly, so von Choltitz had good reason to worry.) Further, von Choltitz was known for obeying orders to the letter. Once he arrived in Paris, however, it was quickly apparent to von Choltitz that the city could not be defended as a fortress. The troops were too few, their morale was poor, as was their training, and there were few heavy weapons. He decided that the best he could do was to keep the transportation and bridge systems as operational as possible—as a highway for the retreating German forces—and to keep the local civilian population under control and smash any attempts by the Resistance to raise revolt in the city. To do this he would establish thirty-six strong points throughout the city. They were designed to overawe the population and maintain essential services. Then, when it was time to go, he would think about obeying Hitler's order to destroy Paris. Until then, though, his relatively meager resources would be dispersed into enclaves: isolated and, as it turned out, subject to capture or destruction, one by one.

Hemingway would play his part in this drama, in the rising of the Resistance and in the liberation of Paris. It would be a small part, but he was there, at the center of events. The idea that Paris might be destroyed lay as heavy on his heart as it did on de Gaulle's—and millions of Frenchmen for whom the Allied avoidance strategy was only a short-term tactical concept that could very easily turn into a long-term catastrophe. Many believed that the Germans would eventually be defeated, but if it came at the cost of the destruction of Paris, and hundreds of thousands of its people, as it did in Warsaw, should not the commanders rethink their plans? Should not they listen to de Gaulle, irritating as he undoubtedly was? And there were many who worried that the reversals of the German army would be eventually themselves reversed. What if the Germans came back, and in force? What if they fell behind their defense line and regrouped? Should not Paris be liberated and defended?

No doubt, too, the idea was intoxicating to Hemingway that he could participate in the liberation of the city he loved beyond all others, just as it was to millions of French people, and millions of others around the world. This had nothing to do with the pedestrian business of his journalism assignments, although every journalist in the shadows of the Allies yearned to be the first into Paris. For Hemingway it had everything to do with reclaiming history, both real and personal. Many people, including many German officers in the west, felt that the Germans were beaten. The question people asked themselves was, would they live to see the peace? Would Paris survive? Would the battle in France be a Pyrrhic victory, at least as far as Paris was concerned?

Of course, Hemingway knew that Paris was a symbol to more people than just himself. And so on the eve of possible liberation, as he and many others trembled at the thought of the city's destruction, they also trembled happily at the thought that the detested *Boches* (a slur for German soldiers) would soon be gone from the city of light. But no one knew where that light would come from—from the victorious celebratory illumination of the Eiffel Tower, or from the explosions and arson of the criminal German occupiers who were intent on destroying yet another monument of civilization—perhaps *the* model of civilization—even as they were retreating.

It's not surprising that the French have nurtured legends about the Resistance. In some ways the legends counterbalance some of the humiliation the French feel because of the speedy collapse of their army. Indeed, de Gaulle would afterward claim that Paris had been "liberated by its people with the help of the French armies, with the support and help of all France, of the France that fights, of the only France, of the real France, of the eternal France!"[11] That this glorious boast obviously overlooks the roles of the US, British, and Canadian armies—as well as the fact that "all of France" included Vichy supporters, the Milice (thirty thousand strong), and a cornucopia of collaborators—is just one small indication of why the Allies viewed de Gaulle as a constant headache. He ceaselessly agitated from his office in London, agitated for resources and recognition of his self-appointed role as head of the Provisional Government of France, agitated for the liberation of Paris—not by the Resistance but by Allied armies with a French division in the vanguard. And there was such a French division available, the 2nd Armored Division under General Philippe Leclerc. That division had been formed in 1940 and had fought usefully in Africa, armed with US tanks and equipment. The 2nd was currently under General Patton's Third Army, and Patton had little use for the idea of being sidetracked into Paris; he wanted to push toward Germany with all possible speed. He famously said that fixed fortifications were monuments to the stupidity of man, or words to that effect. Leclerc and de Gaulle naturally chafed at being thwarted, but they could do little about it except protest the Allied strategy. As for the claim that "all of France" was involved in its liberation, historian Michael Neiberg estimates that only about 10 percent of the French supported the Resistance, at least during the occupation.[12] The other ninety percent consisted of willing collaborators, or ordinary people who were either ambivalent or resigned to a wait and see approach, all the while trying to make it from one day to the next.

There were two phases to the Resistance in France: pre-D-Day and post-D-Day. Before the invasion the Resistance was not a unified force (nor would it really be after D-Day). Instead it was by necessity a collection of small cells, for the possibility of infiltration and betrayal was very real. The pre-invasion Resistance could do little but occasionally assassinate collaborators and Milice, publish clandestine newspapers, and guide Allied aviators who had been shot down, either through Switzerland or across the Pyrenees. Resisters could also sabotage war manufacturing through work slowdowns, activities that fell short of actually damaging equipment and so did not risk severe reprisals. And reprisals were a genuine danger.

In Paris the Resistance was dominated by the Francs-Tireurs et Partisans (FTP). The FTP was a communist organization. Through the courageous efforts of a young French politician, Jean Moulin, who made his circuitous and dangerous way to London to confer with de Gaulle, the FTP and other Resistance groups across the country pledged their support to de Gaulle and his Provisional Government. Aside from their hatred for the Germans and their Vichy allies, the

Resistance groups had little in common with de Gaulle, who they feared would try to establish a dictatorship once France was liberated. But de Gaulle provided access to the British and Americans who were the only source of the weapons the Parisian Resistance desperately needed and continuously called for—to little if any avail. Moulin's diplomacy among the Resistance groups throughout France managed to keep some semblance of discipline. But unfortunately he was arrested in Lyon. Most likely an informer betrayed Moulin to the Gestapo, who tortured him to death.

French leaders in London were desperate to try to establish some greater degree of discipline in the Resistance as a whole. French historian Henri Michel writes: "On 1 February 1944 the French Forces of the Interior (FFI) officially came into being, in principal absorbing all military Resistance formations—the Gaullist Secret Army, the communist Francs-Tireurs et Partisans, and the Army Resistance Organization (ORA) which owed allegiance to Giraud [de Gaulle's rival general based in Algiers]. France was divided into twelve military regions, and an FFI leader was nominated for each region and department, not without difficulty. The ORA in particular wished to be directly subordinate to Algiers, and its leaders only grudgingly accepted the authority of the civil heads of the regions."[13]

There is, not surprisingly, some murkiness about FFI and its formation. The historian Michael Neiberg writes that FFI and the FTP were both active in Paris earlier in the war and that the communist labor leader Henri Tanguy, also known as "Colonel Rol," was selected to command a combined operation of the two groups within the city. This is not the place to try to unravel these complexities, even if it were possible. In the countryside, however, there was still no clear chain of command.

The Paris Resistance groups were right to be suspicious of de Gaulle. They wanted to start a general uprising, but, as mentioned, de Gaulle feared that the results, if successful, would be potentially a springboard for the communists to claim they had defeated the

Germans in Paris, the most important symbol of France. The possibility of mass casualties to the citizens was also a concern to de Gaulle, although it's fair to wonder which worried him more. To liberate Paris was to liberate the soul of France. Trying to keep the Paris Resistance under control was an ongoing and frustrating chore. De Gaulle was helped however by the chronic shortage of weapons among the Paris Resistance. (It no doubt occurred to many that giving weapons to the communists was the last thing on de Gaulle's mind, or on the minds of the British and Americans.) They continually begged for airdrops, but the Allies refused, preferring instead to drop bombs as part of the "transportation plan" designed to degrade the German's ability to move troops and supplies. But because of the notorious inaccuracy of high-level bombing, the French civilians suffered more casualties from their Allies than they did from the Germans. As mentioned previously: "Allied bombardments killed 67,078 French citizens in all, 35,317 of them in 1944 alone."[14] Virtually cut off from their best sources of basic food (meat, dairy, and vegetables from Normandy), robbed by the voracious German army's insatiable supply needs, cruelly rationed by the Germans, and bombed by their Allies, Parisians might well be excused for feelings of despair. Bread lines were a daily ordeal, when there was bread. When there was not, it was worse.

Also, as could be expected in a country of 246 kinds of cheese (though little of any kind was available in Paris), politics was a problem. It is not at all surprising that there was genuine animosity between the communists and the Parisian police. The police had been active agents of political repression, with the communists being their particular targets. Not only were the communists the heart and soul of the Paris Resistance, they also espoused a political philosophy that was repugnant to the much more conservative police force—and to much of the population. Many hundreds of political opponents to Vichy were arrested and imprisoned by the police and their colleagues in the Milice, thereby freeing the Gestapo for the sinister work of interrogation and torture. The police were also useful sources of intelligence for the Gestapo who could not hope to surveil the two and a half million Parisians without the help of the fifteen-thousand-strong Parisian police force and Vichy officials in Paris. The chain of command started with Paris's mayor, Pierre Taittinger, and if that name seems familiar it is because Taittinger's name was also proudly displayed on a champagne label from the company he founded. He also founded a French equivalent to the Hitler Youth, Jeunesses Patriotes (Young Patriots) prior to the war. He was a vehement anticommunist and a willing collaborator with von Choltitz—perhaps, as he later claimed, as a means of protecting Paris from both the Germans and from the communists. Small wonder that the police were presented with moral and political conflicts. As a quasi-military organization, the police were not only used to following orders and the chain of command, they were unaccustomed to and uncomfortable with doing otherwise. De Gaulle therefore saw them as potentially a useful counterweight to the leftist Parisian Resistance.

Even worse, the police had been active in the rounding up and shipping off most of Paris's Jews—men, women, and children who were first sequestered in the appalling conditions of the Drancy prison camp, and then sent off to the death camps. In one two-day period the police arrested 13,152 Jews. Among them, 8,160 Jews, including 4,000 children, were locked up in the Vélodrome d'Hiver, an indoor bicycle racing facility. They languished there for five days, mostly without food or water or sanitary facilities, before being herded into cattle cars and sent to Auschwitz. None of the children survived. In 1940 there were 140,000 Jews in Paris. Almost all of them perished. Many were refugees from Germany and Eastern Europe, and these were the primary targets of the Vichy government and therefore the police. French-born Jews and naturalized citizens had the slight advantage of knowing their neighbors and, in some cases, members of the Resistance, some of whom helped them escape the police and Gestapo dragnets. Others, of course, were not so fortunate.

There is no denying the deep and abiding strain of anti-Semitism among some portions of the French public. The Alfred Dreyfus affair, if nothing else, exposed that. The "willing executioners" among the public in general and the police specifically are proof enough. American expat Elliot Paul quotes one of his Parisian neighbors: "All Jews make a mistake in being born . . . It makes life hard for them and for us."[15] And looking back in 1942 on the Paris of the twenties, the time so cherished and idealized by Hemingway and scores of others, Paul wrote: "Somehow the fall of Jericho does not seem so remote as the carefree 1920's."[16] Indeed it would be difficult to imagine a starker contrast between the twenties and the occupation years. Few in occupied Paris could describe themselves as carefree. Everyone was fearful, and most fearful of all were, of course, the Jews, because they were seen as the enemies not only of the Germans but also of many of their fellow Frenchmen.

Then, too, there was the not unusual tension between the police and the urban poor and working classes—the usual breeding ground for communism—so that politics and economics mingled to create severe discord between the police and the lower classes.

In short, large portions of the Paris citizenry detested the police. And yet, when D-Day finally came, and the Allies finally broke out of their beachhead, there would be some dramatic changes in attitudes within the various Parisian factions.

❖

The Resistance groups in Paris were more of a problem than a solution to Allied planners and de Gaulle. The political differences, to say nothing of their constant pleas for weapons and their calls for the Allies to assist in their liberation, were all problems no one in the Allied high command wanted to address. And de Gaulle, although hardly a member of the Allied inner circle of senior commanders, was just as reluctant to advocate for the Paris Resistance's request—until, that is, the timing was right.

It was different in the countryside. There the Resistance (aka the maquis) were generally scattered into small groups of partisans. And while, being French, they naturally had their share of political differences, there was no organization anything like the communist and leftist structure of the Parisians. This is not to say that the Paris Resistance was a well-led machine but rather to say that the maquis were not a machine at all. Moreover they lived out in the country where it was reasonably safe as long as they kept their heads down and did not attempt to fight any sort of pitched battle, however small. An ambush, yes; a pitched battle, no. As a result the Allies saw these groups as potentially useful, not only for intelligence but, come D-Day, as actual military assets behind German lines, assets that could through sabotage destroy rail and road transportation and thereby retard Germany's ability to move troops from the south and eastern mountains to the battlefields of Normandy and the area of the Seine. (Through sabotage and ambushes, the maquis delayed the 2nd SS Panzer Division for seventeen days, even though the five-hundred-mile trip from Toulouse should have taken at most half that time, if the roads were clear.)[17] Moreover, by hiding in the forests and countryside, the maquis had freedom of movement that allowed them not only to spy on and report German troop activities but also to conduct hit-and-run raids against German couriers and motorized patrols. So the Paris Resistance that the Allies regarded as a mixed blessing and, in fact, as a liability, was a force that was essentially immobile and trapped in a militarily (to the British and Americans) irrelevant city. The maquis in the countryside were regarded as a potentially useful weapon once the invasion began. It may be remembered that civilian resistance was one of Churchill's key strategic ideas (not that his strategic ideas were always very good). And given that fact, plus the fact that the maquis operated with some degree of freedom of movement—certainly in comparison to Paris—the Allies were able to supply them by air drop with weapons (small arms, of course), antipersonnel and anti-armor mines and plastic explosives, and as important, radios, so that they could report German movements and strength as well as receive orders when the time for invasion came. (Small arms are weapons that a single fighter can operate: rifles, submachine guns, pistols, grenades, etc. The most popular was the inexpensively made but useful Sten gun, an automatic submachine gun, of which thousands were dropped to the maquis.)

Since they were actively in the fight, literally fighting "the little war," i.e., as *guerillas*, the great moral dilemma of the maquis was how to deal with their complicity in the resulting German reprisals. German reprisals gave little if any thought to establishing the guilt or innocence of their victims. The aforementioned 2nd SS Panzer Division, which could well have been the most vicious of all German units in France, was traveling north toward the Normandy beachhead, no doubt frustrated by felled trees across the road, altered road signs, and perhaps an ambush or two. Traveling through the village of Oradour-sur-Glane outside of Limoges, the villagers threw some rocks at the troops, who then dismounted from their vehicles, rounded up virtually the entire village, locked them in barns and churches, and set the buildings on fire, killing 425 men, women, and children. France has left the shattered remains of the village just as the Germans left them, as a memorial to the villagers and as a stark reminder of what the Nazis were capable of. There were more abominations to come, specifically in the Vercors Massif, a wild and mountainous country that because of its apparent impenetrability attracted an unusually large contingent of maquis. Almost assuredly alerted to these concentrations by informers, the Germans bombed key areas and then sent in their troops by gliders.

Australian war correspondent T. Southwell-Keely filed this report on the atrocities committed in the Vercors: "WITH THE SEVENTH ARMY: Two members of the maquis were crucified and others had their tongues cut out and their eyes removed in terrible atrocities committed by the Germans. . . . About 4,000 patriots had concentrated in the Vercours Massif in wild rugged country intersected by gorges and few roads. The Germans surrounded the area with one division while an Alpine division was sent up to clear out the maquis."[18]

In the end the Germans killed 830 *maquisards*, their families, and simple villagers who may or may not have been sympathetic to the Resistance but not actively involved. And their use of diabolical torture was not limited to this one-sided battle. Captured Resistance fighters, even caught singly or in small groups were routinely mutilated—eyes and genitals being the most favored targets—all done before executing the victim, often a mere boy. OSS Colonel David Bruce writes about a visit one of his agents made to a French morgue: "[He had] seen the bodies of twelve French boys between the ages of fourteen and sixteen who had been killed by members of the 17th SS Panzer. The Germans had torn out their testicles, gouged out their eyes, and pulled their teeth before dispatching them."[19]

Hanging was another method of reprisal. In reaction to some Resistance activity in Tulle, a small city in central France, the Germans hanged ninety-nine people in the village square.[20] Another 149 were deported to Dachau. Few would survive the war. Not surprisingly, it was the 2nd SS Panzer Division that again was the perpetrator. The SS troops, as distinguished from the regular Wehrmacht, were the usual suspects in most atrocities. It is an example of the power of ideology to corrupt and dehumanize. In the battle for the Cotentin Peninsula the Resistance played a useful part in monitoring German positions and in sabotaging some of their movements. As a result the German fury was unleashed indiscriminately. As historian Colin Beavan writes: ". . . the Germans in their search [for Resistance fighters] had nailed a five-year-old boy to a farmhouse door and bayoneted him in his stomach, leaving him moaning for hours before he finally died. They caught a Resistance liaison girl [a message carrier], lashed her to one end of a rope under her armpits, the other onto the saddle of a horse, and dragged her to her death. Discovering a farm that had been [a Resistance hiding place] the Germans wrenched the live farmer's head off his neck and then stabbed his wife and children."[21] The five-year-old boy is haunting. We all know of course about the Holocaust, but for those who have had a five-year-old boy gamboling around the house, this incident is as powerful an image of evil as anyone could imagine—much like the way the picture of Anne Frank's sweet face haunts us as a symbol of murdered millions.

Of course France was not the only occupied country to suffer atrocities, nor was the SS the only perpetrator. Henri Michel writes: "In addition to the SS, the Wehrmacht initiated seizure of hostages, mass executions, burning of farms and villages. On the slightest pretext the entire population of a locality would be murdered, as at Kragujevac in Yugoslavia, where 7,300 people were massacred including all the schoolchildren with their teachers."[22]

The sadness and the tragedy of this war are beyond description. That is a limp expression of the horrors. There is no adequate description; none exists; none is possible. That is the reason that Dante created a seventh circle of hell—an area Hemingway would investigate in his postwar novel, *Across the River and into the Trees*.

CHAPTER NINE

"Ah, those first OSS arrivals in London! How I remember them—arriving like jeunes filles en fleur straight from a finishing school, all fresh and innocent, to start work in our frowsty old intelligence brothel! All too soon they were ravished and corrupted, becoming indistinguishable from seasoned pros who had been in the game for a quarter of a century and more."
—Malcolm Muggeridge, British Intelligence

William "Wild Bill" Donovan was a highly decorated hero of World War I, a flamboyant and energetic lawyer who amassed a fortune, and having done so, turned his eyes to new challenges, including Republican Party politics. He ran for governor in New York and lost badly. But like many Americans at the time he was concerned about the direction Europe seemed to be taking, and as an unofficial intelligence agent for a group of businessmen and lawyers called "The Room," he traveled to Europe to assess the political climate and the risks to the interests of his colleagues. He met with Franco in Spain and with Mussolini in Italy. He also established connections with the British and in particular with William Stephenson, a member of Britain's MI6, their intelligence agency. A Canadian, Stephenson, who was code-named "Intrepid," was responsible for intelligence activities in North America, and he courted Donovan aggressively to assist him in his efforts to sway American opinion in Britain's favor. There was, as is commonly known, a great divide between the isolationists, like Joseph P. Kennedy and, famously, Charles Lindbergh, on the one side and the internationalists like Roosevelt and, as it turned out, Donovan on the other. From 1938 to 1940, Kennedy was America's ambassador to the Court of St. James. From his vantage point in London he observed the collapse of the French army, the disaster at Dunkirk, and the Blitz, and he came to the conclusion that the Germans were on the verge of winning the war, and that the British could not hope to survive. Kennedy's isolationism and his unconcealed anti-Semitism contributed to his feelings that Hitler held the winning hand, and as a result he said, "Democracy is finished in England." This was not a message Roosevelt wanted to hear; and that statement and others like it cost Kennedy his job. Few, if anyone, in government in England regretted his departure.

Donovan was also in London during the Blitz and he interviewed, no doubt with Stephenson's assistance and approval, a number of British officials, including Winston Churchill. He had dinner with King George VI, who was impressively bellicose and determined to defeat the Nazis. As was Churchill, of course. Also with Stephenson's assistance, Donovan interviewed Stewart Graham Menzies, head of MI6 (Secret Intelligence Service), who went by the code name "C." Menzies explained the workings of MI6 with the understood objective of convincing Donovan that the United States should have a similar operation, even though it was not yet at war. The object was cooperation.

How all this unfolded is still a little vague. As historian Nelson Lankford writes:

"The murky origins of British-American cooperation in intelligence matters are made no clearer by the heroic mythologies surrounding the founding fathers of modern espionage. It appears through Stephenson's reports and Donovan's visits, the British came to believe that 'Wild Bill' had Roosevelt's ear. They also believed that he was the best man to create a covert intelligence organization that could work in tandem with their own hard-pressed service. They revealed to him the operations of their secret agencies with remarkable openness. . . ."[1]

This was red meat to Donovan, and he and a British naval officer working for intelligence named Ian Fleming (the same) drew up a proposal to establish a US variant of MI6.

Donovan returned to the States and conferred with Roosevelt, whom he had known at Columbia Law School, and reported that he believed the British could withstand the German onslaught, if they had help. This was more in line with Roosevelt's thinking. So too was the proposal for a new US intelligence agency. It should be noted that at the time there was no central intelligence agency in the United States. Instead there were intelligence gathering operations within the navy, army, and the FBI—all of which tried to protect their turf and bitterly resisted the idea of a new and centralized agency. As Colonel David Bruce wrote: "[These other agencies] forgot their internecine animosities and joined in an attempt to strangle this unwanted newcomer at birth."[2] A bureaucrat, even one in uniform, is still a bureaucrat and jealous of his portfolio. Not surprisingly, J. Edgar Hoover was one of the most vociferous opponents of Donovan's proposal. Roosevelt agreed with the basic idea of the agency, but he was sensitive to the politics of the situation, and gave Donovan some, but not all, of what he wanted—it would not be a centralized intelligence agency. The rival agencies would retain their independence. But the president did authorize what was called the Coordinator of Information office (COI); Donovan was appointed head. This was on June 11, 1941. Later, when the United States was officially at war, the name would be changed to the Office of Strategic Services, the OSS.

Donovan began hiring. He adopted in many ways the British model of acquiring an Old Boys Network. He was drawn to people he believed could be gifted amateurs, intelligent people who could learn spycraft. In truth he had little choice, because there were few potential candidates who already knew the game, and most of those who did were already attached to the FBI or army and navy. He was essentially building from scratch. His recruiting efforts yielded a mixed bag: "OSS endured its share of criticism in part because of the ample supply of dilettantes who found their way into its ranks. In the early months critics devised endless derogatory permutations for the service's acronym. 'Oh So Social,' or 'Oh, so Silly' being examples of the kinder variety."[3]

It will be remembered that the OSS is the agency Hemingway tried to join but was rejected as being too independent a spirit. There is a glaring irony in this because Wild Bill was nothing if not independent and creative to the point of outshining even Churchill with his various schemes for espionage and covert action. As Evan Thomas writes: "The OSS was . . . freewheeling. 'Woe to the officer who turned down a project because, on the face of it, it seemed ridiculous or at least unusual,' recalled David Bruce. 'His imagination was unlimited. Ideas were his playthings. Excitement made him snort like a racehorse.' In the early days no scheme was too madcap. An OSS psychologist thought that Hitler could be demoralized by exposure to vast quantities of pornography. OSS men dutifully set about collecting smut to be dropped near the Reichsfuhrer's headquarters. Before the plan could be executed an Army Air Corps colonel cursed Donovan and swore he would not risk the life of a single airman on such a boondoggle."[4] (This idea reminds us of the CIA's plots to poison Fidel Castro's beard, so that the loss of its iconic imagery would, if it didn't kill him, diminish him. As mentioned, the CIA is the natural offspring of the OSS—and Wild Bill.)

The command structure of the OSS allowed Donovan to recruit from civilians as well as all the services. That is how he acquired such people as navy commander and filmmaker John Ford, and even ordinary soldiers like army corporal and future historian (and loyal member of the Kennedy family team), Arthur Schlesinger. By the end of the war the OSS employed over thirteen thousand people and was a global operation, although still arguing over turf with domestic rivals, such as the FBI.

This was the organization Hemingway really wanted to join, much more so than the vast machine of the journalistic press. And you would think that Hemingway and Donovan would have been soul mates. Surely their exuberance and appetite for adventure would have bonded them, as well as their ability to be charming or abrasive, depending on the situation or mood. But no doubt Hemingway's application was rejected at a lower level. In retrospect it should have been accepted. Of course, he did not like bureaucracy and did not like taking orders, but he would have been, and in fact was, a useful clandestine agent. As it turned out, another Hemingway, Ernest's oldest son Jack (Bumby), would be accepted into the OSS and would be wounded and captured while on a covert mission in France. (In Hemingway fashion, he parachuted into France carrying a fishing rod—whether a fly rod or a bait casting rod is not clear.) And in another irony, Ernest Hemingway would unofficially operate with the OSS in the liberation of Paris, and with the OSS head of operations in Europe, the aforementioned Colonel David K. E. Bruce.

The Oh, So Social aspect of the OSS could well be personified by David Bruce. A product of Princeton, friend of Fitzgerald, an officer during World War I, married to the daughter of the former banker and treasury secretary, Andrew W. Mellon, and therefore independently wealthy, Bruce was urbane, sophisticated, and socially well connected both in the United States and England. He was the type of American that many Brits were surprised to discover even existed; that such a polished and accomplished character was actually bred in the former colonies was something of a revelation. He would certainly be viewed as the opposite of Joe Kennedy, who was widely viewed as a publicity-seeking parvenu and something of a coward as well. (Kennedy moved himself and his family out of London during the Blitz, and as one MP put it: "I thought my daffodils were yellow until I met Joe Kennedy.") After World War I Bruce traveled widely throughout Europe and developed a taste for differing cultures. He decided to join the diplomatic service, and for a year was vice consul in Rome. But his wife's poor health caused them to return to the United States and private life. His family connections led to offers to sit on the boards of a number of prominent companies, and when the European war broke out he joined the Red Cross as part of their war relief activity. He traveled to the UK and, like Donovan, was there during the Blitz. The two men knew each other, and Donovan appreciated Bruce's abilities and recruited him to become the head of COI's secret intelligence unit, based in Washington. Then in 1943 Donovan sent Bruce to London to expand the European operations of the now-named OSS.

One of the many people Bruce attracted was Raymond Guest, an American naval officer and son of a British diplomat and his American wife. Guest would eventually be in charge of the OSS's small fleet of PT boats. The PTs were one of the ways the OSS used to insert secret agents into France. Interestingly, Guest's brother, Winston, was one of Hemingway's best friends, and he was Hemingway's second-in-command during the U-boat-hunting months in Cuba. When the U-boat hunts were shut down, Winston joined the marines. The Guests were well connected socially, both in the United States and England. They were second cousins to Winston Churchill and distant descendants of the Dukes of Marlborough. But Raymond Guest and his brother Winston were not mere social butterflies or dilettantes. As with Bruce, their wealth and social position did not persuade them to avoid the dangers and rigors of war. Instead, they volunteered, and put themselves in harm's way, like millions of other Americans.

Hemingway's poem "First Poem for Mary" mentions Winston Guest three times by Hemingway's nickname for him, "Wolfie." The beginning of the poem more or less describes Hemingway's attack on a suspected U-boat. They thought they were going into combat. They weren't, but they believed they were.

❖

In a top secret memo to Roosevelt, General Eisenhower said: "We are going to need very badly the support of the Resistance groups in France." This was a position that Churchill thoroughly approved of. In 1940 he established the Special Operations Executive (SOE) to recruit, train, and insert agents into Occupied Europe. "And now set Europe ablaze," he told the fledgling agency.[5] Their role was primarily clandestine sabotage and, when possible, assassination. (SOE was responsible for the assassination of the notorious SS General Reinhard Heydrich in Prague. French historian Henri Michel says that the decision was made by the Czech government in exile—in London—but the assassins were most certainly trained and transported by SOE assets.) Agents also attempted to establish contact with Resistance groups, although in the case of France this was not so easy given the fragmented and squabbling nature of the various groups. SOE agents took their orders from London and communicated back and forth by means of coded radio transmissions. To state the blindingly obvious, this was highly dangerous work, and in France alone over one hundred agents (including thirteen women) were captured and tortured to death or sent to perish in a concentration camp. One hundred-plus deaths may seem coldly insignificant in the context of the millions of casualties in the war, but each of them was also a key to clandestine networks, so that by torturing one to supply information (not all could resist Gestapo torture) meant that scores of unknown fighters would suffer arrest, death, or imprisonment.

SOE headquarters was not especially delighted when the OSS came to London. David Bruce's diplomatic skills helped paper over the resentment SOE felt toward these newcomers, but the resentment was still there (mostly over whose turf was where) and in some ways impeded the cooperation that would in the end prove essential. But early in 1944 the two agencies put their bureaucratic and operational jealousies aside and combined their operations into one organization that was called Special Forces Headquarters (SFHQ). They reported directly to Supreme Headquarters Allied Expeditionary Forces (SHAEF), in other words, to Ike, who had a useful understanding of bureaucratic politics and how to circumvent them, or at least manage them. The object here was to ensure that the French Resistance fighters would operate in line with Ike's strategic plans when the invasion took place. He did not want them running off half-cocked. The essence of his strategy was to immobilize German troops as much as possible, so that reinforcements could not move quickly to the invasion beaches. That meant that specific bridges and rail lines had to be cut. It should not be just random violence. It would not do for the Resistance fighters to rise up and start killing the occasional German or Milice. The targets had to be part of the plan. Therefore they would need specific orders about where and when to attack, or they would be of little use. Nor could the Resistance be expected to know how to blow up a bridge or derail a troop or supply train. For that they would need not only the proper weapons and explosives but also training in how to use them. No doubt during the Occupation some Resistance fighters had learned some of the tricks of the trade, but this ad hoc expertise would not address Eisenhower's need for coordinated attacks designed to clog the transportation facilities of the Germans. Aerial bombing as part of the "transportation plan," was pervasive but notoriously, and sadly, inaccurate. The most effective way to destroy enemy transportation routes and methods was sabotage. If it could be done. And it was not just transportation facilities that needed destroying. The actual columns of German troops streaming toward the invasion sites also needed to be attacked and delayed. That required well-planned ambushes, something the Resistance groups, especially the relatively inexperienced maquis, would find difficult, since they were largely without organization or training. Many were just young men and boys who took to the woods to avoid being sent to Germany as slave labor. Properly armed and led, they could be—and as it turned out, would be—useful combatants and a terror to any German they captured. For when the action came, they often took no prisoners. Given the ferocity of the German reprisals and their random and senseless violence, it is hardly surprising. And so a German clerk who never fired a weapon would pay with his life for a five-year-old boy nailed to a barn door by the SS. No one was concerned with justice; they were only concerned with revenge.

To solve this problem of how best to use the scattered and disunited Resistance, the SOE and the OSS had begun training a special unit of agents. The problem was anticipated early on, during the planning phase for the D-Day invasion. It is part of the marvel of the complex planning that led to D-Day that the planners recognized the strengths and weakness of the Resistance, and created an operation to deal with it. Having to navigate their turbulent politics with de Gaulle's adherents versus the communists in Paris and the countryside did not make matters easy. But ultimately the Allied strategy worked.

An important part of it was Operation Jedburgh. Named for a small town in Scotland, Operation Jedburgh consisted of three hundred highly trained officers and enlisted radio operators. In teams of three—two officers and one radio operator—they would parachute into France and link up with the various Resistance groups and lead them to targets directed by the SFHQ. They would also organize drops of weapons and other supplies. In 1944 the Allies dropped 350,000 Sten guns, 150,000 pistols, and 80,000 rifles as well as ammunition, grenades, bazookas, plastic explosives, and detonators.[6] (A Sten gun could fire 9mm ammunition, the same used by many German weapons. Its magazine held thirty-two rounds and could fire eight rounds a second. Its effective accurate range was one hundred meters.) Since the Resistance was in theory under the unified command of the

FFI, a Gaullist organization, and since many in the Resistance had little if any actual loyalty to FFI, the weapons and supplies, as well as training in how to use them, were crucial motivation for Resistance leaders to follow orders from the Jedburgh agents. Even then it took some persuasion and diplomacy to organize the sometimes unruly mobs of maquis.

The Jedburghs were not the only Allied agents dropped into France; there were 389 SOE and OSS special agents as well. Their mission was sabotage of targets that were deemed too difficult for the amateurs of the maquis. But most were operating on their own or in small groups. The special expertise of the Jedburgh teams was organizing and carrying out guerilla warfare as well as sabotage that did not require too much technical expertise, such as derailing trains by cutting tracks or cutting German telephone lines. They were prepared to lead large numbers of Resistance fighters.

As mentioned the primary mission of the Jedburgh-led Resistance was to immobilize the German divisions and prevent them from moving to the invasion beaches. By sabotaging the railroads and motorways and blowing bridges they could delay if not prevent German reinforcements from counterattacking the Allies' beachhead. And their assignment went beyond simple sabotage. Ambush of the German columns was a vital element of the Resistance tactics. Here the guerilla training of the Jedburgh teams was crucial. First they needed to identify a location that allowed the Resistance fighters to hide and ideally fire down on the German columns, and as importantly, a location that would allow them to escape after a minute or so of rapid firing. They instructed their men when ambushing a column to let the leading motorcyclists pass and then fire a bazooka round into the leading vehicle to block the road. Then hidden in the woods along the road as many as a couple of hundred maquis would empty their Sten guns and rifles into the column of trucks, aiming first for the driver and the officers. And as the troops piled out of the trucks, the Maquis would empty their second magazine, and kill as many as possible knowing that careful aiming was less important than laying down a volume of fire. Then in a matter of mere minutes the Jedburgh officers would signal a retreat and the maquisards would disappear into the woods and head for the designated rendezvous. The selection of the ambush site obviously contributed to it its success. Even the most hardened SS soldier would think twice about going into the forest where the maquis may be lying in wait. Using these tactics one Jedburgh team "estimated that its Resistance killed 15,000 Germans and destroyed seventy-five vehicles in the four weeks beginning on August 20."[7] Body counts are notoriously inaccurate, but it is clear: Ike was right in thinking that the Resistance could be not only useful, but critical.

"The most important Resistance contributions, according to a SHAEF report, included forcing the Germans to chase after maquis groups instead of fighting the Allies; delaying German troop movement to the battlefronts; disrupting German telecommunications; providing military intelligence, and taking over military precautions, such as flank protection and mopping up, so that Allied armies could advance at greater speed."[8]

And in a letter to the head of SOE Ike wrote: "In no previous war and in no other theater during this war, have Resistance forces been so closely harnessed to the main military effort. . . . I must express my great admiration for the brave and often spectacular exploits of the agents and special groups under the control of Special Force Headquarters."[9]

It would not be long before Hemingway joined these Resistance fighters. Or is it that they joined him?

※

On August 18 Hemingway returned to France. His new assignment was to cover Patton's Third Army, units of which were about to participate in Operation Cobra, which was the plan to break out from the narrow ten-mile-deep beachhead. We know that he was at General Bradley's briefing, because, as Antony Beevor writes: "The Soviet war correspondent Lieutenant Colonel Viktor Kraminov, who had a spiteful word for almost everyone, described Hemingway looking over everyone's head. 'The flamboyant, red-headed Knickerbocker . . . was recounting anecdotes as tedious as his numerous and superficial pieces.'" [10] Cobra got underway with two accidental disasters—bombing of Allied troops by Allied airplanes—incidents that Hemingway's hero in *Across the River* would remember with bitterness. One hundred and twenty-six men were killed and five hundred and ninety-four were wounded in the two accidents. [11]

Hemingway linked up with the 4th Division and moved from there to what would become his favorite outfit, the 22nd Regiment under his soon to be good friend, Colonel Charles "Buck" Lanham. Lanham was a wiry, rather short officer who was a fiercely aggressive and thoroughly brave leader who rode his men hard and felt no compulsion about firing battalion or company officers if he felt they were not up to their duties. He also had no reluctance to lead his men in combat from the front, when he thought it was necessary. Profane and irreligious he was the kind of professional soldier Hemingway admired. As has been mentioned, Lanham was the author of the book *Infantry in Battle*. This would turn out to be a fortunate partnership between the two men. Both respected the other's professionalism and courage, and Lanham allowed Hemingway the kind of freedom of movement that Hemingway needed in order to wage his private war against the Germans. Carlos Baker describes the first meeting between Hemingway and Lanham. He writes that Lanham was pleasantly surprised by Hemingway's quick grasp of the military situation and by his manner, which was polite and "deferential." He asked intelligent questions and listened carefully to Lanham's explanations. Lanham also was impressed by Hemingway's "battle sense" and understanding of terrain. [12]

General Barton, commander of the 4th Division, gave Hemingway a jeep and assigned a driver, Private Archie "Red" Pelkey. Later in the period Hemingway would liberate a German Mercedes-Benz and a motorcycle with a sidecar. He had the car painted army green. So he had the mobility he needed to put his plans into action. And he had a useful factotum who would follow orders and be happy to do so.

Following closely behind the 4th Division, Hemingway arrived by motorcycle in the town of Villedieu-les-Poêles, which was being slowly cleared in house-to-house fighting. It was August 3. Snipers were active as Hemingway dodged between the building rubble and interviewed the locals. (He was not gathering material for his articles; he was gathering intelligence regarding German positions.) One of the locals reported that some SS troops were hiding in a nearby cellar; apparently they had been bypassed by the American infantry. The man showed Hemingway and Pelkey where the cellar was, whereupon Hemingway repeatedly called to the Germans to come out and surrender. When he got no response he tossed three grenades into the cellar, saying: "Divide these among yourselves."[13] Strangely, he did not check on the results and therefore never really knew whether there had been any SS troops there at all. Perhaps he did not want to know, so that he could later claim, as Carlos Baker has pointed out, that he had killed "plenty Nazis."[14] Seen in the context of "The Short Happy Life of Francis Macomber," however, there is a certain irony in Hemingway's failure to check on his handiwork. In the story Macomber is revealed as a coward, because he would not go into the tall grass to dispatch the lion he had wounded. He relies on his professional hunter to do the work, even after suggesting that they just leave the lion there to suffer. The hunter is shocked and says, "It's not done." Most likely if the cellar was filled with Germans, or even with just a handful, some of them might not have been killed by the grenades; some might have been just wounded, and wounded enemy troops were routinely treated by US medics. (Except for snipers.) By not checking, Hemingway was violating his own code as a hunter. Of course, there is a difference between the vicious SS troops and a game animal that, while dangerous, is innocent of anything and simply being true to its nature. Still, there remains something of a question about Hemingway's behavior. It is certainly true that Hemingway was violating the Geneva Conventions, whether the cellar was inhabited or not.

The townspeople who watched Hemingway's action were suitably impressed, and not troubled by his behavior. They assumed he was some kind of important character, took him to the *Hôtel de Ville* (city hall), and introduced him to the mayor, who congratulated him and gave him two magnums of champagne. He went back to his motorcycle just as Buck Lanham was coming through town in his jeep on his way back to the command post. Buck remembered his earlier and first meeting with the correspondent, stopped the jeep, and asked what the hell Hemingway was doing and why was he beaming. Ernest told him about the cellar grenade attack and gave Lanham one of the magnums. Undoubtedly, Lanham knew about the rules against correspondents carrying weapons, and just as undoubtedly he didn't care. The champagne was the beginning of "a beautiful friendship." He drove off, a happy commander after a successful and albeit continuing action, and he remembered Hemingway, "standing poised as ever on the balls of his feet. Like a fighter. Like a great cat. Easy. Relaxed. Absorbed. Intent. Watchful. Missing nothing."[15] There was still fighting going on in the streets, but Hemingway seemed unconcerned about exposing himself. In a letter to his wife Lanham said of Hemingway: "He is probably the bravest man I have ever known, with an unquenchable lust for battle and adventure."[16] When it came to bravery Lanham, a West Pointer and professional soldier, knew what he was talking about, and his comments here and elsewhere are a vivid rejoinder to the critics who said Hemingway was a military poseur, someone who was "playing soldier." In that context it's worth revisiting those criticisms. To RAF PRO John Pudney Hemingway seemed like a ham actor playing the role of Ernest Hemingway and doing it badly. His role as the tough guy contrasted glaringly with the youthful RAF pilots whose modesty and quiet courage were in sharp contrast to Hemingway's outsized behavior, like "a bizarre cardboard figure."[17] Pudney was a PRO, which is not to say he was a noncombatant. But it is to say that he might have been the subject of Hemingway's contempt—something no one was likely to forget. There were only a few people he respected; no one else needed to apply.

It was no cardboard figure standing, exposed and watching on a street corner during the house-to-house fighting in Villedieu-les-Poêles. What that PRO officer did not understand, apparently, is that Hemingway really believed what he said. Perhaps it was melodramatic and in its way too much a cartoonish interpretation, but it was what he believed. Truly. And it was the way he acted. There is no gainsaying that.

In an August 30 letter to his wife (whom he wrote to nearly every day) Lanham said: "We've killed a lot of Krauts in the last few days and taken hundreds of prisoners. . . . There is no babying these killers, I'm glad to say. Our prisoners are terrified of the French whom they have terrorized for four years. I may add that they have good reason to be. . . . There are still some dark and bloody days ahead for the French. The village is small but not too small to have its collaborationists and its women who have [illegible] with the Boche. I have just returned from the town's little public square where the women who offended had their heads shaved. It is not a pretty sight but even so these people are more gentle than those of the bigger cities . . . where the shavees were stripped and paraded. One does not see what happens to the men—but one knows."[18]

Not every "horizontal collaborator" was publicly humiliated. Coco Chanel and the film star "Arletty," who both lived in luxury at the Ritz with high-level German lovers, escaped severe censure, perhaps in the case of Arletty because she said, "My heart is French, but my ass is international." Perhaps the French appreciated her feistiness. Or talents. (She did spend a few weeks in prison afterward, but then resumed her career.) As for Chanel, today she is much better known for the perfume and the "little black dress" than for having slept with a high-ranking German official. And they were hardly alone in their adventures. Historian Michael Neiberg estimates that between one and two hundred thousand illegitimate "enfants de Boche" were a product of the four years of occupation.

❖

The details of Hemingway's private war are a little sketchy, most likely because what he was doing was illegal, and he accordingly held his peace thereafter. What's more, his colleague in many of these adventures was OSS Colonel David Bruce, whose memories of much of what went on were, of necessity, best kept to himself. Knowing what we do know of Hemingway's tendency to embellish events, this reticence seems out of character. He did write a story after the war called "Black Ass at the Crossroads." The story suggests he (or his main character) was involved in some ambushes while leading a group of FFIs and implies very strongly that the main character felt a certain sadness, if not guilt, about his role. His striking account of the feeling about shooting a German off a bicycle strikes remarkably true. Shooting at a German vehicle is one thing. They are faceless targets, generally. Shoot an individual German off a bicycle—a very young German at that—generates Black Ass, Hemingway's term for severe depression. Both targets are Germans in uniform, but killing a boy on a bike generates different emotion, always Hemingway's object to create for the reader. The spinning wheel of an overturned bicycle suggests the truth of war, the unpredictable wheel of fortune. Somewhere in Germany a family was dreading the possibility of the news. And the main character here has authored it. He thinks briefly about taking a souvenir, but decides against it. That might bring bad luck, and he wishes he could send some of the boy's effects to his family, but that too is impossible. One of his men stays with the boy as he dies and even kisses him on the forehead. The Hemingway character regrets not doing the same thing. "I should have kissed him myself if I was any good. It was just one of those things that you omit to do and that stay with you." [19]

Whether that incident really happened or not is beside the point. The Black Ass emotions he is feeling during these clandestine operations are as genuine as his happiness that he expressed to Mary in his letters to her. He was feeling happy to be with the 4th Division, including Buck Lanham's regiment. He was on a wild emotional ride, and of course his wild ride was not all that different from those of the people he was working with. But it could be regarded as symptomatic of future troubles. Further, the image of a young soldier ambushed and shot off his bicycle, with the capsized bicycle and its spinning wheels, illustrates Hemingway's achievement of what he wanted to achieve. He wanted us to know how things were—a dead German boy and a spinning bicycle wheel were "how it was." You had killed him. It had been an easy shot. And he was never going to be anything ever again. Because of what you did. You felt the way you felt, and you did not lose those feelings. They would not go away.

It's not known when Hemingway wrote that story. The note introducing it says it was unpublished and written between the end of the war and 1961,[20] so the main character's Black Ass may well have mirrored Hemingway's growing depression, and the closer it was to 1961, of course, the greater that probability. As the main character says: "I don't know how I could feel any worse. But you can all right. I can promise you that."[21] It seems strange, though, that the story was never published. As with *For Whom the Bell Tolls*, the story allows for a complex view of war. It seems to me, at least, a very good story that lacks any pretense to heroism or false notes of the kind that now and then pop up in his World War II journalism.

❖

Hemingway's self-appointed role as guerrilla fighter and intelligence gatherer was apparently highly regarded by General Barton, who supplied Hemingway with weapons. Hemingway gathered intelligence (which he called "gen") primarily by scouting the countryside and talking to the locals. He would then report to Barton or Lanham. Near the village of Saint-Pois, he, Pelkey, and the photographer Bob Capa were tooling down the road looking for Lanham's command post. When they missed the turnoff to Lanham and instead came around a curve they encountered a German tank destroyer (TD). It fired a shell that landed ten yards in front of the motorcycle and blew Hemingway into a ditch where he hit his head on a boulder. Another concussion. The other two men huddled for cover on the other side of the road. The Germans then opened up with the tank destroyer's machine guns and kept the trio pinned down for two hours before withdrawing. In a letter to Mary, Hemingway says that he could hear the enemy talking and making derogatory comments about him, thinking him dead. Maybe. But it seems strange that a contingent from a TD who thought their enemies dead would not peer over the hedgerow to check. After all, there might be useful information on their bodies. But war accommodates all kinds of strange behavior, so perhaps that is how it really happened. And why did the TD pull out? Orders, most likely.

As an aside, a tank destroyer moved by caterpillar treads like a regular tank, but it did not have a turret. The lack of a turret meant it had a lower profile, which was useful in ambushes. Not having a turret, though, meant that the crew was only protected by a three-sided steel shield, or casement. The lack of a heavy turret meant that the TD could support a heavier caliber cannon on a standard tank chassis. The heavier gun was primarily designed to attack enemy armor, hence the name tank destroyer. Various models had different calibers, but by this period of the war the German TDs were armed with 75mm + dreaded 88mm guns, as well as machine guns. The 88 was supremely accurate up to a range of one mile. How they missed Hemingway is a wonder. Perhaps he still had his luck, or most of it.

The United States had a similar weapon, and in his *Collier's* story "War in the Siegfried Line," Hemingway explains how the TD cannon was used to blast the heavy steel back doors of German bunkers, killing or wounding virtually everyone inside. From the front and sides these bunkers were virtually invisible, built into the hillside and heavily camouflaged and protected. But the US troops soon learned to recognize their features and very quickly learned that the best way to attack them was not from the front or side, but from the rear.

After a nerve-racking two hours huddled behind a low wall, Hemingway and the others watched the Germans withdraw and then trudged back to find Lanham's CP (command post). They had to tow the shot-up motorcycle. On the way back Hemingway and Capa argued vehemently. Hemingway accused Capa of hiding in the ditch on the other side of the road, safe from German fire, just so he could take a historic picture of Hemingway's corpse.[22] It's possible there was some truth in that; it's also possible that Capa was just trying to avoid getting killed. The two scenarios are not incompatible.

Speaking of luck, Hemingway freely admitted he was deeply superstitious. He made no bones about it. He said he thought religion was superstition, and that was why he practiced it, after his fashion. He had become a Roman Catholic upon his second marriage, and the mystical elements of the faith appealed to him. This is not to say he was devout but that his imagination was drawn to or compatible with the imagery and rituals of the church. Few romantics are drawn to the Puritans; many to the ritualism and mysticism of the Catholics. As for superstition, Hemingway routinely touched wood at the mention of being lucky or to ward off disaster (as does his main character in "The Undefeated," though much good it does him). And he famously carried a horse chestnut in his right pocket as well as a rabbit's foot that the fur had worn off so that he could feel the claws and know that he still had his luck. And if he had in fact shot that German boy at the crossroads, not taking a souvenir may have in his mind saved him from the TD's 88. Even if the story was made up, his main character would have been carrying some sort of charm; Hemingway does not say it, but it is one of those details you know without having to be told.

❖

And now there would be an interlude of fraternity. After successfully dodging an 88 shell and machine gun bullets, Hemingway took a few days off and, with his new friend Bill Walton, drove over to the newly liberated Mont Saint-Michel. They checked into the one hotel that was open: Hotel la Mère Poulard where Hemingway set about charming the *patronne*, Madame Chevalier, who reciprocated by providing a cornucopia of wine that she had successfully hidden from the Germans. The group of correspondents who gathered at the hotel included Bob Capa, Charles Collingwood, and A. J. Liebling, who assumed the duties as menu organizer, while Hemingway selected the wine for their long lunch hours and sumptuous dinners, courtesy of Madame Chevalier. Also in the group was Helen Kirkpatrick, a reporter for the *Chicago Daily News* and a woman who was as intrepid as Martha Gellhorn. By this time in the war the army had loosened its regulation against female reporters at the front. Had they not, it's likely that Kirkpatrick would have dodged them just as Gellhorn had.

During this period Hemingway wrote an article called "The General" (later called "The GI and the General") using his experience with General Barton. The story contains scenes of Hemingway in close contact during an artillery duel with the Germans, as well as a conversation between some bitter and griping GIs, while the story ends with a scene between Hemingway and the tired general who commands. The contrast favors the general who is plainly concerned about his men and their fatigue. Enlisted men at the front routinely assume that the top brass are somewhere safe behind the lines. One GI, whose wife is cheating on him, says the general is sixty miles behind. The general in this case, however, was only a few thousand yards behind, and like his men he was bordering on exhaustion. What's more, though it is unstated, he has the soul-destroying knowledge of the casualty rates.

Hemingway showed the story to Collingwood and asked his opinion: "I was a very young and very brash war correspondent in those days and made the mistake of thinking he really wanted to know. . . . So I told him it read to me like somebody's parody of Ernest

Hemingway. I don't think he spoke to me again until we got to Paris."[23] This is the second time Hemingway showed his work to colleagues; the first was in London to Roald Dahl. It's interesting to compare this apparent need for approval with his description of reading his drafts of a novel when he was visiting the south of France in the twenties and how they (Gerald and Sarah Murphy, almost certainly) became ecstatic, which he says should have indicated that the stuff was no good. "If these bastards like it, what is wrong with it?"[24] He berates himself for acting unprofessionally by reading his work to others, but he would go on to do the same thing throughout his life.

From his base in Mont Saint-Michel Hemingway drove over to Buck Lanham's new headquarters. The colonel was in the process of organizing an elaborate dinner to celebrate his twentieth wedding anniversary. He was comfortably ensconced in a Norman chateau, and he invited Hemingway to attend the dinner the next night. But something about the scene bothered Hemingway, and he decided to drive back to his hotel. The next day the Germans counterattacked the American positions and shelled the chateau, killing and wounding a number of Lanham's staff and wounding Lanham himself. When asked later why Hemingway had refused to attend the (permanently postponed) dinner, he said, "The place stank of death."[25] Later in the war Lanham was complaining to Hemingway about the performance of one of his officers and said he was intending to replace him. Hemingway said, in essence, "You won't have to; he stinks of death." The officer was killed that day. Readers of *For Whom the Bell Tolls* will remember Pilar's description of the smell of impending death and remember how the gypsies who knew such things would leave a restaurant when a doomed matador entered, as though the stench of death was itself contagious, in the way that the imminent deaths of replacement troops was also considered contagious to American veterans. How Hemingway knew the smell of coming death will remain a mystery. But on at least two occasions during the war, he was apparently channeling Pilar.

CHAPTER TEN

"They started their own goddamned insurrection. Now let them finish it."

—General George S. Patton

"Yesterday the Resistance, having heard we were in Versailles and moving onto Paris, rose prematurely and are said to have suffered considerable losses."

—Colonel David Bruce

S omewhere around the middle of August Hemingway left the 4th Division and headed east. He may or may not have known about the difference of opinion about whether liberating Paris made military sense. Most likely he did not know. But if it happened, certainly he intended to be there when it did.

Traveling in the jeep that General Barton had lent him, and driven as usual by Red Pelkey, Hemingway arrived in Rambouillet, a town that was something like thirty miles southwest of Paris, and that sat along one of the two major roads to the capital. The Germans had only just left and were said to be mining the road to Paris. Knowing the road system as well as anyone, the Germans were most likely to retake the town. There were few if any defenders there.

Bruce had met Hemingway a day or so earlier and, concurring on the strategic value of Rambouillet, agreed to meet him there and assess the situation. When Bruce arrived he found Hemingway ensconced in the local hotel, Le Grand Veneur, although he had acquired along the way a small collection of FFI fighters who succumbed to the Hemingway style and who gleefully put themselves under his informal command. Hemingway's hotel room was a miniature armory, with small arms piled here and there, and a bathtub full of grenades, with his newly acquired guerillas coming in to report what they had been sent to see. As Hemingway saw it, his primary contribution to the next phase of battle would be to send out scouts to gather information about enemy positions, minefields, and other difficulties, such as roadblocks. The scene was very much in keeping with what Hemingway wanted. He was in command of an independent group of fighters, however motley, and he was reveling in it. It was *For Whom the Bell Tolls*; it was the patrols of *Pilar*; it was where and what and how he wanted to be, and imagined himself to be. How often is a person able to recognize much congruence between the image in the mirror and the image in the mind? Hemingway at this point saw what he wanted to see. The lassitude of Cuba was gone now, the difficulties with Martha could be set to the side (though not forgotten or ever forgiven), for after all there was Mary. And he was in his element. Giving orders, not taking them, was more or less always his style.

The Paris police force was in a way a microcosm of Parisian and, more broadly, French politics. After all, the police had been complicit—indeed had been the principal agents—in arresting and imprisoning political opponents and, of course, of rounding up thousands of Jews and shipping them off to the death camps. Some were hand in glove with the Gestapo and the Milice, and no doubt their motives varied, from sincere belief in Vichy to simple self-protection. What's more, the police were very useful to the occupying Germans. They were out and about the city; they understood the neighborhoods and knew the local political leaders and could identify the dangerous ones; they were the only Frenchmen allowed on the streets after curfew; they were in a position to observe clandestine movement and meetings. Besides, since von Choltitz decided on a strategy of establishing thirty-six essentially static strong points, the police were the only force that had complete freedom of movement throughout the city. And they were in a position to observe German movement as well as the comings and goings of the Resistance.

The Germans surely believed that the police were far from popular with the masses of Parisians, especially in the working-class districts. After all, the mayor and the prefect of police were staunch Vichy supporters. They had always been an ally.

But it was not that simple. There were Resistance cells within the police. The group pledged to de Gaulle amounted to 400 members. Then there was the socialist group that consisted of 350 police and another 400 civilian employees. And finally there were the communists, who amounted to 800 members.[1] None of these groups trusted the others, but they all had a common enemy and so managed to coexist, if not fully cooperate. Of the fifteen thousand Paris police only about 10 percent were active in their Resistance groups. But surely many of the police officials were willing to look the other way when an Allied aviator needed false papers to get across the border. (The police were the issuers of identity papers, so that even though the names were false, the papers were genuine and passed the German tests.) What's more, police Resistance activity did not need to be overt. They could simply overlook this and that or walk past a café where there was a meeting going on.

But things were beginning to change after D-Day and the recent Allied drive to the east. In Paris there were strikes against factories that aided the German war machine. Under previous circumstances the police would be used to break these up. But they refused. This led to the possibility of police armed defiance, and von Choltitz considered disarming them entirely. That in turn led to a meeting led by Colonel Rol, the head of FFI, and the leaders of the three police Resistance groups. Not surprisingly the communists were the most aggressive and demanded a general police strike. The others were more cautious but in the end agreed. The three groups distributed information calling for the strike and pointedly declared that any officer who did not join the strike would be considered a traitor. On August 15, the general strike was on.

In retaliation von Choltitz loaded three thousand political prisoners (many of whom had originally been arrested by the Paris police) on cattle cars and shipped these unfortunates to concentration camps, where half would perish. Von Choltitz was not the only one to be disconcerted by the police rebellion. Collaborationists were suddenly frightened that their erstwhile allies and protectors had gone over to the side of the Resistance. They feared that the day of reckoning for collaborators and black marketers and war profiteers was apparently fast approaching. As indeed it was.

Four days later the Gaullist police Resistance staged a coup by arresting the Vichy prefect of police, raising the tricolor for all of Paris to see, and occupying the massive prefecture, "In the name of General de Gaulle and the Provisional government of France . . ." Some two thousand police sang the national anthem in the courtyard of the prefecture and then settled in to await the German response. Word of the seizure spread quickly throughout the city, and shots were fired by random *Résistants* without any orders from FFI or the police. The insurrection was taking on a life of its own.

Von Choltitz's first response was to send two tanks to the Prefecture, which was located on the Île de la Cité—the famous island in the Seine which also was home to Notre Dame Cathedral—a priceless symbol of France and one that was likely to be destroyed if the Germans decided to bombard the island with artillery and airpower (they had some Luftwaffe assets at Le Bourget, the Paris airport). The tanks fired a few shells at the steel doors of the Prefecture, but then, unaccountably, withdrew. The police inside would soon be in a bad way if the tanks returned, for their supplies were limited and of course their armament was inadequate to fight armor. But they did have some advantages. First, once the FFI leaders could be mobilized the Prefecture could be supplied through the Métro (subway) system tunnels. The Métro was not working, so the intricate tunnel system made an ideal avenue for movement and communication. As for weapons, pistols and rifles were no match for tanks, but there was an improvised weapon that was: the Molotov cocktail.

As odd as it may seem, a lumbering tank in a city street is as much a target as it is a weapon. In the narrow, ancient streets in many of the neighborhoods, the tanks could not maneuver. Also, the exploding insurrection meant that Parisians revisited their historic tactics and erected barricades through the city, restricting a tank's mobility even more. Having served in Stalingrad, von Choltitz had learned the bitter lesson that tanks in an urban setting can essentially be sitting ducks. He would revisit that lesson again when his tanks plodded through the streets in Paris and were attacked by partisans with Molotov cocktails—wine bottles filled with gasoline and a flaming rag fuse and dropped into vehicles from the apartments above, and even from the lovely Mansard roofs above. It is impossible to believe that a monstrous metal machine of war could be destroyed by a champagne bottle. But they could; it happened in Paris. And open cars or trucks carrying troops were an obviously even easier target. Even a buttoned-up tank could be set afire, killing the crew by flame, smoke, and heat, or by setting the ammunition alight.

And so it happened at the Prefecture. Von Choltitz sent three more armored vehicles against the Prefecture, and the police, understandably not wanting to be passive targets, set an ambush and used Molotov cocktails to disable the vehicles and capture the Germans in them. The Germans no doubt thought they were only minutes from execution, but in fact the police regarded them as valuable hostages. The Germans, though apparently undecided about how to deal with the uprising, still managed to kill 193 policemen, mostly at the Prefecture and mostly through tank attacks in the first two days of the insurrection.[2]

Recognizing that the insurrection was rapidly getting out of hand, the leaders of the Gaullists and the FFI got together and agreed that the FFI organization was better placed to take command of the entire Resistance. It made no sense for a handful of men with rifles to start shooting random Germans. But that was happening. Resistance leaders understood that the police strike and subsequent takeover of the Prefecture was premature, but the proverbial dogs of war had been released, and there was no restraining them now. The groups agreed to cooperate to bring some semblance of order in the rapidly escalating fighting. Colonel Rol had previously identified "targets of opportunity" in the city, many of them having been guarded by the police and were now unguarded. He sent out orders for the FFI fighters to turn their attention to these as the first coordinated step. But real coordination and command and control were impossible. There were too many Resistance cells in the city, and it seemed all of them wanted to get into the action.

It was chaos.

Von Choltitz's strong point strategy was starting to look very much like a collection of traps, although the Germans did sally forth here and there, capturing and summarily executing any *Résistant* caught carrying weapons. Von Choltitz refused to consider FFI fighters as soldiers; he considered them terrorists who were not entitled to treatment according to the laws of war. But this was war in the streets; individual or small groups of riflemen fired from apartment buildings; the slogan from the newspaper *Combat* was "Chacun son Boche." That meant, everyone should kill a German. And then take his weapons. German armor and SS units fired back. In some cases the Resistance was able to surround a strong point and prevent Germans from coming out. Their greatest coup, however, was the capture of the prisons at Drancy and Fresnes which led to "the freedom from the Nazi clutches of more than three thousand Jews and political prisoners. Their lives were now saved from deportation and incineration in a Nazi death camp."[3]

Feeling increasingly isolated as the fighting accelerated, von Choltitz gradually become receptive to the diplomatic efforts of the Swedish ambassador, Raoul Nordling, who eventually managed to negotiate a truce between the Germans and the Resistance. Von Choltitz had long ago decided that he could not hold Paris as a fortress city, and he did not have the resources to destroy the city, even if he wanted to. He saw no military utility in doing it and so could assuage his conscience about not obeying Hitler's insane orders. Besides, he knew the Allies were coming; he knew he would surrender to them. He would not be going back to Germany; he would not have to explain his actions to a madman. At some point that realization must have been a relief. (As it turned out, von Choltitz spent two and half years in Allied prison. Some was spent in England, some in Mississippi.)

Not surprisingly, the Resistance was split on the value of a cease-fire. The Gaullists were aware that the Allies were near and perhaps coming, albeit slowly. They were also afraid that the Germans would use airpower (they had warplanes at Le Bourget airport) and could easily shower bombs on the Île de la Cité, destroying not only the Prefecture but also Notre Dame, a tragedy that only a Hitler would applaud. There was also the rumor of a possible German counterattack. What if they came back? It would be like a cancer that returned.

The FFI were against the truce because they felt they had gained the initiative, and the communists among them, always willing to sacrifice lives—now and then even their own—for their goals, said that liberating Paris was worth two hundred thousand deaths, if need be. Then there were the SS troops in the city. Oddly, and by Hitler's decree, the SS and the Gestapo were not under von Choltitz's command. It may be remembered that the SS were Hitler's Praetorian Guard, who took an oath to Hitler personally. They were not about to listen to the regular army von Choltitz; they well knew he had no authority over them. Nor did they observe the truce and cease-fire that resulted from Nordling's rather heroic efforts. They were the most dangerous elements, as always.

One of the many problems facing the FFI commander, Colonel Rol, was the lack of weapons. Molotov cocktails were all very well as an improvisation against vehicles, but the Resistance needed rifles and grenades to be effective in street fighting against individual troops. He decided to send his chief of staff, whose nom de guerre was Commandant Gallois, through the lines to the Americans to ask again for a weapons drop. Gallois was assisted in this dangerous mission by a physician who had credentials that allowed him relatively free movement. Gallois was a good choice for the mission, because he spoke excellent English and of course he knew the tactical situation in Paris. After understandable delays Gallois reached the headquarters of General Patton who, when awakened, told Gallois that the American strategy was unchanged, that Paris could look after itself, and that the United States had no interest in supporting the insurrection. The object was not to capture cities but to destroy the German armies, regardless of where they might be. Paris was a strategic sideshow. Which it was. But it was also a symbol of immense importance.

Meanwhile von Choltitz had a problem. His thirty-six strong points had been reduced to twelve, his supplies were running low, and the promised reinforcements did not arrive, and instead were diverted elsewhere. He had been ordered by Hitler to destroy the city, but he knew that was pointless, and besides he did not have the resources to do it. He knew he would have to surrender or fight with the slender resources he had and without the ability to move around the city and consolidate his troops. FFI claimed to control the vast majority of the neighborhoods, but von Choltitz could not in good conscience surrender to the mob of civilians whom he considered terrorists, nor did he feel confident that his troops would be protected by the laws of war, since the FFI were not soldiers. And what's more there seemed to be no central command structure that could restrain the fighters. He came to the realization that his best option was to surrender to the Allies, but there was no knowing of when or even if they intended to come to Paris. Worse, the ragged truce would expire in two days, so the Allies would have to arrive soon. If they were coming, that is.

Von Choltitz called Nordling. The two men met at von Choltitz's hotel. Nordling said that only de Gaulle had the power and stature to negotiate an end to the fighting. And, astonishingly, von Choltitz responded: "Why doesn't someone go and see him?"[4] Nordling volunteered, and von Choltitz wrote out a pass for him to leave the city. He also assigned a German officer to accompany Nordling, in case there was any trouble at a checkpoint. Unfortunately, the stress of the last few days resulted in a mild heart attack, and Nordling was forced to ask his brother to undertake the mission.

Back at Patton's headquarters a crestfallen Gallois was surprised to see the general returning with a bottle of champagne. He had changed his mind, and after a toast he sent Gallois off to US Army headquarters in Le Mans. Gallois told his story to Bradley and his intelligence officers: the Germans were weak and surrounded; FFI controlled most of the city, but the truce was about to expire and there was widespread belief that the Germans would be reinforced, and if that happened, there would be a bloodbath of the kind visited upon Warsaw. Nordling arrived and confirmed Gallois's report.

Bradley changed his mind. Time suddenly became of the utmost importance. He met with General Leclerc and gave him the go-ahead. Bradley may or may not have been aware that Leclerc had already moved some of his units toward Paris. That was borderline insubordination, but at last he had the orders he needed.

The police strike and takeover of the Prefecture sparked the uprising. Had there been no uprising the Allies would have bypassed Paris. Had Gallois and Nordling not succeeded in their missions, the Allies would not have learned of the German weakness, and had Leclerc and de Gaulle not been so persistent in their virtually insubordinate demands, Paris would have been left in the wake of the Allies as they pursued the retreating German army. As it was, Paris was liberated by French troops under the command of a French general. Americans in the 4th Division got there too. As did Hemingway and his "private army."

CHAPTER ELEVEN

*"I was presented to the general there and asked by him to give
all the intelligence I could to his G2, Commander Repiton. This
with the assistance of Hemingway, Mouthard* [a FFI fighter]
and Mowinckel, [an American Lieutenant] *I did."*
— Colonel David Bruce

B uzz off, you unspeakables." This was Hemingway's G-rated
(and perhaps exaggerated) version of his meeting with General
Leclerc in Rambouillet—the same meeting that David Bruce
described as a request to provide whatever intelligence the guerillas
had regarding enemy positions to Leclerc's G2. (The G2 is the staff
intelligence officer.) That procedure would have been entirely routine
and appropriate; it would have been the G2's job to evaluate the information and advise the general of its merits and make some suggestions

about what to do with it. Bruce does not imply or suggest that he was offended by Leclerc's responses. After all, that was how things were done. But Hemingway was for some reason offended by his encounter with Leclerc and forever after referred to him as "that jerk, Leclerc." And, he further interpreted Leclerc's brusqeness with nervousness. It's not hard to discern the reasons for Hemingway's reaction. Hemingway felt that he deserved respect, and no doubt he had good reasons, not for his writing, but for the intelligence about German movements and positions that he and his irregulars had risked themselves to gather. It is also entirely possible, and even likely, that Leclerc was offensive in his manner. He was an aristocrat whose nom de guerre was designed to protect his family. In fact he was Philippe Francois Marie, Comte de Hauteclocque, a graduate of the French military academy at Saint-Cyr and the scion of a family that had been in arms for France since the Crusades. He had been in action since 1940 (mostly in Africa until D-Day in Normandy). He had been captured twice—and escaped both times—until he traveled a difficult road to London to join de Gaulle. He was a man de Gaulle trusted and a man and officer who had earned that trust. If Hemingway thought he was nervous, then Hemingway probably got it wrong. There is after all a difference between nervousness and the strain created by urgency. Leclerc was in a hurry; the Americans had delayed his movement toward Paris until the last possible minute. And there is little doubt that Leclerc's personality could be difficult; his American corps commander called him "that miserable man."[1] It's also easy to accept the possibility that the general viewed with some reservations the information provided by these amateur intelligence-gathering people. Only Bruce would have merited much respect; he was after all an American colonel. But Leclerc did not know him and did not have an estimation of his abilities. Aside from Mowinckel, who was an American lieutenant assigned to the OSS, the rest of this crew were little more than civilian rabble. Whether Leclerc had read anything by Hemingway is irrelevant. Leclerc was a professional soldier; Hemingway was a war correspondent, an amateur who had gone off the reservation. The fact that he had written some books would not have impressed Leclerc in this context. So if Leclerc was rude, it was probably not because he was nervous; it was because he was busy.

❖

The problem now is how to tell the story of Hemingway's famous road to Paris. There is legend—always seductive—and there is truth, even more elusive, especially when recounted by the author himself. Fortunately for the record, or at least most of it, there were reliable witnesses who were with Hemingway at least much of the time: Colonel Bruce, Lieutenant Colonel S.L.A. Marshall (an army historian and later Brigadier General), and, improbably, a Frenchman named Jean-Marie L'Allinec, who was one of the Private Army and traveled with Hemingway and his ragged band of resisters all the way to the Ritz Bar in Paris.

About Hemingway, whom he met in a shattered café outside of Rambouillet, Marshall wrote: "Many tall tales have been written about 'Force Hemingway.' The real story is good enough. [A comment that applies to many of Hemingway's adventures.] As a war writer Hemingway spun fantastic romance out of common yarn. But he had the courage of a wild ox, and he was uncommonly good at managing guerillas."[2]

Marshall, Bruce, Hemingway, and a handful of irregulars attached themselves to Leclerc's column and were on the way to Paris. Leclerc's armor fought at least two sharp actions against German artillery and tanks, and Hemingway was there for both. After Hemingway somehow annoyed a French junior officer, who told him he could not advance with the column until the entire column had passed, Hemingway retreated to a shattered café where he met Marshall and his driver, Captain John Westover. They had retreated here too because they had just been shelled by German artillery.

"Marshall, for God's sake, have you got a drink?" bellowed Hemingway. It so happened that Marshall did in fact have a fifth of Scotch. Also present was an eighteen-year-old Spanish girl. (Bruce and his men had become temporarily separated. Perhaps because of his rank Bruce had been permitted to stay with the advance units.) Thin and unkempt, the girl, Elena, would later be described in glowing terms by Hemingway in his article about the liberation of Paris. Physically she hardly matched Hemingway's romantic descriptions, but Marshall later wrote that her courage made her seem "almost beautiful." She was on her way to Paris to join her man, who was with the FFI. They decided they had better take her along. She joined Marshall and Westover in their jeep.

Bruce meanwhile had run up against a roadblock and diverted to a nearby farmhouse where they were treated to omelets and a bottle of wine provided by villagers along the route. (Bruce always seemed to do himself pretty well when it came to eating and drinking; his diary has many descriptions of his meals.) They were nine kilometers from Versailles, and when they finished their meal they ran into Hemingway and his merry gang, once again following the column. Despite the occasional contact with German opposition, Bruce wrote: "It was evident that relying on intelligence furnished by us and others to them that the French were bypassing those points where any determined opposition could be expected."[3] Whether this was self-congratulatory or not is a question. But surely some of the intelligence the OSS et al. provided was at least useful, if not vital.

Aside from having to deal with occasional small pockets of German resistance, the French were trying to move quickly, but they were delayed time and again by German roadblocks of felled trees, mines, and booby traps, to say nothing of the delirious crowds who lined the roads and showered the vehicles with flowers and wine and fruit, as well as the attentions of the young women who jumped on the trucks and tanks. There was welcoming on both parts.

Both Bruce and Hemingway recount that the most hazardous part of the journey was having to go past a German ammunition dump that retreating troops had set on fire. Ammunition was exploding; bullets were whizzing in all directions. As Bruce writes: "I for one found this part of the journey terrifying."[4] They were past the dump in less than a minute, but it seemed longer. As they approached the outskirts of the city the streets were mobbed with jubilant crowds, all shouting "Vive La France" and showering the troops with flowers, fruit, and wine; Bruce says they were kissed by men, women, and children, all of whom were nearly hysterical with joy. US, British flags were everywhere, along, of course, with the tricolor. The crowds and an occasional roadblock of felled trees made the going very slow. By the time darkness fell they were still a mile from the Pont de Sèvres over the Seine. The French were also encountering some stiff resistance from a factory on the other side of the river; one of von Choltitz's strong points, most likely. The Allies would have to wait until the next day for their triumphant entry into a city that was still occupied by German troops who were increasingly under siege in their strong points. Hemingway found an unoccupied house, and the Private Army settled in for the night.

Leaving the next day around noon, they crossed the bridge after the French army and were immediately engulfed once again by cheering civilians. Worse, there was a great deal of sniping, although it was not clear who was shooting whom, or why. As Bruce writes: "The streets are really dangerous, for everyone with a firearm is trying to use it. The police are impotent, and the whole situation is disorganized."[5] Elsewhere he says: "The French Forces of the Interior are well out of hand and draw on anybody whom they consider suspicious."[6] Given the sniping it's useful to remember the internecine squabbles among the Paris Resistance groups. And there were still elements of the detested Milice scattered around the city, to say nothing of von Choltitz's regulars and the SS. Immobilized in his hotel, von Choltitz had no control over the situation and was probably counting the minutes until he could surrender to an Allied officer and so preserve his dignity, such as it was. Much of the sniping came from the rooftops, hence the expression *guerre des toits*—war of the roofs. Who was fighting whom was a question. And still is. Most observers felt that the snipers were poor shots, which may indicate a degree of amateurism that could absolve the Germans (most of whom were bottled up in their strong points). It could point the finger toward the French, who were settling old scores, political or otherwise, such as the Milice versus FFI, and FFI versus known collaborators. Perhaps it was the action of a long-frustrated Parisian who wanted to erase the bitter taste of four years of occupation from his or her psyche; to be able to do something, if only to shoot indiscriminately was irresistible. He had a gun and wanted to use it. But the chaos and lack of leadership certainty validated de Gaulle's firm insistence that the French army needed to liberate and establish control in a city that was teetering on the brink of civil war and anarchy. De Gaulle was a frustrating and maddening personality to his Allies, but he knew his people, as events demonstrated.

Dodging German tanks and taking back streets, Hemingway and Bruce arrived at the Arc de Triomphe and the Tomb of the Unknown Soldier, which was being "guarded" by six French veterans and a seventh, sadly mutilated, seated in a wheelchair. (Elena had slipped away in the commotion, no doubt to search for her husband.) They climbed the Arc and were greeted by squad of *pompiers* (firemen). For some reason he could not fathom, Bruce was presented with a pompier's medal. The view from the roof was in Bruce's words "breathtaking. One saw the golden dome of the Invalides, the green of the Madeleine, Sacré-Coeur, and other familiar landmarks. Tanks were firing in various streets. Part of the Arc was under fire from snipers. A shell from a German 88 nicked one of its sides."[7] It seemed to be a good time to leave.

They could see that the Champs-Élysées was oddly free of traffic—oddly, given the commotion everywhere else. They jumped into their jeep and dashed down the Avenue and stopped at the Travellers Club, an exclusive men's (at the time) club housed in an opulent home that had been built by one of the Belle Époque's most notorious courte-sans, a woman known as "La Grande Horizontale." She married two wealthy aristocrats and used their money to build her "Love Palace." After a celebratory bottle of champagne with the club president, Hemingway and the rest headed for the Ritz Hotel; to get there they drove through the Place de l'Opéra, in which a mob of jubilant Pari-sians clogged their way by kissing them seemingly by the thousands. They made a quick stop at the Café de la Paix, an ironic name given the continuing fighting and small-arms firing going off all around the city. But this sniping did not seem to dent the Parisians' jubilation. When there was a shot the crowds would scatter into doorways, or shelter behind or under vehicles.

They were finally able to get their vehicles through the mob scene and drive a few blocks to the Ritz Hotel. Bruce writes: "Except for the manager, the imperturbable Ausiello, the Ritz was completely deserted, so we arranged to quarter there as well as to take lodging for the private army. This was done. Ausiello asked us what he could immediately do for us and we answered that we would like fifty mar-tini cocktails. They were not very good, as the bartender had disap-peared, but they were followed by a superb dinner. During the night there was almost incessant shooting."[8]

One of Hemingway's private army was Jean-Marie L'Allinec. He had met Hemingway and Bruce in Rambouillet and had been involved in scouting and intelligence gathering under the two Americans' orders. And he was with the others when they went to Paris. In 2004 he was still living in Rambouillet, and an enterprising American journalist who was retracing Hemingway's steps in France was fortunate enough to learn of L'Allinec and went to see him. "I'll bet you're here to talk about Hemingway. Of course you know we went to Paris together. To the Ritz. . . . It was all he could talk about. It was more than being the first American in Paris. He said, 'I will be the first American at the Ritz. And I will liberate the Ritz.' He was wonderful to be with. He was *sympathetique*, he was loud, he was drinking . . ."[9]

When asked about Hemingway's role in fighting, the old veteran said: "Sure, he always had a pistol, but he never killed any Germans." This contrasts strongly with Hemingway's claims; after the war in a 1950 letter to Chink Dorman-O'Gowan he claimed he had killed 122 enemy in combat and executed a number of others.[10] It is probably obvious that this is Hemingway at his worst "apocryfying," to borrow Martha's word. Dorman-O'Gowan was a close friend and a professional soldier, a man whose respect Hemingway would value. Why anyone would inflate or even invent the number of people he had killed is a legitimate question. But in war, of course, body counts count. Hemingway was in harm's way and occasionally significant danger—witness D-Day and his scouting missions with the private army. And to repeat S.L.A. Marshall's comment: "The real story is good enough." But it never seemed that way to Hemingway. It's entirely possible that he never killed anyone, aside perhaps from the Germans in the cellar—if they were actually in there. But the body count should not matter; being there and doing what he was doing should have been "good enough." He was already stretching—in fact breaking—the rules of a war correspondent. And his was valuable service. According to Bruce their intelligence allowed the Allies to bypass, at least in some cases, enemy concentrations. Hemingway didn't need the pile of imaginary enemy corpses. At least, that need should not have been there. But apparently something inside of him needed those bodies—anonymous men whom he later, and oddly, referred to as "deads."

On the other hand, Hemingway was not the only one to inflate his role in the liberation of Paris. It's possible that L'Allinec's recollections are accurate and not simply the exaggerated memories of a veteran. Few veterans are innocent of remembering more than there was. Conversely, many of those who were really there want to forget as much as they can.

Happily ensconced at the Ritz, Hemingway hosted a number of lunches and parties for American correspondents and military.

Elements of "Hemingway's Division," the 4th, had arrived to an equally joyous reception from the crowds of Parisians, many of them young women. Young Andy Rooney was there to observe it all, as was Ernie Pyle, about whom Rooney wrote: "I had become friendly with Ernie coming through Normandy, so I made my way across the street and up the stairs to his room. He was still out on the balcony with several other reporters. Ernie's language was more refined compared to that of many of the correspondents, but he looked down, as French girls threw themselves with wild abandon at American boys, and said: 'Any GI who doesn't get laid tonight is a sissy.'" [11] The correspondents were lodging at the Hotel Scribe, the official location where the army had set up a mess hall for them. But Hemingway and his private army stayed at the Ritz. Colonel Bruce and the OSS were funding their upkeep. In his diary, Bruce makes a cryptic remark about wanting to keep the gang together for some special purposes he had in mind. He did not specify what those special purposes were.

The day following liberation Hemingway went for a reunion with his old friend and sometime benefactor, Sylvia Beach—who, of course, owned the bookstore and lending library Shakespeare and Company. In her memoir Sylvia describes their meeting: "There was still a lot of shooting going on, and we were getting tired of it, when one day a string of jeeps came up the street and stopped in front of my house. I heard a deep voice calling 'Sylvia!' And everybody in the street took up the cry 'Sylvia!' 'It's Hemingway! It's Hemingway!' cried Adrienne Monnier [Sylvia's longtime companion]. I flew downstairs; we met with a crash; he picked me up and swung me around and kissed me while the people in the street cheered.

"We went up to Adrienne's apartment and sat down. He was in battle dress, grimy and bloody. A machine gun clanked on the floor. He asked Adrienne for a piece of soap, and she gave him her last cake.

"He wanted to know if there was anything he could do for us. We asked him if he could do something about the Nazi snipers on the roof-tops of our street, particularly on Adrienne's roof. He got his company out of the jeeps and took them to the roof. We heard firing for the last time in the rue de l'Odéon. Hemingway and his men came down again and rode off in the jeeps—'to liberate,' according to Hemingway, 'the cellar at the Ritz.'" [12]

Beach's account of the meeting suggests strongly that it took place as Hemingway was entering the city. His "bloody" and "grimy" appearance does not suggest the appearance of a man who had just spent the night at the Ritz. And you would think he would not need a bar of soap—surely the Ritz could provide that. (Although there were shortages of everything after four years of occupation and rationing.) But biographers Carlos Baker and Michael Reynolds both write that the meeting did in fact take place on the morning after the Ritz was "liberated." And they make no mention of clearing out the snipers. So there's something of a mystery about what happened and when. Judging from where Hemingway and Bruce crossed the Seine at the Pont de Sèvres they would have to recross to return to the Left Bank to get to the rue de l'Odéon and then cross again to get to the vicinity of the Arc de Triomphe. It's also unlikely that Hemingway would have left the courtly Colonel Bruce outside in his jeep while there was firing going on. It seems more likely that Baker and Reynolds have the truth of the story. It's entirely speculative, but it's possible Sylvia wrote to Hemingway to freshen her memory of the day. She wrote her book twelve years later. (At least it was copyrighted in 1956.) If so, it's also possible that Hemingway remembered the events a little differently. In any case, it's not at all surprising that there is more than one version of a story involving Hemingway.

❖

August 25 was a momentous day for Paris. Von Choltitz was in his office in the Hôtel Meurice when he must have heard the explosion in the lobby. The French under the command of Lieutenant Henri Karcher had thrown white phosphorous grenades into the lobby causing billowing smoke though which six German officers emerged to surrender. (As an aside, white phosphorous is a particularly nasty explosive that causes not only thick white smoke but fire that cannot be extinguished until it burns itself out, whether on objects or flesh. It is used in artillery shells as well as hand grenades.) Karcher demanded from the Germans the whereabouts of von Choltitz, and then he hurried up to the general's office, demanding that he surrender and accompany him to the Prefecture where Leclerc was waiting. No doubt relieved to some extent to see an officer in uniform, von Choltitz agreed, as long as he could be guaranteed that he and his troops would be treated according to the laws of war. Karcher had a bit of trouble getting von Choltitz through a crowd of screaming and jostling Parisians, one of whom stole von Choltitz's suitcase. Invectives and spittle flew along with a few stones. But by four o'clock they arrived at the Prefecture, where Leclerc was joined by his commanding officer, General Barton of the 4th Division and Colonel Rol of the FFI, as well as Charles Luizet, prefect of police and a de Gaulle supporter. The signing of surrender terms was delayed while Leclerc and Rol argued about whether Rol should be allowed to sign. If he did not sign, said Rol, FFI would not be bound by the terms. This was a microcosm of the rift between the Gaullists and the mostly communist FFI. Finally, Luizet convinced Leclerc to let Rol sign to avoid potential internecine strife. Leclerc agreed. (This would later infuriate de Gaulle, who wanted the surrender to be only to the Provisional Government, not the Resistance, which had no official political standing. Nor did the surrender terms mention the other Allies, for similar reasons. This was to be—and to be seen as—a triumph of the Free French Army, which was under the command of the French Provisional Government. De Gaulle was building his own legend, and more importantly laying the groundwork for France's republican future, which in de Gaulle's mind was simply the return of the pre-Vichy government. General Barton was at the surrender by courtesy. Sensing a delicate political situation, Barton left the room while Leclerc and Rol were arguing. He did not want to get the United States embroiled in French domestic politics by appearing to take sides. It was bad enough that he had been sent into the city and diverted from the primary job of chasing the retreating Germans.)[13]

The luckless, but perhaps relieved, von Choltitz's next stop was the Gare Montparnasse where he would meet the arriving de Gaulle and sign a second set of surrender documents. Meanwhile teams of French and German officers spread out to the last remaining strong points to announce the surrender. Not all cooperated, and fighting around the German strong points continued until it became clear to the Germans that all hope was lost. In one case, the holdouts refused to surrender to the French and demanded to surrender to the Americans, whereupon officers from the 4th Division were rushed to the scene at the Palais Bourbon, which was home of the French Parliament's lower house and which was on fire from post-surrender fighting. Finally convinced by the American officers, 530 Germans surrendered. Not surprisingly the last strong point to surrender was the Palais du Luxembourg, defended by the SS, but by 7:30 P.M. even they saw that there was no hope, and gave up.

At most strong points the disarmed Germans were subject to the abuse of hysterical crowds as the Germans marched into captivity. Parisians spat on the captives, hurled stones, punched and kicked, tore clothing. The shoe was on the other foot now, and the newly liberated wanted to take some measure of revenge. Some forty German captives were killed marching under guard.[14] It was small change, in view of the casualties and cruelties of the past four years—unless of course you were one of the forty, or one of their families, waiting and fearfully praying.

Paris was now free, but at a cost. The "butcher's bill" for the uprising and subsequent liberation was 1,482 FFI and 581 French civilians killed, 3,467 FFI and 2,012 civilians wounded; German losses were 2,887 killed, 4,911 wounded, and 4,312 captured.[15] The rest of von Choltitz's initial thirty thousand had been withdrawn earlier or had escaped. The battle for Paris was over. More or less.

❖

August 25 was a good day for Hemingway. Not only did he "liberate" the Ritz, it marked the day that his new passion would arrive. Mary came to Paris, like "a cat in heat."[16] It's not clear whether she was talking about her journalistic desire to be where the action was or whether she was longing for a reunion with her new paramour. But it's an interesting simile that suggests the latter more than the former. She also probably knew that cats were Hemingway's favorite animals. The Finca had a formidable population of them.

She had lived in Paris before the war, and so had her own memories. Even so, she would come to be absorbed into Hemingway's memories. They would develop a romantic scenario that was, as usual, dictated by Hemingway. Even better from Hemingway's point of view, he would have a new audience for some of his old stories about life in Paris in the twenties. And if you're going to have a romance with a new and sexually responsive lover (something of a change after Martha), what better place than Paris? Between bouts in the bedroom at the Ritz, there were restaurants and cafés, and although the food was mostly scarce and of poor quality, there was enough wine, and there were sidewalk tables where you could to sit and enjoy the intoxicating feeling of being in love and, for the moment, being out of harm's way. And there were friends, some who had survived the Occupation and some who had come with the invasion.

They spent long afternoons walking through the city, and especially through the Left Bank arrondissements that were Hemingway's favorites. They visited with Picasso, a Hemingway friend from the old days. Picasso had stayed in Paris, steadily working throughout the Occupation. The Germans left him alone. "They didn't like my work but they did not punish me for it," he said.[17] Mary did not especially appreciate all of the work Picasso showed them on the afternoon of that visit: ". . . many of the forms I don't understand at all," she said to Ernest after they left. "He's pioneering," Ernest said. "Don't condemn them just because you don't understand them. You may grow up to them. . . . If you understand easily, the thing may be spurious."[18] This is ironic given the fact that Hemingway was famous for the clarity of his prose; but maybe he was suggesting that in his art there was more going on beneath the surface of his simple sentences. Perhaps he was; often, he was right. If Mary resented the rather condescending "you may grow up to them," she didn't say so in her memoir. She did say, "Later Ernest wrote me on his views on understanding art. 'There is a real aesthetic blindness in some people. . . . I suppose like true tone deafness in music . . . But a certain amount of knowledge and appreciation of pictures, writing, and music makes a fine backlog of civilized understanding between people."[19] Hemingway's complexity is on display here. Few would argue with what he said; to some the odd part is that he said it at all, since these kinds of ideas are at variance with the image of him as a brawling war lover, an image that so many people tried to impose upon him and an image that he did little to discourage. Very little has been written about his astute appreciation of modernist painting, other than the usual reference to his statement that he learned a great deal about writing from looking at Cézanne's pictures. But he had a good eye for quality, no doubt derived in part from youthful conversations with Gertrude Stein. While her fiction is generally, if not universally, unreadable, she knew good art when she saw it.

There was a subsequent meeting with Picasso. Hemingway and Mary took Picasso and his mistress, the stunning Françoise Gilot, to dinner. Françoise was forty years younger than Picasso and an artist herself. They would live together for ten years, and in that time Francoise would give birth to two children. On the evening of the dinner Hemingway violated his pledge not to eat in a black market restaurant, because he could not bring himself to offer Picasso the wretched fare of legitimate places. Even the Ritz was still subpar. The dinner was amiable, although Mary suggests she was a bit left out of the conversation. With two larger-than-life personalities such as Hemingway and Picasso, it is hardly surprising; and perhaps she took it that way. Besides, she had little in common with Françoise and may, in fact, have felt the difference between them, physically. In any event, she wrote a *Time* story about Picasso, so she was at least compensated for being somewhat ignored. But did she realize that this was symptomatic of something? Perhaps. As she wrote in her memoir: "The heat of exuberance he engendered in any group around him seemed to me to melt away my identity."[20] That feeling was the basis for her ambivalence about a future with Hemingway. It would be overcome by that same heat of romantic exuberance, but if we are to believe her memoir, it never disappeared completely. Indeed, it got worse. But she stayed with him, until the end.

Regardless of any lurking uncertainties, to Mary and Hemingway both, the Paris days were mostly blissful, as indeed how could they not have been? Paris was at last free of the detested Boches and the pervasive fear that their presence engendered. Now they were gone, and Paris was itself again, more or less. Sorting out the toxic politics was something that could be postponed, for a time, and they were largely irrelevant as far as Hemingway and Mary were concerned. French politics was not their business. Their business was each other: "We lived those few days far out beyond the usual reaches of our senses. 'This is it,' Ernest said solemnly one morning. 'Our one and only life.'"[21]

Soon Hemingway would abandon the feeling of romance and happiness in the streets of his well-loved Paris, and he would return to the war, where he would expose himself to the loss of his "one and only life."

CHAPTER TWELVE

"Hang yourself brave Crillon; we fought at Arques, and you were not there."
— King Henry IV of France in a letter to his good friend, the Duke of Crillon

King Henry IV was the founder of the Bourbon dynasty and was born a Protestant but converted to Catholicism in order to become king, famously (or apocryphally) saying that Paris was "worth a mass." (Something of a phrasemaker, he also said he wanted every French peasant to have "a chicken in every pot," thereby beating Herbert Hoover by several centuries.)

Colonel Buck Lanham was a fluent French speaker and a student of history, so he knew what he was doing when he sent a note to Hemingway at the Ritz: "Go hang yourself, brave Hemingstein. We have fought at Landrecies and you were not there." Hemingstein was one of Ernest's self-made nicknames. Another was "Ernie Hemorrhoid, the Poor Man's Ernie Pyle." He was fond of using nicknames. Martha was Mooky, Mary was Pickle, among other things.

Landrecies is a French town just south of the Belgian border. The 4th Division was chasing retreating Germans who were frantically retreating across the Belgian border so that they could then turn east to their Siegfried Line, behind which they could regroup and reorganize in anticipation of a future counterattack—an attack that would come to be known as the Battle of the Bulge. But that was months away, in December. As it was now, many units were disorganized and there were many stragglers and small units bypassed by the charging Allies. The routes between Paris and the Belgian border were therefore extremely dangerous to any small units traveling them. Snipers and roadblocks and pockets of Panzers and artillery were among the hazards. Some Germans were even intent on ambushing travelers and stealing their vehicles, military or civilian, in order to speed up their flight to the German border.

While Lanham and his colleagues were pressuring the retreating Germans, engaging them now and then, as in Landrecies, Hemingway was enjoying his time at the Ritz, not only with Mary but also with a group of well-wishers and old acquaintances, such as André Malraux, who appeared in a sparkling uniform of a French colonel, and who irritated Hemingway with his haughty manner. A young private named J. D. Salinger also made a call and was thrilled when Hemingway was kind and encouraging about the young man's stories. Jean-Paul Sartre and his long time mistress Simone de Beauvoir came to call also, although this was later in the year. Sartre wanted to know what Hemingway thought of William Faulkner, and in an apparently uncharacteristic evaluation Hemingway said Faulkner was a better writer. This seems incongruous given Hemingway's well-documented competitiveness with current and past writers. In a 1949 letter to Maxwell Perkins he tells of how he could beat Tolstoy and Cervantes and Maupassant and Henry James and a variety of other prominent writers.[1] And although both Faulkner and Hemingway won the Nobel Prize, both produced some work that was uneven.

But the charms of Paris and the charms of his latest love could not override the challenge that Buck Lanham's letter had presented. Besides, he knew in his deepest heart that he was happiest when he was with the infantry, and with the friends he had made among the officers and enlisted men of the 22nd. Romance was all very well, but war was the reality of life, invigorating and tragic at the same time. He wanted to be with people who understood that perception and could live in the appalling conditions of combat and endure it, ultimately win it, and emotionally survive it. He wanted to be back with his friends in the 22nd, not entertaining a strutting Malraux or a Sartre who had managed to sit out the Occupation while pondering literary merits, constructing existential rationalizations, and doing little else. Mary could and would wait. She would be there when he returned. She was a war correspondent, too, and would understand. No doubt part of her also felt a sense of relief to be given a respite from Hemingway's manic ardor. As she wrote of this period: "I was beginning to feel that I was being swallowed up by him."[2] This was a feeling that Martha Gellhorn would have understood.

Hemingway and his self-appointed body guard, Jean Decan, headed for the Belgian border. In the French village of Wassigny Hemingway's jeep attracted the attention of a handful of Resistance fighters. As in Rambouillet, Hemingway's presence somehow appealed to the French, and they more or less placed themselves under his command, calling him *mon capitaine*. They told him that the road ahead was blocked by a German antitank gun. The fighters asked Hemingway if he thought they should attack the gun, but Hemingway said it was not necessary because the American infantry was in the area and would deal with the Germans. Carlos Baker picks up the story. The young man spat on the ground as if to question Hemingway's courage. Hemingway lost his temper and told the men to try the attack, if they thought they could.[3]

The unsuccessful attack lasted only a few minutes and left six dead Frenchmen and two wounded and the gun still intact. Hemingway did not claim to have participated. (Is it cynical to wonder if the attack had been successful, he might have?)

But did it happen that way? Did anything happen at all? In a letter to Carlos Baker, Buck Lanham expressed skepticism, saying essentially that if something like that happened Hemingway would have told it to Lanham when they finally reunited. Lanham had closely questioned Hemingway about what he saw during his travels, because he was concerned about Germans in the rear. Hemingway never mentioned the antitank gun and only told the story later.[4]

The 22nd had been a part of a task force that had achieved its objectives along the Belgian border. Seeing that there would now be a lull in the action, Hemingway and Jean returned to Paris. He would have a delightful reunion with Mary involving champagne and the delights unique to Paris, including the sharing of memories of prewar times there. Hemingway would later write that these weeks, alternating between Paris and Mary on the one hand and the 22nd infantry on the other were the happiest of his life. It's easy to understand why the Paris chapters were blissful, but only someone with Hemingway's particular outlook on war would find it so in the other side. But he did. It was comradeship with people he respected, as well as his fascination with violence and courage. There were no emotional complexities. You did your job or you didn't. You survived or you didn't. And there was something else. It was that private language that Hemingway would try to reproduce in the memories of his Colonel Cantwell in the novel *Across the River*. Hemingway had been there; he knew "how the weather was." He had seen the casualties of the 22nd Regiment, his adopted unit. In his imagination he spoke the private language of the infantry. Like the Picasso paintings that Mary did not care for or understand, the private language of the infantry veteran was complex, and to the outsider, difficult to understand. Impossible, really. Hemingway prided himself on his inclusion in this group and on his ability to understand. As a noncom and diarist in the 22nd, Sergeant David Rothbart wrote: "The front is a perpetual nightmare in which men converse in a language all their own, understood only by those who continuously wallow with them in this border of hell. . . . Only they know precisely what they mean."[5] This is another reflection of the alienation that Hemingway, as well as the frontline soldiers, felt from the rest of society, even from those elements in the army that did not undergo the rigors and horrors of combat. This sort of brotherhood against the internal and emotional opponents, as well as the enemy, fit well within Hemingway's personality and worldview. It explains to some extent the binary views of his behavior, his life, and his work. There were those he accepted and admired and treated with deference and affection—those who understood the private language—and there were those who were in his view essentially worthless and therefore treated accordingly. Mix in the generous helpings of alcohol to dull inhibitions, and you end up with wildly differing descriptions of his behavior, not only in combat but also in the Ritz Bar in Paris. And it seems fair to suggest that the language of *Across the River* reflects this separation between people who knew how it was, and everyone else. It's no different from the point of his story "A Way You'll Never Be." Colonel Cantwell's internal monologues as well as his inability to explain the truth to his (admittedly) unlikely nineteen-year-old mistress, underscore his isolation, the same isolation and alienation that the men, who had been in combat and understood it, felt when dealing with anyone else, even once they had returned home. *Across the River* is generally regarded as a failure, but it does reflect the main character's alienation from almost all of civilian and military society, in tragic combination with his impossible love for his Italian muse. It is a combination of bitter experience and doomed romanticism, with background voices telling him, "And in my back I always hear Time's winged chariot hurrying near." Besides, how much more isolated can a fifty-year-old wounded soldier feel than to have a fatal heart condition and a differently fatal passion for an exquisite girl? In Venice, with hints of Thomas Mann.

The novel is not very pleasant to read, but it's not difficult to understand when you know what he saw in the war, especially when the 22nd hit the Siegfried Line. Of course, a work of art, even one that has its flaws, must stand apart from its author's biography. But Hemingway's writing had always, rightly, or now and then wrongly, been associated with his own adventures. It seems fair to understand that his experiences in the horrific battles along the Siegfried Line are worth keeping in mind when evaluating his subsequent work, especially *Across the River*. He said he was reborn in those battles; into what new form, one wonders. But his young Italian lover is named Renata. It means "reborn." The great irony, and perhaps the tragedy of the novel, is that he has come together with her at the moment he is in the process of dying. The lovers on the Grecian Urn abide, but Colonel Cantwell and Renata cannot.

But all of this was in the future. The novel would not appear for five years. Perhaps it was a heavy burden to unload.

❖

It was a short reunion with Mary in Paris, for on September 7 Hemingway left to rejoin the 22nd. The 4th Division had penetrated eighty-five miles into Belgium hard on the heels of the retreating Germans. This time Hemingway had more company: Captain Marcus Stevenson, a PRO handpicked by General Barton to keep an eye on Hemingway. It was a good choice, for Stevenson was a tough Texan with taste for being at the center of action. He was therefore well suited for "herd guarding Ernie," as Barton put it. Jean Decan and two other Resistance fighters were part of the group as well as a correspondent for London's *Daily Mail*. Archie Pelkey had once again been assigned to Hemingway. And finally there was a half-comic, half-annoying Brazilian correspondent who babbled endlessly in mangled English and borrowed incessantly any items he forgot to pack, which covered a lot of territory. Typewriters were the particular objects of his desire. Hemingway would label him "the Brazilius" and later "the Pest of the Pampas."

Their journey was not without its pleasures. Cows killed by artillery or by stepping on a mine provided steaks for the merry group, and no one commented on the difference between a milk cow's tenderloin and that of, say, a black Angus. The job of butchering these milk cows fell to Archie and Jean. The group wound their way along the main road, now and then diverting to side roads to avoid the mines, on the advice of the locals, so that their luck did not run out, yet. They arrived in the Belgian village of Saint-Hubert, where beef tenderloins were harvested from the dead, stiff-legged cows by Archie and Jean, happy factotums to the traveling correspondents. Jean was no doubt especially happy, because he spent the night with the hotel owner's daughter, who is described in the various memoirist literature as "tall"—not exactly the description of a Helen of Troy, but, after all, this was war. Hemingway described himself as a "target of opportunity" in his "Poem to Mary." A tall Belgian girl may have felt the same. And besides, maybe Jean was also "tall," in a similar metaphorical way. At a time when any future at all was more than a little doubtful, many hearts became targets of opportunity.

Hemingway, feeling the onslaught of a chest cold, went to bed in the inn and spent a comfortable night, without someone's daughter, tall or otherwise. He had committed himself completely to Mary. His letters to her were ardent and persuasive, emphasizing their lovely although impermanent time. It was a classic romantic perception—intense love in the context of fleeting time. It was Mary who was now and then ambivalent about the relationship, but she did not have the romantic imagination of Hemingway, nor his emotional volatility. She lacked his ability to imagine a dream, perhaps not knowing—or possibly more likely knowing—that she was only in the first verse of that dream and that, inevitably, that dream must fade in subsequent verses.

Only the lovers on the Grecian Urn live on; everyone else loses, one way or the other, sooner or later. Things fade. It was only a question of time. And there was only so much of that. Mary may have glimpsed that future. Yet, despite his own experience, Hemingway, apparently, did not. Or more likely, he did but did not want to acknowledge it. Relationships always seemed to bring with them "a short imper-manence." In his heart of hearts, he knew this to be true, whether that impermanence came from violent death in a catastrophic war, or simply the inevitable withering away of love. Though their styles and personalities were different, Hemingway and Fitzgerald shared a similar romanticism. As Fitzgerald once said, in so many words, the difference between a sentimentalist and a romantic is the sentimen-talist believes that passionate love and happiness can last, the romantic knows that it cannot. Hemingway during this period may have told himself that this "one and only life" would endure, but it's hard to believe that he believed it—especially as experience, time, and events provided rebuttal.

The German collapse at the Battle of the Falaise Pocket and their subsequent retreat toward their Westwall, the line of defenses known to the Allies as the Siegfried Line, meant that the Allied armies were moving faster than they expected. That, in turn, meant that their supply lines were becoming increasingly stretched. Their primary supply depots were still in Normandy, and Cherbourg was still the primary port to receive supplies from English ports. Gasoline was in short supply at the leading edges of the "rat race," as the pursuing Allies called the chase. Ammunition was also at a premium, both for small arms and artillery. Moreover the heavy list of casualties meant that the replacement system was also strained. Merely transporting replace-ments to the constantly moving Front was a major logistical problem.

Hemingway and his merry band caught up with the 22nd and Colonel Lanham just outside the Belgian village of Houffalize some thirty-five miles south of Liège. They could see the retreating German armor fleeing toward the relative safety of the Westwall. Lanham ordered the platoon of tank destroyers to fire at the Germans. When the last German vehicle crossed the little bridge in the center of the village, they blew it up using enough explosives to damage not only the bridge but several adjacent houses. Lanham's engineers were still far to the rear—a frustrating situation for Lanham, who needed that bridge in order to continue pursuit. As with almost all liberated villages the locals were ecstatic and showered the Americans with food and wine, and when they learned of Lanham's predicament, they set out to repair the bridge—a feat they accomplished astonishingly in less than an hour, as Lanham and Hemingway sat on a fence and watched. It must be assumed that the German charge of TNT sent a blast upward and then outward in a kind of mushroom cloud, thereby destroying the nearby houses, but leaving a break in the bridge that was easily repaired. The chase was on again.

Their next objective was the German border and the little village of Hemmeres. In the afternoon of September 12 Hemingway watched as the first American tanks entered Germany.

The villagers understandably approached the invading Americans with wariness. Hemingway described them as "ugly women and ill-shaped men." Some offered schnapps; others merely emerged with their hands raised.

Hemingway commandeered an abandoned farmhouse just outside the village, sent Jean and Red to find someone to milk the suffering cows, and gathered a flock of chickens for dinner that evening. According to Carlos Baker, he shot the chickens' heads off with his pistol. (Baker got this information from a letter Hemingway wrote to Mary from Hemmeres; he mentioned a "fine dinner from offhead shot pistol chickens" [sic].) This seems like something Hemingway would say, and perhaps it's true. But his sidearm was a .45 Colt, a weapon that is not terribly accurate much beyond twenty-five yards or so, but devastating when it does hit the target, and it's amusing to think of Hemingway standing in a walled farmyard blasting away at a flock of terrified chickens that were running helter-skelter in all directions.

Shooting their heads off is not as easy as it sounds, nor is it very efficient. More likely he gathered them up one by one and wrung their necks, which would have been faster with less chance of damaging the meat. In any event, he found a German woman who accepted the job of cleaning and stewing the chickens.

That night Hemingway hosted a dinner for his friend Buck Lanham, his executive officer, his three battalion commanders, and others of his staff. Hemingway and his team listened as Lanham and his officers outlined plans for the coming day, a day that would send the 22nd against the vaunted Westwall. Then they all sat down to dinner. Lanham writes:

"The food was excellent, the wine plentiful, the comradeship close and warm. All of us were heady with the taste of victory as we were with the wine. It was a night to put aside the thought of the great Westwall against which we would throw ourselves within the next forty-eight hours. We laughed and drank and told ourselves horrendous stories about each other. We all seemed for the moment like minor gods, and Hemingway, presiding at the head of the table, might have been a fatherly Mars delighting in the happiness of his brood."[6]

Small wonder that this life appealed to Hemingway. He was with friends he admired and who admired him in return. He was doing something that was useful—not the reporting, especially, which was only a means to an end—but simply being there to gather material and to support his comrades. And at its most basic, simply being there. What's more, he had organized this festive dinner, and he was sharing the wine and the laughter with men who would soon go into a desperate battle. And he was at the head of the table.

There were no phonies in that room that night, no "ballroom bananas," no rear-echelon types, no women with their complicated sets of needs and emotions. These were men who knew the special language of the combat soldier and who knew the way their experience separated them from everyone else, and at the same time bonded them together. They were all at the moment living together in a clean, well-lighted place.

❖

Hemmeres was not part of the Westwall, which was still to the east, although not far. Hitler had ordered villages that were within the Westwall to be evacuated so that the barns and houses could be converted into defensive positions that were integrated with the pillboxes and trench systems of the formidable Siegfried Line.

The supply problem would get worse once the Allies engaged the now dug in Germans along the Westwall, a major problem because the casualty rate would accelerate dramatically as the Americans assaulted the deeply and cleverly entrenched Germans, who had stopped running and had turned to fight from behind their defensive installations. Major Edward D. Miller describes the German defenses:

"The Westwall stretched from the Dutch-German border near Kleve to just north of Basel, Switzerland. It consisted of thousands of mutually supporting concrete bunkers and other positions emplaced in depth. Some bunkers were built into the sides of hills overlooking important roads. Others were designed to resemble buildings and power stations. The original purpose of the Westwall was to delay an enemy until the Germans could bring up mobile reserves. By 1944, however, such reserves no longer existed.

"Construction began in 1936, and by 1938, 500,000 men worked on the project day and night. The typical machine gun bunker had a reinforced concrete roof nearly seven feet thick, a front wall about four feet thick, and a rear wall about eight feet thick. The average size was about 30 by 36 feet. The Americans later found that it took 400 pounds of TNT to destroy one bunker.

"A row of antitank obstacles the Americans called 'dragon's teeth' blocked the approaches to the Westwall where terrain might support a tank attack. These obstacles consisted of multiple rows of reinforced concrete pyramids nearly five feet high, at a depth of about thirty feet . . ."[7]

Approaching one section of the Westwall which the 22nd was assigned to breach, Hemingway described the gloomy forest of the

Schnee Eifel as where the dragon lived. Hemingway was obviously aware of the story of the young Siegfried, a hero of German mythology and the man who slew the dragon, Fafnir, by hiding in a hole covered with branches and stabbing the dragon as the creature passed over the hole. And given the dragon teeth obstacles, Hemingway also knew of the travails of Jason in pursuit of the Golden Fleece; Jason encountered a field of dragon teeth that metamorphosed into a horde of enemy soldiers. Jason solved the problem by throwing a jewel to the soldiers, so that they would fight amongst themselves. The US troops would have to offer something far more deadly.

Hemingway wasn't at the Schnee Eifel when the 22nd breached the Westwall on September 14, 1944. He was back at 4th Division HQ laid low with a powerful cold. As an aside, it's one of the curious aspects of Hemingway's career that he was susceptible to minor illnesses that could disable him for days. He returned on September 18, after the initial attack had been made. Lanham was happy to walk Hemingway through the battleground, explaining what they did and how they did it. Three companies of riflemen made the initial attack, supported by five tanks and nine tank destroyers. Once through the wheat fields surrounding the village, the attackers had to climb a heavily wooded hill that was dotted with pillboxes, many of them camouflaged with logs and earth so that the soldiers could walk past them and never notice until they opened fire. In some cases the German tactics were to let the attackers pass by and then fire on them from the rear. Things went according to plan in the first stages, but then the German artillery opened up with fast-firing antiaircraft guns used in this case against ground forces. These were bad enough but then the 88s opened up too. A lead TD hit a mine and was disabled. Then artillery hit another TD and a tank. The infantry scattered, and the armor reversed course and started retreating. Seeing that the attack was faltering, Colonel Lanham, Captain Howard C. Blazzard, and a sergeant ran into the woods to rally the infantry, most of whom had grouped together, unwisely, and taken what shelter they could find. Waving his .45 and shouting to his men, Lanham got them going again, even though they were under fire from a pillbox. "Let's go get these Krauts. Let's kill these chickenshits. Let's get up over this hill now and get this place taken." (In order not to shock *Collier's* readers, Hemingway, or more likely an editor, changed *chickenshits* to *chickensplitters*.) The Americans (and one FFI boy, who was killed) were in a sharp firefight with Germans who were in their rear. Lanham killed one with his .45, Blazzard another with his pistol, and the sergeant two more with his carbine. The rest of the Germans disappeared into the forest. Lanham was able to get a TD into a clearing behind the pillbox, and loading the gun with armor piercing shells, they fired point-blank into the steel door at the pillbox's exit. They fired six times and finally destroyed the door and most of the Germans inside. The inside was an unholy mess with blood and body parts scattered everywhere. Hemingway reports that the 22nd destroyed eighteen pillboxes in that battle.

Hemingway turned the information into his story "War in the Siegfried Line." Biographer Michael Reynolds attributes the style of the story, in which Hemingway gives the distinct impression that he was an eyewitness, to "*Collier's* editing."[8] Maybe. But it seems dubious that an anonymous editor at a weekly magazine would change the tone of a Hemingway piece. It seems more likely that Hemingway wrote it more or less exactly as it appeared. It sounds that way, anyway. A paragraph in particular raises these sorts of doubts. The dialogue is between Hemingway and Captain Blazzard, Lanham's S2: "Now I company was back so far they couldn't get up. You remember everything that was happening that day. *(Plenty. Plenty was happening.)*"[9] Hemingway's italicized remarks suggest that he was actually there during the attack. And in more than one instance Blazzard says something to the effect that "you remember how it was." Maybe Hemingway was there during the planning, but he was not there during the execution—a word that carries more than one meaning. By having the story organized as a conversation with Captain Blazzard, it appears as if Hemingway was really there.

He would be, though, in future action with the 22nd. There was more action to come; it was coming soon.

Hemingway commandeered a small farmhouse on the side of the hill in a small village called Buchet. He named it Schloss Hemingstein and used it as his headquarters as he observed the artillery battering the German positions in a village called Brandscheid, in the company of an artillery spotter. Spotting for artillery is a dangerous business. The enemy knows you are there somewhere and that you are the prime cause of the misery they are enduring under fire. Finding you and eliminating you are the surest ways to eliminate the menace of being shelled. It's not clear that Hemingway was in fact with a spotter; perhaps he was simply observing the results of the shelling. But the other scenario is also possible.

When Captain Stevenson arrived at Schloss Hemingstein along with an artist from *Esquire*, John Groth, Hemingway told them there was a danger of an enemy counterattack. After giving the artist two hand grenades, Hemingway bade him goodnight with the further admonition to drop the grenades from the upstairs window in the event of an attack. Hemingway sat up most of the night, reading, with a Thompson submachine gun in his lap.[10]

The danger of counterattack was very real, because it was an element of German doctrine as expressed by one German division commander: "A retreat from prepared positions will take place only on explicit and confirmed orders. Responsible officers and noncommissioned officers of strong points will be sworn in by battalion commanders to defend their position to the last breath. Local reserves will go into action immediately to counterattack local penetrations of the enemy. The battalion counterattack will be led by the battalion commander personally. All guns will fire to the last shell, and once the last shell is expended, the gun crews will fight as infantry. Only when there is no longer ammunition for the infantry weapons will an order be given to destroy the gun. Even if such an order were given, an investigation to determine whether it was necessary will be conducted. If it was found that the order was not absolutely required, appropriate action will be taken against the responsible person."[11]

This explicit threat against an officer who surrendered to the enemy carried with it a threat to the soldier's family back home. The Gestapo was pitiless in rounding up the families of deserters or those who surrendered by choice. There was no secret about this, for in fact the Nazi propagandists wanted the troops to understand what could happen if they did not give their all and fight "to the last breath."

Hemingway's worry about a counterattack—a worry shared by Buck Lanham—was in no way melodramatic; counterattacking is what the Germans routinely did whenever their enemy penetrated their positions. Looking at it from his perspective it's not surprising that he sat up with his Thompson submachine gun.

After a day of observing artillery, Hemingway attended a dinner at Buck Lanham's command post. Steaks were on the menu, no doubt harvested from local cattle, some already dead, others most likely victims of occupation or targets of opportunity. Lanham's staff was there, too, and what follows has added a significant chapter in the Hemingway legend. As the men were seated and served their steaks, an 88 shell crashed through the farmhouse wall and exited the rear without exploding. Either it was an armor-piercing shell that was not impressed by the farmhouse wall or it was a dud. (An 88 shell traveled at the speed of sound, and so did nothing to announce itself, incoming.) When the shell crashed through the wall and exited, Lanham and his men headed for the cellar, but Hemingway did not budge. He kept calmly cutting his steak. Lanham expostulated, but Hemingway would not move. Another shell came through the house, and Lanham came back to the table to talk some sense into Hemingway, who expressed his favorite opinion that when under artillery fire you were as safe in one place as another because they weren't firing at you personally. Lanham told him that it seemed to him that that was precisely what they were doing. But he was stubborn, and Lanham was not to be outdone, so he sat at the table and continued the meal. Finally a third shell came through the wall; it did not explode either, and that was the end of it. The other officers came back to the table and the dinner recommenced. Had the shells been high explosives with a contact fuse, they would have put an end to Hemingway and the staff of the 22nd. It will always remain a mystery why they did not explode. It will also remain a mystery—what was Hemingway thinking? Surely, he had nothing to prove to the men he was with. Bravado was irrelevant and even false in this context. Did he have, as he wrote to Mary, an old and welcome feeling of invulnerability in combat; or did he just not care anymore? Perhaps he alternated between the two. Here and there he felt that his luck had run out, so what was the use of taking cover? In other moods he felt immortal. He was not the only one whose emotions were on a roller coaster. Most of the men were, for good reasons. But he was one of the few who felt occasional blasts of romantic euphoria. Mary was responsible for that. The rest of the 22nd would have settled for some dry socks and a respite from the German artillery, though no doubt most, if not all, harbored feelings for a faraway sweetheart.

As for why the shells did not explode and put an end to Hemingway's career, the invaluable Sergeant Rothbart's diary may shine some light. When he, as part of the 22nd Normandy fight, encountered a Frenchman who had been forced to work in German ammunition factories, he was told the man was part of the French underground who participated in the war effort "by sabotaging artillery shells, producing many duds. I heard an instance from our troops of a shell that landed, fell apart without exploding and a note fell out reading 'We did our part, now you do yours.' None of the shells that came in my direction failed to explode, but one soldier said he owes his life to three 88 duds that fell near him."[12]

Perhaps more than one owed their lives to an anonymous French slave laborer and saboteur. In any event, Hemingway survived three 88 artillery shells and finished his steak dinner with his comrades. Surely, his luck was still in. Maybe.

He would need it, because in early October he received orders from Third Army headquarters to report to the inspector general. He knew what that meant; the ballroom bananas who disliked him had reported his activities in Rambouillet and the army was poised to investigate the truth. He drove by jeep to the city of Nancy where the inspector general was headquartered and reported to a Colonel Clarence C. Park who would be his interrogator. The charges against Hemingway were fairly extensive: that he had removed his correspondent patches, that he carried and used weapons in Rambouillet, that he commanded FFI fighters and accompanied them on patrols, that his hotel room was a veritable arsenal, and that Colonel Bruce was his chief of staff. Having read the charges Colonel Park dismissed Hemingway and told him to report back in the morning where he would have to answer these charges under oath. Furious and apprehensive, Hemingway at least had the evening to think through his response. It would have to be artful, or Hemingway could be stripped of his correspondent credentials and sent home.

It was artful, and like many of Hemingway's stories his defense contained more than a little fiction, and, since he was under oath, what he said amounted to perjury. He said he had stripped off his correspondent tunic because of the hot summer weather. He had not carried weapons in Rambouillet (although he made no mention of carrying them outside the village). The arsenal in his room was merely storage for the FFI. As for commanding the FFI he repeatedly declined the honor and merely gave them advice about their patrolling, and though they called him "Colonel," it was purely an honorific. He only served as a translator for Colonel Bruce and any army officers who passed through the town. He asserted that General Barton and Colonel Lanham would vouch for him, and also reported that much of the time during the Allied breakout and liberation of Paris, Hemingway had been accompanied by Captain Stevenson, the

4th's PRO, who would also attest to Hemingway's adherence to the Geneva Conventions.

The charges were dropped, leaving Hemingway relieved but bitter, since he had been forced to deny action that he was most proud of, all because of what he perceived as the jealousy and envy of the correspondents who turned him in. Since the 22nd was pulled off the line to rest and reorganize in Belgium, Hemingway decided to stay in Paris, and he resumed his old quarters at the Ritz. He would spend most of October there. Seeing old friends and comrades and, of course, Mary.

CHAPTER THIRTEEN

"At the time my mental anguish was beyond description. My magnificent command had virtually ceased to exist. These men had accomplished miracles . . . my admiration and respect for them was . . . transcendental."

—Colonel Charles T. Lanham
writing to Carlos Baker

It was November and gray winter had come to Germany. The Hürtgenwald is a pine forest seventy square miles south of the German city of Aachen. The pine trees are practically entwined with each other, and it was impossible to see more than a few yards. Even on the rare days when the sun came out, however briefly, the forest floor was dark and gloomy, like something out of a frightening German folk tale.* The trees were growing a hundred feet high in some cases, and they were thickly packed in a forest that also consisted of steep ridges, at the bottom of which were rushing streams. There were few roads and few firebreaks. Those that existed were well-known to the German defenders and often nearly impassable because of incessant rain and the resulting mud. The soil was clay and therefore slippery to man and vehicle. Well positioned through this forest maze were German concrete pillboxes supported by machine-gun bunkers and connected to each other by slit trenches. Logical fields of fire had been cut in the forest. Just outside these defenses were rows of concertina barbed wire, sometimes several levels thick and several levels high, protecting the approaches to the pillboxes and bunkers. Worse, the wire was festooned with booby traps. And in front of the wire was a minefield. There were few roads through the forest, and those that were there were buried in mud and, worse yet, mined and registered by German artillery and mortars, so that if and when the Americans crept into the open along these roads, the German artillery need not worry about range, for they had already figured that out in preparation. The German artillery spotter's only job was to radio when the Americans entered a preregistered artillery target.

Here and there, small farming villages existed like islands in a maze of forest. Around the villages were grain fields that had long since been abandoned as the Germans evacuated the peasants and turned their stone cottages into machine gun and mortar positions as part of the Westwall. These would ultimately have to be taken house by house, or rather, cellar by cellar, once the upper structures had been destroyed by artillery. In the cellars, it was hand-to-hand combat.

After a period of rest and refit, the 22nd moved east with the rest of the 4th Division. They would encounter the Westwall again, in

---

* It may be interesting to note that the Brothers Grimm were not the authors of their fairy tales. Rather they were folklorists who collected the stories from the German country folk and then published them.

the forest south of Aachen and north of the Ardennes. The attack was scheduled for mid-November, and it would involve the entire 4th Division plus elements of other units, and it would be a head-on fight against the Siegfried Line, where another dragon awaited. The Americans had been butting against these defenses since September, and they had not made much, if any, progress. The Germans were determined to resist and defeat the invasion, and they were well positioned to do it. Field Marshal Walter Model issued the following instructions to his troops:

"The long awaited enemy offensive has begun. . . . Disappointed peoples stand behind the mercenaries of American and England. Peoples who had promised Germany's collapse this year. Behind them stand the greedy Jew, lusting after gain, and the murderous, blood-thirsty Bolshevist. Capture of the Ruhr, the collapse of the Reich, the enslavement of all Germans are but stages in their will to destroy. We must shock these hypocritical benefactors of mankind out of their expectations of a cheap victory. With terror they shall realize that here German soldiers battle stubbornly and tenaciously for the German home soil. Our women and children look on us. With blasting hatred and unceasing courage we will fight for the honor and security of the German fatherland. Every combat squad must be a repository of fanatic battle spirit in our holy struggle for life. Then the bitter strife . . . will end with our success. Faith in the Führer will guarantee our victory."[1]

They very nearly pulled it off, and in the process, essentially destroyed Hemingway's favorite regiment, the 22nd infantry.

It was a battle that many on both sides wondered about, both at the time and in retrospect. What was the point? What was the objective? The Americans were buoyed by their success in the "rat race" chase across France and Belgium. There was talk of ending the war by Christmas. Hemingway himself predicted that result, although the infantrymen he said it to had their doubts. Commanders were optimistic, overly so as it turned out. Beyond the Western Wall lay the valley of the Ruhr and the industrial heartland of Germany. Beyond that lay the Rhine Valley, and most commanders defined the Rhine as their immediate objective. Protecting the Ruhr and the Rhine was the Siegfried Line, and in it lay the most difficult terrain in northern Germany, and perhaps the most difficult terrain at any place on the entire Line—the Hürtgen Forest. And yet with their eyes on the prizes to the east and with their confidence at perhaps the highest level since D-Day, the American commanders decided to take the Hürtgen Forest defenses head-on. The battle would more closely resemble World War I attacks against trenches or even a Civil War–era battle in the confusion of the Wilderness than an integrated, combined operation in which infantry, armor, artillery, and airpower joined to overwhelm static defensive positions. In the event, combined operations were virtually impossible. The weather grounded air support for most of the battle, and the thick woods hid the pillboxes and bunkers from the artillery air spotters even on those rare days when the weather broke and permitted some flights. The lack of serviceable roads meant that tanks and TDs were severely restricted. They simply could not get through the densely packed pine trees, some towering as high as one hundred feet. Armor was therefore pretty much restricted to using the few roads and firebreaks, and of course these were heavily mined, and those that avoided the mines often were bogged down by the sea of sticky and slippery clay mud. German artillery spotters called in fire from 88s and mortars, making the tank commanders and TD commanders reluctant to move forward. The artillery also made American infantry reluctant to get too close to the tanks, and that opened opportunities for hidden Germans to use their *panzerfausts* against the tanks. (The panzerfaust was a shoulder-mounted weapon in concept like a bazooka but carrying greater punch.) US Army engineers tried to clear the roads of mines but had to do it often under artillery fire. Moreover, in some cases the Germans had laid mines inside wooden boxes to foil the metal detectors. In other cases they piled one mine on top of another and booby-trapped the upper mine.

Why did the Americans choose to fight on terrain that nullified their greatest advantages? Why fight in the gloomy forest of Hürtgenwald? Even the Germans who benefited from the American decision to attack nearly impregnable defensive positions were puzzled, albeit gratified. According to Major General Rudolf Christoph von Gersdorff: "There was no use in the Americans going through the Hürtgen Forest. . . . Had [they] gone around it on both sides [they] would have had almost no opposition."[2] Another German general, Friedrich Kochling, commander of LXXXI Corps, did not believe the Americans would attack through the forest: "A push, possibly south and north of the forest . . . would have brought the German troops fighting in the Hürtgen Forest into the danger of being locked up."[3]

In fact, the Americans were playing into the Germans' hands; beyond and to the south of the Hürtgen Forest defenses, the Germans were organizing their massive counterattack through the Ardennes forest, an attack that would be known as the Battle of the Bulge. The defenses in the Hürtgen Forest prevented Allied penetration of the German northern flank. Had the Americans gone around they would have been able to strike the German positions and perhaps destroy or cripple the Ardennes offensive before it began. American commanders were worried that if they bypassed Hürtgenwald that would leave German units in their rear, and invite a counterattack. But the Siegfried Line in Hürtgenwald was purely defensive. Its guns were mostly fixed in the pillboxes and pointing west, and although formidable as defenders, the German army there was not strong enough to mount an effective counterattack in large numbers had the Americans simply gone around the forest.

The battle for the Hürtgen Forest began in September. It would last until after the New Year, and it would cost more lives and more casualties than it was worth. It would embitter more than one field officer, like Colonel Lanham, and it would achieve only questionable results, especially given the availability of alternatives. It would later require some revisionist and unconvincing analysis by the senior officers who ordered the attacks. And these same senior officers would come under intense criticism because they rarely visited the front and had little if any understanding of the difficulty the terrain posed. They demanded more progress but received little as a result, aside from casualty reports. And though he was friendly with General Barton of the 4th Division, Hemingway soon began referring to him as "our lost leader," for Hemingway, like Lanham, was well aware of the chasm between the field officers and the headquarters. In stark contrast to divisional and corps commanders, Lanham, as Hemingway had noted in his story about Schnee Eifel, liked to lead his troops personally. As historian Robert S. Rush writes: "Lanham led from the front, even to the point of foolhardiness, and expected his leaders to do the same. His first words to officers on assuming command were if they retreated one step without permission, they would be court-martialed. . . . Emphasis on heroic leadership had a cost. From 10 July to 16 November, four battalion commanders and eighteen rifle company commanders were killed, wounded, or relieved of command."[4] It's not surprising then that Lanham and Barton clashed frequently over issues of tactics. Nor is it surprising that Lanham increasingly resented Barton's calls for more progress and his continued absence from the front, an absence that greatly contributed to Barton's issuing impractical, if not impossible, orders. They even disagreed on the regiment's objectives, with Barton ordering the 22nd to take on one of the villages in the forest (Grosshau) while Lanham argued it was actually the road beyond the village that led out of the forest that was the proper objective, not the heavily defended village, which could be bypassed.[5]

Hemingway was there when the 22nd Regiment fought in the Hürtgenwald, from November 16 to December 3. He saw the virtual destruction of the 22nd. He saw the reasons a regimental commander like Lanham became permanently scarred by sorrow and bitterness—scarred in a way that would reappear in *Across the River and into the Trees*. And despite his previous encounter with military law, Hemingway fought there, too, often alongside his friend, Buck Lanham. In one incident, Lanham had moved his regimental command post—a plywood trailer—into a small clearing in the forest. A German platoon that had been bypassed attacked and completely surprised Lanham and his staff. The Germans killed Captain Mitchell, Lanham's HQ commandant. Hemingway came bursting out the door and began firing his Thompson submachine gun. He and the others of the HQ staff fought off the attackers. Jean Decan, Hemingway's self-appointed bodyguard, was in the action too. As Lanham wrote in his unpublished memoirs: "Men were firing and advancing and dropping and firing . . . Then I saw E.H. He was standing bolt upright watching the fight with intense interest. He was moving with the moving wave but I never saw him hit the ground. And this time there was no question at all that he was armed and using those arms."[6]

The GIs would be facing not only a difficult German defensive position but also unique ways to get wounded and killed. The regiment had turned over since D-Day. Nearly 4,600 had become battle casualties,[7] and given that the regiment's authorized strength was 3,698 enlisted and 209 officers, it's obvious that the regiment that had moved across France and Belgium and arrived at the Hürtgenwald was not the same as the one that hit the beaches in Normandy. Many of the wounded casualties who recovered were returned to their original units. The invaluable Sergeant Rothbart describes one such replacement: "Today we received a man returned to duty from a hospital where he had been recuperating since D-Day when he was evacuated with two bullets in his stomach. His life had hung on a thread as he underwent a series of delicate operations that eventuated in a miraculous recovery and a tribute to the great skill of army surgeons. We were certain he would be returned to the States when his condition permitted and were amazed to see him returned as a front line replacement. He was weak and obviously unfit for anything strenuous. Nobody along the way had interested himself sufficiently to at least designate him for 'Limited Assignment.'"[8]

Whether an even slightly wounded returnee would ever have the same spirit and unreasonable sense of immortality granted to a nineteen-year-old rookie rifleman was unlikely, to put it mildly. New replacements were hardly as well trained as the original troops of the 22nd Regiment of the 4th Division. As mentioned earlier, many were clerks and cooks and drivers who were pressed into rifle companies because of the severe attrition. Many were shoved into rifle squads without any training at all. Many, if not most, did not last. As one company commander said: "If a replacement lasted a day, it was fantastic."[9]

When the 22nd and the other regiments of the 4th got to the Hürtgen Forest they were faced with a combat situation that did not resemble even their scanty infantry training. There was little if any armor support, little if any air support, and the artillery support was now and then as dangerous to the GIs as to the Germans. The lines were close together, and, worse, communications were difficult and in some cases impossible. The engineers ran telephone lines between the front and headquarters, but these lines were frequently broken by German artillery or by German patrols infiltrating US lines and cutting the telephone lines. The battery-operated walkie-talkies rarely worked in the dense forest where the radios worked best in line of sight. Batteries were often in short supply. Runners who carried messages could measure their lives in minutes.

Aside from his M1 rifle, the favorite piece of equipment for the infantryman was his trenching tool. But even this old reliable failed him in Hürtgenwald, because the ground was so saturated, and the rain so incessant, that a foxhole quickly filled with water. Still men hid in them as best they could, sheltered from the blast and shrapnel of artillery and mortar shells. The troops were constantly wet and cold, and to make matters worse, German forward observers often called in mortar fire against individual foxholes, not moving on until they scored a direct hit. But there was another deadly enemy to the men in foxholes: tree bursts. German artillery targeted the trees and blasted them to create an explosion of splinters that rained down on the men huddling in foxholes. The Germans used contact fuses and time fuses to create this storm of deadly splinters mixed with shrapnel. The foxhole therefore became a liability, and the men soon learned that the best way to escape was literally to stand and hug the trees, hoping that their helmets would fend off any stray splinters or jagged hot steel. But standing up then exposed them to the vicious shrapnel of mortar fire. (This technique of using shot to create splinters is as old as the days of fighting sail, when ships fired solid shot into the wooden hulls of their enemy. It was not the shot so much that did the damage to the crews, but the explosion of splinters.) And the danger was not just from splinters and shrapnel; a tree that was hit lower in the trunk might topple over and crush anyone in its path. At the very least, felled tree trunks made movement that much more difficult.

With perceptive accuracy Hemingway called the Hürtgenwald battle "Passchendaele with tree bursts," after the World War I battle that was not only bloody (over a half million casualties combined) but also fought in wet winter conditions in which the mud made movement almost impossible. Indeed, the soldiers who fought there called it the "Battle of the Mud." The troops in the Hürtgenwald also suffered from the weather and the mud. They slept in their foxholes, usually drenched to the skin, and in some cases woke to find the rainwater frozen. The mud also meant that resupplying the frontline troops was very difficult and generally had to be done on foot; vehicles like trucks and jeeps simply could not travel through the mud even assuming that the German artillery would not soon spot them and seek them out. On one occasion an officer reported that his company was down to one day's worth of ammunition and food.

The lack of transportation also meant that evacuating the wounded was a matter of carrying them back on litters. The trip from the front lines back to the aid stations was often a mile or more, and even though medics were unarmed, that did not stop the Germans from firing at them. (In one rare event, four Germans guarding a bridge over the Kall River allowed US litter bearers to cross without harm. That incident, however, indicates that the lines between the Americans and Germans were often mixed together.)

It was not just the German defenders who inflicted casualties on the Americans. "Units throughout the [22nd] regimental received artillery fire that they attributed to American artillery units. Incoming friendly artillery fire hit the regimental command post during the day, killing Corporal Harold Watkins, Colonel Lanham's old Regular Army orderly, who had recently returned for duty after being severely wounded in September, and wounding several others. Able company in the rear area also complained of short rounds from friendly artillery." [10] "Eightball" Watkins was a Hemingway favorite, and his death, like so many other senseless deaths, troubled Hemingway deeply. As Carlos Baker noted, Hemingway was severely distressed not only about Eightball Watkins but also about the meaningless deaths of the men of the 22nd. These casualties would be the subject of his nightmares for years going forward. [11] Colonel Cantwell's brooding bitterness in *Across the River* comes into sharper and perhaps more sympathetic focus when placed in the context of the bloodshed in Hürtgenwald.

Accidents, too, were a continuing menace. One man dropped a grenade that went off and killed or wounded seventeen of his comrades. Rifles with safeties left off fired accidentally. And of course friendly fire casualties from artillery and occasional bombing were a continuing worry to troops and commanders alike. Then, too, in the gloom of the forest where visibility was measured in yards, GIs could be killed by their comrades who were not sure of whether the approaching figure in the dripping mist was a GI or a German and who, being nervous and, most likely, a replacement, preferred not to take any chances. Or, more likely, did not think anything and merely fired reflexively and hoped for the best.

Of course in the wretched conditions, and weather, of the war in the forest, illness was a common problem. Respiratory diseases as well as frostbite and the truly severe and disabling trench foot were major causes of noncombat casualties. "Trench Foot is a condition caused by prolonged exposure to damp, cold, unsanitary conditions. The foot becomes numb, changes color, swells, and starts to smell due to damage to the skin, blood vessels and nerves in the feet. It can take three to six months to fully recover and prompt treatment is essential to prevent gangrene and possible foot amputation."[12] There is obviously a grim irony in this disease to an infantry soldier. Not only is he the most exposed to violent death, but his very feet can betray him—all of which should imply that the weather conditions at the Westwall were appalling; the pleasant autumn weather that Hemingway had enjoyed in his travels back to the regiment was replaced by incessant rain, snow, and seemingly bottomless mud covering the few roads. The skies rarely cleared, which meant the American superiority in airpower was nullified, and it's fair to wonder whether airpower could be effective even in good weather, since the German pillboxes and bunkers were well camouflaged and protected by the dense evergreen forest. They would be mostly impossible to see from the air. Bad weather also meant that the American single engine Piper Cub–like artillery spotter planes were equally useless, most of the time. That in turn meant that US artillery had no eyes beyond what they could see themselves or that the infantry could call in—always a risky proposition because of the proximity of the two front lines. Friendly fire accidents as well as mistakes in reading coordinates were a problem. This situation was in stark contrast to the Germans who had occupied these areas since 1938 and who had already registered the likely targets: the few roads, narrow trails, and firebreaks, and who only needed a single spotter to observe when the Americans entered a firebreak or came to a crossroads. The gunners already had their targets defined, the ranges calculated.

By comparison the Americans were virtually blind. In the battle for the Hürtgen Forest, one unit observed German infiltration of a high ground position and called for artillery support, but the artillery officer responded that that area was held by US troops and refused to fire. He misread a map, or misunderstood intelligence reports that might also have been faulty. On the following day the Americans were shattered by a flank attack from these very Germans who were judged not to exist. Intelligence mistakes like this were common, because reconnaissance patrols could rarely penetrate the forest beyond a few hundred yards. Poor intelligence also meant that the divisional commanders and above had little knowledge of the true state of affairs and issued orders that were unrealistic.

The tactics for taking pillboxes varied. In some cases the riflemen would provide mass fire at the pillboxes' firing embrasures to keep the defenders' heads down while a combat engineer ran to the pillbox and dropped a satchel charge or grenades in one of the openings. Alternatively, using a TD to put a hole in the exit door, a man with a flame-thrower would first spray unignited naphtha through the hole and then send a blast of flame afterward.[13] The pillboxes that the German engineers thought were virtually impregnable became death traps—a hideous death, at that—to the men trapped inside. But it was dirty and difficult business for the GIs too. It required a few brave men to approach within yards of the pillbox. Bombing from fighter-bombers was virtually impossible, for the pillboxes were well camouflaged and hidden in the forest. So too for artillery. Further, as mentioned, the weather during these final months of 1944 tended to be abysmal, limiting not only aggressive bombing but aerial spotting for the artillery. What's more, the lines between the two armies were not distinct; the troops of the 22nd often found that the Germans were in their rear.

The situation in one of the fortified villages, Grosshau, offered differing problems to the attackers. The village sat in the middle of farm fields, and so could be targeted by American artillery and, when the weather permitted, aerial attack. Tanks, when available, could also be used. On the other hand, those barren fields meant the infantry (and armor) would have to traverse a thousand yards of coverless ground and be subject to German mortar and machine gun fire. The three battalions of the 22nd (each of which had lost its original commanders, killed or wounded) assembled in the woods surrounding the town and made several attempts to take the town, which was heavily defended. As Lanham reported to Barton by radio: "Blue (3rd Battalion) is on its objective. Grosshau is filled with Krauts, and we are firing lots of artillery in town. White (2nd Battalion) has suffered heavy casualties."[14] One company commander said of November 16–21: "These five days so far were the roughest and bloodiest I have seen. It was a nightmare."[15]

One example tells much of the tale. A GI was walking along one of the trails and stepped on a mine, which blew off his foot. The wound was cauterized by the heat of the explosion and so did not bleed very much. German troops snuck up on the wounded GI, stripped him of anything valuable or useful, and placed a booby trap under his back. The GI stayed conscious for nearly seventy hours, and was able to warn the medics before they lifted him up and set off the booby trap. These kinds of tricks and tactics by the Germans made the GIs reluctant to take prisoners, especially when they came across dead GIs who had been mutilated. In the battle for Grosshau Lanham told his battalion commanders not "to take too many PW's. If they want to fight to the death, then see that it is their death."[16] He later told the commander of the first battalion "not to take more PW's from Grosshau."[17]

If the GIs were suffering, and they were, the ordinary German soldier did not have it any better. As one wrote in his diary: "This morning we had a terrible artillery barrage. The beasts are firing phosphorous shells and smoke. The 1st and 2nd platoons had casualties already. While standing my post I am thinking of my brother who died three years ago. I am wet through and through and freezing. Now I am sitting in my foxhole and wish the only possible thing, either get slightly wounded or become a PW. The latter would be the much more appreci-ated solution. If only this whole swindle would be over."[18]

The suffering soldier would have no doubt been aware of his army's guidelines for behavior: "Don't surrender to the enemy unless you are severely wounded and can't shoot anymore. . . . Every act of treason will be known at home and not forgotten there. For traitors there will be no homecoming. The families are responsible for cowards and deserters. Their names will be placed on the 'blacklist.'"[19]

It will be remembered that shells or grenades carrying white phospho-rous started fires on flesh that could not be extinguished. Carlos Baker writes of Hemingway's discovery of a dead German who had been hit and "roasted" by a white phosphorous shell or grenade and was being eaten by a ravenous dog. Such images, to a man who dealt in images, never left him.[20] Nor would he forget the dead GI lying in a road, flat-tened by his own army's vehicles. This was the stuff of nightmares.

Yet despite the terrible images and smells, despite the constant danger from German artillery and despite the hideous weather and mud, Hemingway was buoyantly alive and engaged. He and Bill Walton made their way through shell fire to catch up with the 22nd, which was in the process of clearing out the Germans in house to house fighting in Grosshau. The Germans were hiding in the cellars of the mostly ruined village, so it was with rifles and hand grenades and flamethrowers that the GIs gradually and painfully took the town. Tanks, too, played their part, when they could find their way across the open fields. Two were hit by German antitank guns, two others mired in the mud and could not move, but the ones that did make it to Grosshau flattened the remaining buildings with high explosive shells. The foot soldiers were aided by the shell holes that were everywhere; they used them as they crossed the open fields and into the village, running from one to the next.[21]

In the end the GIs took the village, such as it was. The road out of the forest was almost theirs, so they thought. But Lanham knew his enemy and feared a counterattack, and after getting no support in the form of reinforcements from Divisional HQ, he organized his regimental command personnel into two more or less complete rifle companies. Cooks and clerks were issued weapons and told to keep them close by. By this time Hemingway and Walton were in the town, having arrived uninvited but welcome at a battalion commander's cellar HQ. Hemingway was wearing a fleece-lined white jacket taken in one way or another from a dead or captured German, since the Germans used white-camouflage coats in the snow-covered fight in the Schnee Eifel. While this made him rather a conspicuous target, he was probably more concerned with maintaining his warmth and health than he was worried about Germans. Besides, the greatest risk in the Hürtgen Forest had to this point been from the incessant German artillery, and Hemingway's theory of artillery attacks told him that he could wear any color he liked. Death came randomly, regardless of what one wore. Apparently he was not concerned about snipers, who would welcome a well-defined target. Since he survived the battle, perhaps we can credit his judgment.

Lanham had good reason to fear a counterattack. It came at night, and the battalion commander on the receiving end phoned Lanham for reinforcements while, as Baker writes, he was shooting Germans with one hand and holding the field telephone with the other. Lanham called Hemingway, who joined him immediately as they ran to the point of the attack, leading the makeshift companies. Then after a sharp firefight involving not only riflemen but tanks, the counterattack was beaten, and dozens of Germans surrendered. Perhaps the wet and shivering German *Landser* who wanted to be captured was among them. (*Landser* is a German term for a low-ranking soldier on the level of the American GI.)

After eighteen days of incessant combat, the 22nd was relieved. The toll on the regiment was 2,678 casualties of all kinds: 233 killed, 1,730 wounded, 184 missing, 531 non-battle casualties, mostly from illnesses, such as trench foot. Though Hemingway stayed with the 4th Division and primarily the 22nd Regiment, the battle for Hürtgenwald involved also "the 1st, 8th, 9th, 28th, 78th and 83rd infantry divisions, the 505th and the 517th parachute regiments, the 2nd Ranger battalion, the 5th armored division, and some attached special tank, engineer and artillery units."[22] In the end this mighty force was able to break through the forest but at the cost of twenty-four thousand dead, wounded, or missing soldiers—casualties that seriously weakened these units, which in turn contributed to the initial success of the German counterattack through the Ardennes, an attack that came to be known as the Battle of the Bulge. They launched their attack on December 16. The unhappy 22nd, already bled white, was thrust into the battle along with the rest of the 4th Division, and helped prevent the Germans from retaking Luxembourg City.

Analysis of the battle for Hürtgen raises a number of questions, the first being the obvious one: why do it at all? As the chief of staff of the German 7th army told General James Gavin (Martha Gellhorn's soon to be lover): "The German command could not understand the reason for the strong American attacks in the Hürtgen Forest. . . . The fighting in the wooded area denied the American troops the advantages offered them by the air and armored forces, the superiority of which had been decisive in all the battles waged before."[23]

There is no easy explanation. In his monograph at the US Center of Military History, Major Frederick T. Kent explains that the successes of the swift "rat race" across France and Belgium convinced the generals that the German armies were on the verge of collapse, hence cracking the Siegfried Line in the Hürtgen would be relatively painless. They also worried that by going around the forest they were leaving a strong German contingent in their rear, troops that could attack the Americans where they were most vulnerable. But as many historians have pointed out, the Siegfried Line was designed for defense; it did not offer a platform for attack. Most of its heavy artillery was fixed in pillboxes. Once committed, the American high command did not understand the difficulties the terrain caused, and few if any bothered to investigate the scene, and relied instead on maps. Not understanding the problems posed by terrain and weather they pushed for faster progress and ordered attacks that would result in little other than mounting casualties. Kent further argues that the 22nd was given too wide a zone of action: 3,500 yards, roughly twice what it should have been. The result was that in order to follow commands to attack, the three battalions had to concentrate to have a sufficient mass. That in turn exposed their flanks and bypassed German positions, which accordingly could attack from behind (as in the case of the attack at Lanham's CP), and worse, left many German artillery spotters in place to call in fire. And as has been mentioned it was artillery and mortar fire that caused the greatest number of US casualties. It was virtually incessant. As Sergeant Rothbart wrote: "Every infantry attack we make is pounced on by German artillery and practically stopped cold."[24] The weather, the mud, and the mines meant that supplies were difficult to send and casualties were difficult to evacuate. In both instances these jobs were done by men carrying their burdens by hand. There were not enough engineers to locate and disarm mines in the roads and not enough to repair the roads (often involving "corduroy" patches using logs). Had there been enough engineers, both supply and evacuation of wounded would have been vastly more efficient. Tactics were also questionable, specifically Barton's order to take Grosshau by frontal attack even though Lanham objected and provided an alternative plan. Barton refused, and it was one of the many heated disputes between the two. Barton even sent an army psychiatrist to evaluate Lanham in the hopes of getting him relieved with combat fatigue.[25] Lanham, however, was a favorite of Barton's boss, General "Lightning Joe" Collins, VII Corps commander, who said Lanham was "a shining example to all division officers in [my] command" and further that the performance of the 22nd was "exemplary and an inspiration to all."[26] Major Kent also criticized high command for not relieving the 22nd sooner because of the hideous number of casualties they were enduring.

The fighting in the forest from September into December delayed and drained the US divisions and provided time for the Germans to organize and launch their attack through the Ardennes.

Finally, some historians have criticized high command for not understanding the strategic value of the dams on the Ruhr River. The great danger was that the Germans could open the floodgates and inundate the entire valley, preventing the Americans from getting across the river or possibly cutting off any US units that had crossed downstream.

In sum, the Battle for the Hürtgen Forest seems to have been the wrong fight in the wrong place. Hemingway was there for the worst of it, and he said he was "reborn" in that battle. If it was a rebirth, it's fair to ask: a rebirth of what? And what would the newborn do with the experience? Or is the better question, what would the experience of this rebirth do to him? Was the sight of so many men being blasted apart by artillery traumatizing? Was the witnessing of a frontal attack on a fortified village that resulted in heavy casualties the basis of future fiction, or rather more likely the source of existential despair? Was the physical misery of the troops a subject for a magazine article? Such a thing may have seemed to him as obscene. There's no way of knowing, but we do know that he never wrote a nonfiction article about the Hürtgenwald, even though that was his most intense and personally dangerous action of the war.

Hemingway was not the only one, of course, to be affected emotionally and physically by the action in the forest. As 22nd Regiment Chaplain William S. Boice wrote afterward: "Part of us died in the forest, and there is a part of our mind and heart and soul left there."[27] Most of the surviving men of the 22nd were "burnt out cases," humans who had confronted the dragon and been seared, eternally.

❖

Hemingway, Walton, and Red Pelkey headed back to Paris in a jeep, but they came very close to becoming casualties. Driving along a muddy road Hemingway suddenly heard a familiar sound. He told Pelkey to stop and then said "Jump!" He and Walton landed in a pile in the ditch next to the road. Hemingway hit his head on a rock. Another head injury. The familiar sound grew louder and suddenly a 1930s-vintage German fighter appeared and strafed the jeep. Hemingway had recognized the sound from his days in Spain. That's the story, anyway, and it has some ring of truth. But vehicles traveling on the muddy roads in the battle zone would have been well advised to halt and have the occupants hide when they heard *any* incoming airplane engines, for American fighter-bombers were just as likely to strafe any vehicle they saw. And the Americans dominated the skies above the battle zones. They were as capable of inflicting friendly-fire casualties as the heavy bombers and the artillery. In a similar situation to Hemingway's, on another road, Lanham himself narrowly escaped an attack from an American fighter-bomber when Lanham's vehicle was strafed. War is a dangerous business, even when you are on the same side.

To celebrate their escape Hemingway offered Walton a drink. His canteen was full, and contained one large martini. Walton later said more or less that he never had a better one in his life. (According to biographer Michael Reynolds, Pelkey got a swig too. It would have been out of character for Hemingway to exclude him.) At other times he carried two canteens, one of schnapps and one of cognac.

As mentioned earlier, Hemingway's oldest son had been wounded and taken prisoner, although Hemingway did not know the details and suffered with the army's designation, Missing in Action. The uncertainty was more than difficult. Back in Paris Hemingway learned from the army that Jack was wounded, although not too dangerously, and was a prisoner of war. Hemingway was more than a little relieved. In a coincidence worthy of a Dickens novel, the officer who interrogated Jack was an Austrian who had known Ernest and Hadley and two-year-old Bumby in Schruns, the Hemingways' winter getaway village. Seeing that Jack was bleeding badly the officer ended the interrogation and sent Jack to a hospital in Alsace.[28]

Hemingway's luck was apparently still with him.

CHAPTER FOURTEEN

"Admittedly, Papa had gone to war—under duress—when he hadn't needed to, and he had added to that hairy-chested 'Hemingway legend.' But he had remained what he had always been ever since he had first sprung to fame in the late 1920's: the rich American, cut off by his money, fame and influence from the European world and that of the common soldier. An American staying in a grand hotel. Yes, Papa had gone to war, but in the final analysis, he had been simply a tourist in a helmet."
—Charles Whiting

C harles Whiting's quote above is, to put it as politely as possible, rubbish. First of all, Hemingway was in the thick of one of the worst battles of the war. His experience in Hürtgenwald alone would by itself disqualify him as a "war tourist."

He was personally involved in combat both on the road to Paris and in the Hürtgenwald. And when he was not actually fighting he was dodging bullets, artillery shells, antiaircraft flak, and strafing in order to gather material for his articles and, more importantly, for the novel he was gradually working out in his imagination, a book that he told Maxwell Perkins would cover the land, sea, and air war. It's true that he would later write to his friend, professional soldier Chink Dorman-O'Gowan, that he had personally killed 122 Germans—most certainly an egregious exaggeration.[1] But Whiting's description of him as a war tourist reeks of malice as well as blatant inaccuracy. As for being a rich American, he wrote to Hadley in July 1942 that he had to borrow $12,000 to pay his taxes ($103,000) last year, and he had to pay that back and get enough ahead so that he would not be broke when he came home from the war.[2] Of course to owe $103,000 in taxes implies a large income. But it's well to remember that the top bracket during the war was 94 percent, so Hemingway's tax bill would have far exceeded what he borrowed, with the difference being made up from his cash. Two years later in a letter written to Mary from the front, he gives her a rundown on his financial situation saying that he has $15,000 in the bank, and expects "25-35 G" in royalties for *For Whom the Bell Tolls* as well as $3,000 in expenses from *Collier's*. This is hardly the profile of the stereotypical "rich American," and although the dollar certainly went much farther in 1944, Hemingway was hardly a plutocrat. Moreover he had expenses; he owed monthly alimony to Pauline (which he bitterly resented because Pauline's family was very wealthy); he was supporting his mother, whom he detested; the Finca Vigia house needed repairs after a hurricane, and as anyone who has ever owned a boat knows, boats are money pits. *Pilar* was no exception, and it's worth noting that Hemingway bought *Pilar* with cash given to him by Pauline's wealthy Uncle Gus, not from his own pocket. What's more, Hemingway's anti-U-boat adventure led to extensive repairs on *Pilar*'s engines and hull.

As for Hemingway's stay at the Ritz, *Collier's* was paying his expenses, as noted above. And as Gellhorn biographer Caroline Moorehead writes: "The Allies . . . commandeered 700 hotels for their use. . . ."[3] No doubt the Ritz was one of them.

Whiting goes on about Hemingway's failure to interact with the common soldiers. This is contradicted by several accounts of his behavior. Sergeant Rothbart quotes 4th Division journalist Lin Streeter, who had comments about the civilian journalists he encountered: "Some of them were pretty arrogant. . . . Ernest Hemingway and Ernie Pyle were among the unassuming."[4] Later Rothbart writes: "He [Hemingway] spends a lot of time right up front with the companies, but he is afraid of falling into German hands. He's positive they have it in for him on account of his writings from Spain during the Spanish Civil War when Germany supported General Franco."[5] Carlos Baker references a 22nd Regiment battalion commander. Hemingway stayed in the frontline command post for several days. The weather was miserable with rain, snow, and sleet, and the dangers from enemy attacks were constant. He was right in the thick of the heaviest fighting, looking for a story.[6] Hemingway's friend and colleague in the Hürtgen, William Walton, said that Hemingway was at his best in the Hürtgenwald battle. He was happy to be with his friends in the regiment, happy to share their dangers and suffering, happy to be free "of the complications of women,"[7] happy in the knowledge that he was doing something worthwhile. And yet the horrifying casualties he was witnessing were leaving an impact on his emotions and would continue to do so after the battle was long over. Indeed, the juxtaposition of happiness in the comradeship of battle with the attendant existential despair over casualties—and horrific images—suggests that Hürtgenwald is a metaphor for Hemingway's complex personality and imagination. And it may be a broader metaphor for a pitiless universe in which sharks inevitably devour a great fish.

To put a period on this riposte to Whiting, there is throughout his book a quite noticeable distaste for most, if not all things, American. This is a common strain in some British circles. The novels of Graham Greene and John le Carré display some of this attitude, but not to the extent of Whiting. His screed is a reflection of his dislike for Hemingway and the Hemingway public persona, and creates not only a caricature of the writer but also a sneering caricature of Americans in general.

Hemingway was back in Paris suffering badly from yet another chest cold, yet not badly enough to curtail his rounds of entertaining. (It was during this time that Sartre and de Beauvoir had the discussion comparing Faulkner and Hemingway.)

While still suffering from his cold, Hemingway learned of the German breakthrough in the Ardennes and called General Barton to see if the "show" was worth his effort to get to the front. (He had been exploring ways to get back to the United States and from there to Cuba. He had had enough of the war after Hürtgenwald, although he did miss his comrades in the 4th Division and the 22nd Regiment.) Barton, in Luxembourg, answered that yes indeed there was a "pretty hot show" on; this was putting it mildly, but Barton could not be more specific for security reasons. Sweating, running a temperature, and bundled into two fleece-lined jackets, Hemingway was able to borrow a jeep and a driver, and headed for the 4th Division HQ. By the time he got there, the Allies had blunted the German attack; the 4th Division had been in the thick of the fight and had prevented the Germans from retaking Luxembourg City. The very real fear that the Germans would be back in Paris began to recede. Still suffering from his cold, which could easily have degenerated into pneumonia, Hemingway and Bill Walton went to Buck Lanham's HQ. Lanham immediately ordered Hemingway to see the regimental doctor and be dosed with sulpha drugs, put to bed, and ordered to stay there. The house he and Walton shared was that of a priest who had collaborated with the Germans. In one of his more juvenile stunts, Hemingway drank the sacramental wine, urinated in the empty bottles, and then labeled the bottles "Schloss Hemingstein, 1944." He later claimed that he had used the bottles as a chamber pot because the night air was frigid and he was worried about his cold—the lamest possible excuse. There was after all a convenient window. And it's worth remembering that Hemingway was a nominal Catholic and had been so since his marriage to the extremely devout Pauline. (As an aside, Hemingway's quite real superstitions and his attraction to the mystical ritualism of the Catholic faith stayed with him throughout his life, even though he was not a faithful practitioner.) In this case, it may have been karma, or something, but Hemingway woke in the night and mistakenly took a swig from one of the bottles.

Although Buck Lanham knew of the deteriorated relationship between Martha and Ernest—Lanham later said that in effect it was fearsome to hear his hatred of her—not everyone did. One of the officers of the 22nd heard that she had come to Luxembourg on Christmas Eve, and thinking to do a favor for Hemingway, sent a jeep to collect her and bring her to the 22nd HQ. As Carlos Baker reports, the officer intended to provide a pleasant surprise for Hemingway. It didn't work out that way.[8]

That same night Ernest attended a men's-only dinner hosted by General Barton, who was being relieved because of persistent health problems. It was also a Christmas party, complete with all the usual trimmings. Significantly, Colonel Lanham was not invited, a clear indication of the bitterness between Barton and Lanham. But Lanham was not alone in his criticism of divisional command. There was more rancor during the dinner, no doubt fueled by alcohol and smoldering resentment about tactics and losses, as well as simple fatigue—and, perhaps, a species of moral collapse or demise, given the disastrous bloodletting of the Hürtgen. No one who survived that battle (which was still raging) emerged unscathed emotionally. Though he was there that night at the dinner, Hemingway was not involved in the arguments; that was army business. But he was with the Lanham camp, and he would remember and address it later, in his novel. Finally, when things got too heated, he took the offending, outspoken officer, Colonel Luckett, whom General Barton ordered out, to a champagne party at another battalion celebration. It's fair to wonder if that gesture was symbolic. Luckett's criticisms no doubt mirrored the uninvited Lanham's, and Hemingway's as well.

Oddly, Hemingway and Gellhorn later returned to Barton's HQ where they sat around the Christmas tree, too well versed in irony to overlook the contrasts among the Holy Child, Joseph, and Mary, a loving couple on the one hand, and the childless couple who now hated each other, all in the context of brutal and ongoing combat. Peace on Earth, good will to men, and women for that matter, were in short supply that evening, both on the larger stage on the battle-grounds where men of both sides were being blown into shreds, and on the smaller stage, the one arranged around General Barton's Christmas tree. Afterward, Ernest and Martha drove to Lanham's HQ, and although Lanham was well aware of the poisonous relationship between the husband and wife, he offered them his HQ bedroom and slept in his chilly trailer. Whether their being together in Lanham's bedroom resulted in any romantic intimacy seems more than a little unlikely. A man like Hemingway may be able to make love to a woman he hates, or does not even know, but a woman may find it more dif-ficult, especially a woman like Martha who didn't particularly care for the whole business to being with: "It was never any good."

There would be more unpleasantness. The next day Lanham, Hemingway, and Gellhorn made a driving tour of the 22nd's battalion headquarters. As Carlos Baker writes, Martha was annoyed at what she thought was Ernest's "supreme arrogance," and dressed him down in French so that Lanham would not hear. Unbeknownst to Martha, Lanham spoke very good French, and Hemingway told her so when she finished her remarks. It was awkward.

Bill Walton arrived at the Luxembourg hotel where the Heming-ways were staying (not in the same rooms) and met Martha for the first time. Walton was charmed, and would not waste too much time falling in love with her and having an affair with her. But for now he merely took her sledding and then invited her to dinner. Learning of this, Hemingway invited himself too, and the evening soon degener-ated into nasty and loud recriminations, originating from Hemingway and directed at Martha. Later Walton reproached his friend for his boorish rudeness, to which Hemingway responded that hunting an elephant with a bow and arrow was impossible.[9] It's an odd metaphor, for there was nothing about Martha that would suggest an elephant except, perhaps, her memory, because for the rest of her long life she detested the remembrance of her life with Hemingway, saying in a letter to her beloved mother, "A man must be a very great genius to make up for being such a loathsome human being."[10] She did not think of Hemingway or his later works as the product of a "very great genius." Far from it. That same night, Hemingway stripped down to his skivvies, found a bucket and mop in a maid's closet, put the bucket on his head and the mop on his shoulder, and marched to Martha's room. He pounded on the door, but she refused to open, telling him to go away, because he was drunk. And he did, eventually.

The image of a comic knight-errant, a drunken Don Quixote, the role of a fool, does not fit Hemingway, nor would it fit his own self-image. But he undoubtedly played it that night. If he remembered it, it was most likely not with any pleasure. Martha on the other hand remembered it vividly, and she remembered it without any pleasure either.

The Battle of the Bulge was winding down, and Hemingway decided to go back to Paris, fully intending to return to the United States and thence to Cuba. Before he left, though, he was tempted to go on a mission with former sergeant and newly promoted Lieutenant Rothbart. The object was to arrange a truce with the Germans to allow time for a German field hospital containing not only German wounded but also Americans to pack up and leave the area. It was a delicate negotiation that was ultimately successful. Hemingway wanted to go along, but it was at this point that he confided in Rothbart his worry about falling onto the hands of the Nazis. The Ardennes offensive was his last exposure to World War II combat. He was ready to go home. And unlike many millions of others, he could arrange it. But the domestic wars were not over quite yet.

The Rothbart mission was on January 9, and soon after that Hemingway returned to Paris where his better self lately seemed to go missing. Mary was there and his room at the Ritz was waiting for him, a room that he used to entertain all and sundry and especially any soldiers from the 22nd who were there on leave. There was an unseemly brawl between Hemingway's party (including Peter Wykeham-Barnes) at the George V Hotel versus William Saroyan's group—not anyone's finest hour, although Hemingway seemed to enjoy it. There was another disturbing incident when Buck Lanham came to Paris on leave and presented Ernest with two German machine pistols—something that delighted Hemingway. But during an alcohol-fueled party Hemingway took a framed photo of Mary's husband, Noel Monks, and set it up as a target in the fireplace so that he could try out the new weapons. He was about to fire off a few bursts when Lanham stopped him. Hemingway then took the photo into the bathroom, closed the door, and fired, destroying not only the photo but also the toilet and causing a small flood. When management arrived he blamed it on a mysterious spontaneous explosion. They made the repairs, but anyone who witnessed the incident could well be excused for thinking that something was not quite right. And indeed there was not.

Returning to London Hemingway met briefly with Martha to discuss the terms of divorce. Martha was in bed with the flu, hence the brevity of the meeting. Hemingway and Martha Gellhorn never saw each other again. (Martha lived a long life, and with her eyesight and health failing, she committed suicide in February 1998, a few months short of her ninetieth birthday. No longer able to read, write, travel, or do any physical activity, suffering from cancer of the liver, life no longer seemed worth living. Given the way she had lived her life and her career, her final choice seems perfectly in keeping with who she was and always had been.)

Hemingway was conflicted about whether to return to the 22nd or to go home. There was work to be done in Cuba, both writing and repairing the Finca. Knowing that Jack/Bumby was safe and wanting to reconnect with his other two boys, Hemingway made what he thought was a sacrifice: instead of being where he wanted to be, he would go home and take up his responsibilities, both professional and familial. He left a brief note to Mary explaining how best to get to Cuba, where they would begin their life together. Given his antics in Paris, Mary undoubtedly had some reservations about whether this was such a good idea, although of course she eventually gave in and joined him, only to be presented, both immediately and forever after, with additional reasons to doubt the whole enterprise.

In London, Hemingway arranged transport on a bomber leaving for the United States on March 7. From there he would return to Cuba. Hemingway's war against the fascists was over. His personal war against whatever was bedeviling him—his fight against recurring Black Ass—was not only not over, but appeared to be intensifying. The internal fight against growing depression was made more difficult from the trauma of the Hürtgen Forest, where it should be remembered he said he was "reborn"—and into what, it's fair to ask. Surely he suffered vicarious agonies along with Buck Lanham as the two of them watched the 22nd Regiment attack against almost impregnable defenses and leave more of itself than it could replace on the floor of the dripping forest, torn to shreds and gone forever—men and boys, as Ernie Pyle said, "for whom there would be no homecoming, ever." And ten times the number of dead were the wounded, men who would be wounded in more than their bodies. Hürtgen was more than a tragedy. Worse even, it was hell. It's seems fair to say Hemingway, having seen the worst of it and been a part of it, left the front lines more seriously damaged than he or anyone else understood—although there were those who suspected, and worried. Buck Lanham was a professional soldier and a part of him had inured himself to this kind of slaughter, much as he resented the reasons for it. But even he was seared by the casualties. Hemingway was an artist and, although he was familiar with combat, he was also a gatherer of images. Something of the imagery of the Hürtgen Forest disturbed him; there was too much blood and too many shards of flesh, too many fresh-faced innocents sent into certain death, replacements who were killed the day they arrived. He would not publish anything about it for another five years. When he did, it was a novel called *Across the River and into the Trees*.

CHAPTER FIFTEEN

". . . they all have bad dreams."
—Sergeant David Rothbart, 22nd Regiment

Although he could not know it at the time, Hemingway's *Across the River and into the Trees* had its genesis in Cuba, during the lonely months when Martha was away covering the war in Europe. Often unable to sleep without company, he endured four months of solitude, aside from his cronies and hangers-on. But that was during the day. The nights were visited by his nightmares. He may have made use of the Havana prostitutes, but they were no substitute for a loving wife—something he began to think was becoming impossible, at least not with Martha.

Acrimony ensued when Martha returned to Cuba from London. Their arguments were bitter and violent. "I had thought Ernest would drive me mad with cruelty," she wrote to a subsequent lover, David Gurewitsch.[1] On the other side it was not surprising that Hemingway resented Martha's fierce ambition that led her to desert him for months at a time. Had Martha been content to express herself in another work of fiction, had she done so in Cuba while showing at least moderate interest in the management of the Finca, it seems likely that Hemingway would never have gone to the European war. He therefore never would have exposed himself to the atrocities of the Hürtgen Forest and thereby avoided adding to his already extensive inventory of nightmares and concussions. Of course, once he went to Europe he plunged into the action with gusto and plunged into the dissipation of wartime London and Paris with equal gusto. In the company of men he admired and in combat itself, he was at his best. His heightened awareness of his surroundings and the action were the fuel for future fiction. But it was more than that. It was the exhilaration of danger. Back in Paris and earlier in London he was often at his worst; his drinking dulled even his normal awareness. His need to be the center of attention displayed the worst sides of his personality. His treatment of Martha was shameful, and his courtship of Mary ardent to the point of being manic. Small wonder that the thought of life with him in Cuba was accompanied by some well-warranted reservations about the future.

The six articles he wrote for *Collier's* were mediocre and gave the impression of being dashed off just, as he said, to prevent his being sent home. On the other hand, Hemingway never took kindly to any sort of criticism. (He was not alone in this, of course.) And it should be said, though, that he must have thought his stories had some merit, since he showed one to Roald Dahl and another to Charles Collingwood, expecting their enthusiastic response. He was disappointed when neither detected much in the way of value. What's more, he exaggerated his own role in several of these six stories, implying that he was closer and more involved in the action than he was in fact. As was habitual with Hemingway, reality was never enough, although it should have been. There is some irony in this because his closest and most dangerous combat was in the Hürtgenwald—action that would be impossible to overdramatize; indeed it would take him another five years to come to terms with the horrors and to turn them into fiction.

In London he wrote two "poems" to Mary, which biographer Jeffrey Meyers called: "two intolerably sentimental poems (the worst things he ever wrote)." Not many would argue with that assessment, even though Hemingway was himself proud of these efforts and routinely read them to admiring cronies and people like *New Yorker* correspondent Janet Flanner, who should have, and probably did, know better. But they were all comrades together then, and that feeling would paper over the manifest deficiencies of the actual work—that and the fact that Hemingway himself with his outsized personality was himself doing the reading. The photo of Hemingway and Flanner in uniform and in a café shows the man himself reading his poetry and Flanner leaning toward him in a state of imminent rapture, or something.

Having seen enough of the war and needing to get home to look after the necessary repairs and get the Finca ready to receive Mary, Hemingway flew back to the United States in March and from there traveled to Cuba where he would spend busy but lonely weeks waiting for Mary to arrive.

His war was over, and he would have every right to think he had contributed to its success. Few if any of the millions of soldiers on the Allied side had seen as much combat or exposed themselves to harm's way as Hemingway had. Tragically, the anonymous riflemen of the 22nd as well as the officers who were friends of Hemingway did not, most of them, live long enough to appreciate what he would write about them. Nor would they know how deeply their sacrifices would sear his memory and imagination. After the Hürtgenwald, he would never be the same. In some ways it was his finest hour; in other ways it was the source of continuing nightmares.

That contradiction is perfectly compatible with Hemingway's imagination and personality, which Carlos Baker describes as Manichean.

❖

The general consensus is that *Across the River and into the Trees* is not a very good novel; probably his worst until the posthumous release of *The Garden of Eden*. The main character, a bitter and much-wounded colonel, is unpleasant and pretty much unlikeable, and while there is no requirement that fictional characters must have some redeeming qualities, it certainly does not hurt. Though Cantwell is facing death bravely, he does not inspire much in the way of sympathy. The love of his life, a young Italian countess named Renata, is two-dimensional for the most part—a device to allow Cantwell to tell his story. She is every poet's dream girl. There is a great deal of repetitive conversation and virtually no story, although Carlos Baker attempts to explain that by calling it a prose poem, not a narrative. Still, even if you accept Baker's analysis, that does not relieve the essential dullness of the novel.

On the other hand, for those who are interested in Hemingway's Manichean sensibilities, the novel is a useful and perhaps even important indication of Hemingway's state of mind. He used Buck Lanham's experience as well as his own, coupled with his alternating romantic and Black Ass moods, and as such has given the reader perhaps a greater insight into the man as artist than any of his previous works. And to some extent the novel is a glimpse not only into Hemingway's state of mind at the time but also a glimpse into the increasingly darkening future, something that Martha recognized: "To me it has the loud sound of madness and a terrible smell as of decay."[2] Of course, when the book came out in 1950, Martha was still in the process of trying to forget her life with Hemingway, and could hardly be considered an objective critic. Still, she knew about the process of creative writing, and she knew a great deal about the man, so although her criticism should be taken with a pinch of salt, it should not be dismissed as mere spitefulness.

⁂

Biographer Michael Reynolds writes: "[Hemingway's] son Gregory firmly believed that his father changed during that 1943–1944 period into a different person."[3] Certainly Hemingway suffered from Martha's abandonment of the marriage for career reasons (as well as her quite natural resentment of her husband's mostly verbal abuse). It was the only time in his four marriages that he was the one who was left. There can be no doubt that his ego was bruised. And certainly he was to an extent traumatized by the abattoir of the Hürtgen, for as he told Mary, he had frequent nightmares about being surrounded by Germans. The several concussions that he suffered also contributed to his mental distress. Any and all of these factors contributed to the changes Gregory noticed. And of course these changes could also be understood as a gradual worsening of the manic-depressive illness that would eventually lead to his death by his own hand.

Yet ironically Martha had done him a favor: she had gotten him to the war. He was reluctant at first but soon plunged into it enthusiastically. There were two alternating phases to his war: the first was his interaction with cronies in Paris and London, the second his actual contact with combat in the war in Europe. He would alternate between the two during his seven months in Europe—back and forth between the two sides of his personality. To say the least, his activities in London and Paris often were not his finest hours: heavy drinking parties, boastful conversations with junior officers, frequent brawls. As Peter Wykeham-Barnes wrote in the *Times* of London: "He impressed me as the sort of man who spends his whole life proving that he is not afraid. . . . I met Hemingway through a lifelong friend of mine, the poet John Pudney. I think he was in charge of Hemingway being in the RAF public relations department. . . . He was like a gentle man who's accidentally found himself leading a rampaging bull. He got into more drunken parties, fights and wrangles, being thrown into fountains, ejected from hotels and locked in people's rooms."[4] Not a pretty or heroic picture. It's quite likely however that Wykeham-Barnes moderated his opinion after taking Hemingway up in a Mosquito fighter-bomber during a V-1 attack. Hemingway showed then that his personal courage was not bravado, and he would go on to display that courage over and over in actual combat situations, both in the air and more extensively on the ground in France and Germany.

It was infinitely better when Hemingway got to the front and could spend his time with men he admired. In an August 28 letter to his wife Buck Lanham wrote: "Ernest Hemingway and I were discussing [battle] yesterday over a bottle of wine in the CP. He is probably the bravest man I have ever known, with an unquenchable lust for battle and adventure." As mentioned Lanham was in a position to know about courage in battle, having displayed it himself on many occasions, and having observed Hemingway in action. Nor did he have any reason to embellish his opinion of his friend; it was after all expressed in a private letter to his wife.

Hemingway was at his best in combat, in situations that shattered both the bodies and the minds of many around him. He was at his worst in domestic and social situations that suffering GIs like Willie and Joe could only dream of and long for. The Manichean dark side for most people—war—was where he found his light. As a man in rebellion against death, he put himself in death's path and so became his best self. War, like hunting or big game fishing, was a place to test himself, and it must be assumed that he felt he passed each test, and then some. Buck Lanham's good opinion of him was worth more to him than all the good wishes of numerous cronies, toadies, and hangers-on put together. The phonies and the ballroom bananas were not part of his combat fraternity and were well behind the frontlines. They were objects of contempt, and he did nothing to disguise what he felt. In combat he was with his own kind, men he could admire and with whom he could share their mortal danger. He said he was reborn in the Hürtgen Forest. On the surface that could be understood to mean he was traumatized by the slaughter; but it also could mean that he was now released from the pettiness and acrimony of his domestic life, cleansed from the jealousies of journalistic rivals, and reborn into the stark realities of war in which there is no equivocation—a man either performs to his hopes and standards, or fails himself once and for always. If he lives. Either interpretation of his experience in Hürtgenwald is plausible; both together are more plausible, still.

But when his war was over and he had to return to Cuba and temporary loneliness again, the Black Ass darkness began to reemerge. He would try to rekindle the emotion of comradeship by staying in touch with Lanham and others from the 22nd, but of course this was no substitute for being there. And that time was over for them all, anyway—those few who survived.

⁂

In 1947 Hemingway was awarded a Bronze Star. The citation reads:

> Mr. Ernest Hemingway has performed meritorious service as a war correspondent from 20 July to 1 September, and from 6 November to 6 December, 1944, in France and Germany. During these periods he displayed a broad familiarity with modern military science, interpreting and evaluating the campaigns and operations of friendly and enemy forces, circulating freely under fire in combat areas in order to obtain an accurate picture of conditions. Through his talent of expression, Mr. Hemingway enabled readers to obtain a vivid picture of the difficulties and triumphs of the front-line soldier and his organization in combat.

Carlos Baker writes that Ernest believed the period between mid-August 1944 and the end of the war had been the happiest of his life.

The war provided comradeship with men he could respect and admire, and it offered a chance to prove himself to himself without the complications of turbulent personal relationships. There was nothing false about the life at the front; the job to be done was clear. It was difficult, but it was not complicated. You either did it or you did not. In his own mind he could believe that he had in fact done his share.[5]

It seems fair to say that he never again would achieve that level of happiness. War had liberated him from the mundane—and, one suspects, from depressing self-absorption. The presence of death had sharpened his sense of awareness, of being alive, just as the alcohol-fueled parties in Paris and London had dulled those same senses. Now the war was over, and his personal battles were back again. They would get worse as time passed, and there would be no more wars to go to and so escape them. For the rest of his life, the darkness would continue to blight his life and work, off and on in accelerating doses until, in the end, like time's winged chariot, it overtook and overwhelmed him.

ENDNOTES

CHAPTER ONE

1. *The Paris Review Interviews, I* (New York: Picador, 2006), 44.
2. Caroline Moorehead, *Gellhorn: A Twentieth Century Life* (New York: Henry Holt, 2003), 41.
3. Ibid., 78.
4. Caroline Moorehead, *Selected Letters of Martha Gellhorn* (New York: Henry Holt, 2006), 42.
5. Caroline Moorehead, *Gellhorn: A Twentieth Century Life* (New York: Henry Holt, 2003), 113.
6. Scott Donaldson, *Fitzgerald and Hemingway: Works and Days* (New York: Columbia University Press, 2011), 447.
7. Michael Reynolds, *Hemingway: The 1930s* (New York: W.W. Norton, 1997), 262.
8. Scott Donaldson, *Fitzgerald and Hemingway: Works and Days* (New York: Columbia University Press, 2011), 425.
9. Ibid., 424.
10. Caroline Moorehead, *Gellhorn: A Twentieth Century Life* (New York: Henry Holt, 2003), 111.
11. Ibid.

12. Caroline Moorehead, *Selected Letters of Martha Gellhorn* (New York: Henry Holt, 2006), 125.

13. Antony Beevor, *The Battle for Spain: The Spanish Civil War 1936–1939* (New York: Penguin, 2001), 197.

14. Caroline Moorehead, *Selected Letters of Martha Gellhorn* (New York: Henry Holt, 2006), 126.

15. Caroline Moorehead, *Gellhorn: A Twentieth Century Life* (New York: Henry Holt, 2003), 24.

16. Ibid., 81.

17. Caroline Moorehead, *Selected Letters of Martha Gellhorn* (New York: Henry Holt, 2006), 236.

18. Ibid., 313.

19. George Orwell, "Politics and the English Language," in *Essays* (New York: Everyman's Library, 2002).

20. Carlos Baker, *Ernest Hemingway, A Life Story* (New York: Collier, 1969), 268.

21. Ibid., 315.

22. Caroline Moorehead, *Selected Letters of Martha Gellhorn* (New York: Henry Holt, 2006), 85.

23. Larry W. Phillips, ed., *Ernest Hemingway On Writing* (New York: Touchstone, 1999), 111.

24. *The Paris Review Interviews, I* (New York: Picador, 2006), 59.

25. Caroline Moorehead, *Selected Letters of Martha Gellhorn* (New York: Henry Holt, 2006), 309.

26. Caroline Moorehead, *Gellhorn: A Twentieth Century Life* (New York: Henry Holt, 2003), 135–136.

27. Ibid., 68.

28. Ibid., 55.

29. Caroline Moorehead, *Selected Letters of Martha Gellhorn* (New York: Henry Holt, 2006), 207.

30. Ibid., 116.

31. Ibid., 158.

32. Carlos Baker, *Ernest Hemingway, A Life Story* (New York: Collier, 1969), 334.

33. Ibid., 142.

34. Caroline Moorehead, *Gellhorn: A Twentieth Century Life* (New York: Henry Holt, 2003), 173.

35. Caroline Moorehead, *Selected Letters of Martha Gellhorn* (New York: Henry Holt, 2006), 102.

36. Ibid., 389.

37. Ibid., 82.

CHAPTER TWO
1. Terry Mort, *The Hemingway Patrols* (New York: Scribner, 2009), 71.
2. Ibid., 123.
3. Ibid., 100.
4. Nathan Miller, *War at Sea: A Naval History of World War II* (New York: Scribner, 1995), 190.
5. Michael Reynolds, *Hemingway: The Final Years* (New York: W.W. Norton, 1999), 91.
6. Ibid., 229.
7. *The Hour* (Norwalk, Conn.), July 2, 1999.
8. Scott Donaldson, *Fitzgerald and Hemingway: Works and Days* (New York: Columbia University Press, 2009), 15.
9. Caroline Moorehead, *Selected Letters of Martha Gellhorn* (New York: Henry Holt, 2006), 102.
10. Terry Mort, *The Hemingway Patrols* (New York: Scribner, 2009), 103.
11. Michael Reynolds, *Hemingway: The Final Years* (New York: W.W. Norton, 1999), 91.

CHAPTER THREE
1. A. J. Liebling, *World War II Writings* (New York: Library of America, 2008), 751.
2. Ibid., 752.
3. Ernie Pyle, *Brave Men* (New York: Grosset & Dunlap, 1944), 271.
4. A. J. Liebling, *Between Meals: An Appetite for Paris* (New York: Modern Library, 1995), 42.
5. A. J. Liebling, *World War II Writings* (New York: Library of America, 2008), 139.
6. Ibid., 477.
7. *The Hour* (Norwalk, Conn.), July 3, 1999.
8. A. J. Liebling, *World War II Writings* (New York: Library of America, 2008), 874.
9. Timothy Gay, *Assignment to Hell: The War Against Nazi Germany with Correspondents Walter Cronkite, Andy Rooney, A. J. Liebling, Homer Bigart, and Hal Boyle* (New York: New American Library, 2012), 68.
10. A. J. Liebling, *World War II Writings* (New York: Library of America, 2008), 738.
11. Ibid.
12. Timothy Gay, *Assignment to Hell: The War Against Nazi Germany with Correspondents Walter Cronkite, Andy Rooney, A. J. Liebling, Homer Bigart, and Hal Boyle* (New York: New American Library, 2012), 65.

13. John Keegan, *The Mask of Command* (New York: Penguin, 1988), 305.

14. Timothy Gay, *Assignment to Hell: The War Against Nazi Germany with Correspondents Walter Cronkite, Andy Rooney, A. J. Liebling, Homer Bigart, and Hal Boyle* (New York: New American Library, 2012), 26.

15. Bill Mauldin, *Up Front* (New York: W.W. Norton, 2000), vii.

16. Ladislas Farago, *Patton: Ordeal and Triumph* (Yardley, Pa.: Westholme Publishing, 2005), 752.

17. Ibid., 751.

18. Bill Mauldin, *Up Front* (New York: W.W. Norton, 2000), vii.

19. Timothy Gay, *Assignment to Hell: The War Against Nazi Germany with Correspondents Walter Cronkite, Andy Rooney, A. J. Liebling, Homer Bigart, and Hal Boyle* (New York: New American Library, 2012), 66.

20. Ibid., 239.

21. Ibid., 109.

CHAPTER FOUR

1. Joseph Balkoski, *Omaha Beach: D-Day, June 6, 1944* (Mechanicsburg, PA: Stackpole Books, 2004), 7.

2. Samuel Eliot Morison, *The Invasion of France and Germany: 1944–1945* (Champaign: University of Illinois Press, 2002), 5.

3. Ibid., 16.

4. Ibid., 28.

5. Jewish Virtual Library website: http://www.jewishvirtuallibrary.org/.

6. David Johnson, *V1-V2 Hitler's Vengeance on London* (New York: Scarborough House, 1991), 18.

7. Michael Reynolds, *Hemingway: The Final Years* (New York: W.W. Norton, 1999), 93.

8. Ibid.

9. Mary Hemingway, *How It Was* (New York: Knopf, 1976), 143.

10. Carlos Baker, *Ernest Hemingway, A Life Story* (New York: Collier, 1969), 392–393.

11. Caroline Moorehead, *Gellhorn: A Twentieth Century Life* (New York: Henry Holt, 2003), 216.

12. Caroline Moorehead, *Selected Letters of Martha Gellhorn* (New York: Henry Holt, 2006), 163.

CHAPTER FIVE

1. B. H. Liddell Hart, *The Rommel Papers* (Cambridge, MA: Da Capo, 1953), 465–466. Italics are the author's.

2. Ibid., 469.

3. Samuel Eliot Morison, *The Invasion of France and Germany: 1944–1945* (Champaign: University of Illinois Press, 2002), 38.

4. Michael Neiberg, *The Blood of Free Men: The Liberation of Paris, 1944* (New York: Basic Books, 2012), 13.

5. Samuel Eliot Morison, *The Invasion of France and Germany: 1944–1945* (Champaign: University of Illinois Press, 2002), 42.

6. Joseph Balkoski, *Omaha Beach: D-Day, June 6, 1944* (Mechanicsburg, PA: Stackpole Books, 2004), 38.

7. B. H. Liddell Hart, *The Rommel Papers* (Cambridge, MA: Da Capo, 1953), 469.

8. Ibid., 468.

9. Ibid., 468 (note).

10. Ibid., 467.

11. Ibid.

12. Ibid., 457.

13. Ibid., 458.

14. Ibid.

15. Samuel Eliot Morison, *The Invasion of France and Germany: 1944–1945* (Champaign: University of Illinois Press, 2002), 114.

16. B. H. Liddell Hart, *The Rommel Papers* (Cambridge, MA: Da Capo, 1953), 439.

17. Joseph Balkoski, *Omaha Beach: D-Day, June 6, 1944* (Mechanicsburg, PA: Stackpole Books, 2004), 23.

18. Samuel Eliot Morison, *The Invasion of France and Germany: 1944–1945* (Champaign: University of Illinois Press, 2002), 138.

19. Joseph Balkoski, *Omaha Beach: D-Day, June 6, 1944* (Mechanicsburg, PA: Stackpole Books, 2004), 58.

20. Ibid., 63.

21. Ibid., 62.

22. Ibid., 64.

23. Ibid., 289.

24. Ibid., 288.

25. D-Day Overlord—*Encyclopedie du Debarkment et de la Bataille de Normandie* website: http://www.dday-overlord.com/bataille-normandie/after-action-reports/amphibie/uss-dorothea-l-dix.

26. Samuel Eliot Morison, *The Invasion of France and Germany: 1944–1945* (Champaign: University of Illinois Press, 2002), 138.

27. Carlos Baker, *Ernest Hemingway, A Life Story* (New York: Collier, 1969), 395.

28. *The Paris Review Interviews, I* (New York: Picador, 2006), 44.

29. Mary Hackett, *William "Bill" Walton: A Charmed Life* (Wellesley, MA: Branden Books, 2013), 70.

30. Ernest Hemingway, *The Complete Short Stories* (New York: Scribner, 1987), 111.

31. *The Paris Review Interviews, I* (New York: Picador, 2006), 61.

32. *The New York Review of Books* Oct. 11, 2011.

33. Caroline Moorehead, *Gellhorn: A Twentieth Century Life* (New York: Henry Holt, 2003), 221.

34. Carlos Baker, *Ernest Hemingway, A Life Story* (New York: Collier, 1969), 395.

35. Caroline Moorehead, *Gellhorn: A Twentieth Century Life* (New York: Henry Holt, 2003), 221.

36. Caroline Moorehead, *Selected Letters of Martha Gellhorn* (New York: Henry Holt, 2006), 170.

37. Ibid., 210.

38. Ibid., 173.

CHAPTER SIX

1. RAF Website, http://www.raf.mod.uk/.

2. David Johnson, *V1-V2 Hitler's Vengeance on London* (New York: Scarborough House, 1991), 38.

3. George Orwell, *Essays* (New York: Everyman's Library, 2002), 676.

4. Andrew Roberts, *The Storm of War: A New History of the Second World War* (New York: Harper Perennial, 2012), 485.

5. David Johnson, *V1-V2 Hitler's Vengeance on London* (New York: Scarborough House, 1991), 42.

6. Ibid., 79.

7. Ibid., 72.

8. Ibid., 64.

9. Ibid., 195.

10. Ibid., 82.

11. *London Daily Telegraph* June, 23, 2015.

12. *Air Power Journal*, Summer 1989.

13. Ibid.

14. David Johnson, *V1-V2 Hitler's Vengeance on London* (New York: Scarborough House, 1991), 104.

15. Ibid.

16. Carlos Baker, *Ernest Hemingway, A Life Story* (New York: Collier, 1969), 396.

17. Ibid., 397.

18. RAF website, http://www.raf.mod.uk/.

19. *Watford (UK) Observer*, Aug. 12, 2012.

20. Carlos Baker, *Ernest Hemingway, A Life Story* (New York: Collier, 1969), 399.

21. Ibid.

22. Ibid.

23. Ernest Hemingway, *A Moveable Feast* (New York: Scribner, 1964), 104.

24. Scott Donaldson, *Fitzgerald and Hemingway: Works and Days* (New York: Columbia University Press, 2009), 311.

25. Charles Whiting, *Hemingway Goes to War* (Stroud, UK: Sutton Publishing, 1999), 61.

26. Carlos Baker, *Ernest Hemingway, A Life Story* (New York: Collier, 1969), 400.

27. Andrew Roberts, *The Storm of War: A New History of the Second World War* (New York: Harper Perennial, 2012), 518.

28. Ibid.

CHAPTER SEVEN

1. Martin Blumenson, *The Duel for France, 1944* (New York: Da Capo, 2000), 17.

2. Ibid.

3. David K. E. Bruce, *The OSS Against the Reich*, ed. Nelson Lankford (Kent, OH: Kent State University Press, 1991), 85.

4. Antony Beevor, *D-Day: The Battle for Normandy* (New York: Viking, 2009), 254.

5. Ibid., 252.

6. Ernie Pyle, *Brave Men* (New York: Grosset & Dunlap, 1944), 302.

7. Antony Beevor, *D-Day: The Battle for Normandy* (New York: Viking, 2009), 253.

8. David K. E. Bruce, *The OSS Against the Reich*, ed. Nelson Lankford (Kent, OH: Kent State University Press, 1991), 196.

9. Antony Beevor, *D-Day: The Battle for Normandy* (New York: Viking, 2009), 258.

10. C.T. Lanham, *Infantry in Battle* (Whitefish, MT: Kessinger Publishing, 1939), 324.

11. Antony Beevor, *D-Day: The Battle for Normandy* (New York: Viking, 2009), 224.

12. Samuel Eliot Morison, *The Invasion of France and Germany: 1944–1945* (Champaign: University of Illinois Press, 2002), 215.

13. National 4th Division Assoc. website, http://www.4thinfantry.org/.

14. Michael Reynolds, *Hemingway: The Final Years* (New York: W.W. Norton, 1999), 122.

15. Carlos Baker, *Ernest Hemingway, A Life Story* (New York: Collier, 1969), 400.

16. Chrisinger, David. "General Patton, Combat Fatigue, and World War II." Stronger at the Broken Places, July 7, 2014. http://strongeratthebroken-places.com/general-patton-combat-fatigue-and-world-war-ii/.

17. Robert Rush, *GI: The US Infantryman in World War II* (Oxford, UK: Osprey Publishing, 2002), 52.

18. Michael Reynolds, *Hemingway: The Final Years* (New York: W.W. Norton, 1999), 127.

CHAPTER EIGHT

1. Ernest Hemingway, *A Moveable Feast* (New York: Scribner, 1964), 210.
2. Michael Neiberg, *The Blood of Free Men: The Liberation of Paris, 1944* (New York: Basic Books, 2012), 34.
3. Ibid., 104.
4. Ibid., 107.
5. Colin Beavan, *Operation Jedburgh: D-Day and America's First Shadow War* (New York: Penguin, 2007), 278.
6. Ibid., 188.
7. Ibid., 192.
8. Ibid., 84.
9. Ibid., 85.
10. Ibid., 84.
11. Michael Neiberg, *The Blood of Free Men: The Liberation of Paris, 1944* (New York: Basic Books, 2012), 237.
12. Ibid., 34.
13. Henri Michel, *The Shadow War* (New York: Harper and Row, 1972), 308.
14. Michael Neiberg, *The Blood of Free Men: The Liberation of Paris, 1944* (New York: Basic Books, 2012), 13.
15. Elliot Paul, *The Last Time I Saw Paris* (London: Sickle Moon Books, 2001), 15.
16. Ibid.
17. Colin Beavan, *Operation Jedburgh: D-Day and America's First Shadow War* (New York: Penguin, 2007), 155.
18. *Sydney Morning Herald*, Sept. 1, 1944.
19. David K. E. Bruce, *The OSS Against the Reich*, ed. Nelson Lankford (Kent, OH: Kent State University Press, 1991), 142.
20. Michael Neiberg, *The Blood of Free Men: The Liberation of Paris, 1944* (New York: Basic Books, 2012), 25.
21. Colin Beavan, *Operation Jedburgh: D-Day and America's First Shadow War* (New York: Penguin, 2007), 163.
22. Henri Michel, *The Shadow War* (New York: Harper and Row, 1972), 289.

CHAPTER NINE

1. David K. E. Bruce, *The OSS Against the Reich*, ed. Nelson Lankford (Kent, OH: Kent State University Press, 1991), 11.
2. Ibid., 205.
3. Ibid.
4. Evan Thomas, "Spymaster General," *Vanity Fair*, March 2011, http://www.vanityfair.com/culture/2011/03/wild-bill-donovan201103.

5. Colin Beavan, *Operation Jedburgh: D-Day and America's First Shadow War* (New York: Penguin, 2007), 11.

6. Ibid., 293.

7. Ibid., 272.

8. Ibid., 293.

9. Ibid., 293.

10. Antony Beevor, *D-Day: The Battle for Normandy* (New York: Viking, 2009), 345.

11. Ibid., 345–346.

12. Carlos Baker, *Ernest Hemingway, A Life Story* (New York: Collier, 1969), 403.

13. Ibid., 404.

14. Ibid.

15. Michael Reynolds, *Hemingway: The Final Years* (New York: W.W. Norton, 1999), 192.

16. Lanham letter Aug. 28, 1944.

17. Carlos Baker, *Ernest Hemingway, A Life Story* (New York: Collier, 1969), 392–393.

18. Lanham letter (undated).

19. Ernest Hemingway, *The Complete Short Stories* (New York: Scribner, 1987), 588.

20. Ibid., 579.

21. Ibid., 588.

22. Carlos Baker, *Ernest Hemingway, A Life Story* (New York: Collier, 1969), 405.

23. Ibid., 407.

24. Ernest Hemingway, *A Moveable Feast* (New York: Scribner, 1964), 209.

25. Carlos Baker, *Ernest Hemingway, A Life Story* (New York: Collier, 1969), 407.

CHAPTER TEN

1. Michael Neiberg, *The Blood of Free Men: The Liberation of Paris, 1944* (New York: Basic Books, 2012), 113.

2. Ibid., 146.

3. Ibid., 147.

4. Ibid., 145.

CHAPTER ELEVEN

1. Michael Neiberg, *The Blood of Free Men: The Liberation of Paris, 1944* (New York: Basic Books, 2012), 99.

2. *Spokane Daily Chronicle*, June 2, 1962.

3. David K. E. Bruce, *The OSS Against the Reich*, ed. Nelson Lankford (Kent, OH: Kent State University Press, 1991), 170.

4. Ibid., 171.

5. Ibid., 175.

6. Ibid., 174.
7. Ibid., 173.
8. Ibid., 174.
9. Taylor, Michael. "Liberating France Hemingway's way: Following author's 1944 reclaiming of the Ritz Hotel." *San Francisco Chronicle*, August 22, 2004. http://www.sfgate.com/travel/article/Liberating-France-Hemingway-s-way-Following-2731590.php.
10. Terry Mort, *The Hemingway Patrols* (New York: Scribner, 2009), 166.
11. Andy Rooney, *My War* (New York: PublicAffairs, 2000), 215.
12. Sylvia Beach, *Shakespeare and Company* (Lincoln, Neb.: Bison Books, 2004), 218.
13. Michael Neiberg, *The Blood of Free Men: The Liberation of Paris, 1944* (New York: Basic Books, 2012), 231.
14. Ibid.
15. Ibid., 246.
16. Mary Hemingway, *How It Was* (New York: Knopf, 1976), 107.
17. Ibid., 117.
18. Ibid.
19. Ibid.
20. Ibid., 121.
21. Ibid., 114.

CHAPTER TWELVE

1. Carlos Baker, *Ernest Hemingway: Selected Letters 1917–1961* (New York: Scribner, 1981), 673.
2. Mary Hemingway, *How It Was* (New York: Knopf, 1976), 121.
3. Carlos Baker, *Ernest Hemingway, A Life Story* (New York: Collier, 1969), 412.
4. Ibid., 640 (note).
5. David Rothbart, *A Soldier's Journal* (New York: I Books, 2003), 257.
6. Carlos Baker, *Ernest Hemingway, A Life Story* (New York: Collier, 1969), 425.
7. Edward Miller, *A Dark and Bloody Ground: The Hurtgen Forest and the Roer River Dams, 1944–1945* (College Station: Texas A&M University Press, 1995), 8.
8. Michael Reynolds, *Hemingway: The Final Years* (New York: W.W. Norton, 1999), 112.
9. Ernest Hemingway, *By-Line Ernest Hemingway* (New York: Scribner, 1967), 394.
10. Carlos Baker, *Ernest Hemingway, A Life Story* (New York: Collier, 1969), 426.
11. Robert Rush, *Hell in Hurtgen Forest: The Ordeal and Triumph of an American Infantry Regiment* (Lawrence: University Press of Kansas, 2001), 118.
12. David Rothbart, *A Soldier's Journal* (New York: I Books, 2003), 198.

CHAPTER THIRTEEN

1. Robert Rush, *Hell in Hürtgen Forest: The Ordeal and Triumph of an American Infantry Regiment* (Lawrence: University Press of Kansas, 2001), 144.

2. Edward Miller, *A Dark and Bloody Ground: The Hürtgen Forest and the Roer River Dams, 1944–1945* (College Station: Texas A&M University Press, 1995), 210.

3. Ibid., 96.

4. Robert Rush, *Hell in Hürtgen Forest: The Ordeal and Triumph of an American Infantry Regiment* (Lawrence: University Press of Kansas, 2001), 92.

5. Ibid., 325.

6. Michael Reynolds, *Hemingway: The Final Years* (New York: W.W. Norton, 1999), 120.

7. Robert Rush, *GI: The US Infantryman in World War II* (Oxford, UK: Osprey Publishing, 2002), 59.

8. David Rothbart, *A Soldier's Journal* (New York: I Books, 2003), 264.

9. Edward Miller, *A Dark and Bloody Ground: The Hürtgen Forest and the Roer River Dams, 1944–1945* (College Station: Texas A&M University Press, 1995), 137.

10. Robert Rush, *Hell in Hürtgen Forest: The Ordeal and Triumph of an American Infantry Regiment* (Lawrence: University Press of Kansas, 2001), 195.

11. Carlos Baker, *Ernest Hemingway, A Life Story* (New York: Collier, 1969), 437.

12. "Trench Foot," Foot-Pain-Explored.com, last modified July 19, 2016, http://www.foot-pain-explored.com/trench-foot.html.

13. Robert Rush, *Hell in Hürtgen Forest: The Ordeal and Triumph of an American Infantry Regiment* (Lawrence: University Press of Kansas, 2001), 45.

14. Edward Miller, *A Dark and Bloody Ground: The Hürtgen Forest and the Roer River Dams, 1944–1945* (College Station: Texas A&M University Press, 1995), 133.

15. Ibid.

16. Ibid., 157.

17. Ibid., 158.

18. Robert Rush, *Hell in Hürtgen Forest: The Ordeal and Triumph of an American Infantry Regiment* (Lawrence: University Press of Kansas, 2001), 191.

19. Ibid., 202.

20. Carlos Baker, *Ernest Hemingway, A Life Story* (New York: Collier, 1969), 437.

21. Edward Miller, *A Dark and Bloody Ground: The Hürtgen Forest and the Roer River Dams, 1944–1945* (College Station: Texas A&M University Press, 1995), 156.

22. Gerald Astor, *The Bloody Forest: Battle for the Hürtgen: September 1944– January 1945* (New York: Presidio Press, 2000), 356.

23. Ibid.

24. David Rothbart, *A Soldier's Journal* (New York: I Books, 2003), 264.

25. Michael Reynolds, *Hemingway: The Final Years* (New York: W.W. Norton, 1999), 121.

26. Robert Rush, *Hell in Hürtgen Forest: The Ordeal and Triumph of an American Infantry Regiment* (Lawrence: University Press of Kansas, 2001), 178.

27. Ibid., 282.

28. Carlos Baker, *Ernest Hemingway, A Life Story* (New York: Collier, 1969), 443.

CHAPTER FOURTEEN

1. Carlos Baker, *Ernest Hemingway: Selected Letters 1917–1961* (New York: Scribner, 1981), 612.

2. Ibid., 536.

3. Caroline Moorehead, *Gellhorn: A Twentieth Century Life* (New York: Henry Holt, 2003), 225.

4. David Rothbart, *A Soldier's Journal* (New York: I Books, 2003), 227.

5. Ibid., 272.

6. Carlos Baker, *Ernest Hemingway, A Life Story* (New York: Collier, 1969), 435.

7. Ibid., 437.

8. Ibid., 440.

9. Ibid., 441.

10. Caroline Moorehead, *Gellhorn: A Twentieth Century Life* (New York: Henry Holt, 2003), 230.

CHAPTER FIFTEEN

1. Caroline Moorehead, *Selected Letters of Martha Gellhorn* (New York: Henry Holt, 2006), 206.

2. Ibid., 204.

3. Michael Reynolds, *Hemingway: The Final Years* (New York: W.W. Norton, 1999), 91.

4. Jeffrey Meyers, *Hemingway, A Biography* (New York: Harper & Row, 1985), 398.

5. Carlos Baker, *Ernest Hemingway, A Life Story* (New York: Collier, 1969), 424.

BIBLIOGRAPHY

BOOKS

Astor, Gerald, *The Bloody Forest: Battle for the Hürtgen: September 1944–January 1945*, (New York: Presidio Press, 2000)

Baker, Carlos, *Hemingway: The Writer as Artist*, (Princeton, NJ: Princeton University Press, 1952)

———, *Ernest Hemingway, A Life Story*, (New York: Collier, 1969)

———, *Ernest Hemingway: Selected Letters 1917–1961*, (New York: Scribner, 1981)

Balkoski, Joseph, *Omaha Beach: D-Day, June 6, 1944*, (Mechanicsburg, PA: Stackpole Books, 2004)

Beach, Sylvia, *Shakespeare and Company*, (Lincoln: Bison Books, 2004)

Beavan, Colin, *Operation Jedburgh: D-Day and America's First Shadow War*, (New York: Penguin, 2007)

Beevor, Antony, *The Battle for Spain: The Spanish Civil War 1936–1939*, (New York: Penguin, 2001)

———, *D-Day: The Battle for Normandy*, (New York: Viking, 2009)

———, *Paris After the Liberation 1944–1949*, (New York: Penguin, 1994)

Blumenson, Martin, *The Duel for France, 1944*, (New York: Da Capo, 2000)

Bruce, David K. E., *The OSS Against the Reich*, edited by Nelson Lankford. (Kent, OH: Kent State University Press, 1991)

Donaldson, Scott, *Fitzgerald and Hemingway: Works and Days*, (New York: Columbia University Press, 2009)

Farago, Ladislas, *Patton: Ordeal and Triumph*, (Yardley, PA: Westholme Publishing, 2005)

Gay, Timothy, *Assignment to Hell: The War Against Nazi Germany with Correspondents Walter Cronkite, Andy Rooney, A. J. Liebling, Homer Bigart, and Hal Boyle*, (New York: New American Library, 2012)

Glass, Charles, *Americans in Paris: Life and Death Under Nazi Occupation*, (New York: Penguin, 2010)

Hackett, Mary, *William "Bill" Walton: A Charmed Life*, (Wellesley, MA: Branden Books, 2013)

Hemingway, Ernest, *Across the River and Into the Trees*, (New York: Scribner, 2003)

———, *The Complete Short Stories*, (New York: Scribner, 1987)

———, *To Have and Have Not*, (New York: Scribner, 1937)

———, *For Whom the Bell Tolls*, (New York: Scribner, 1940)

———, *A Farewell to Arms*, (New York: Scribner, 1995)

———, *By-Line Ernest Hemingway*, (New York: Scribner, 1967)

———, *The Fifth Column and Four Stories*, (New York: Scribner, 1989)

———, *A Moveable Feast*, (New York: Scribner, 1964)

———, *Complete Poems*, (Lincoln: University of Nebraska, 1992)

Hemingway, Mary, *How It Was*, (New York: Knopf, 1976)

Johnson, David, *V1-V2 Hitler's Vengeance on London*, (New York: Scarborough House, 1991)

Keegan, John, *The Mask of Command*, (New York: Penguin, 1988)

Lanham, C. T., *Infantry in Battle*, (Whitefish, MT: Kessinger Publishing, 1939)

Liebling, A. J., *Between Meals: An Appetite for Paris*, (New York: Modern Library, 1995)

———, *World War II Writings*, (New York: Library of America, 2008)

Liddell Hart, B. H., *The Rommel Papers*, (Cambridge, MA: Da Capo, 1953)

Mauldin, Bill, *Up Front*, (New York: W.W. Norton, 2000)

Meyers, Jeffrey, *Hemingway, A Biography*, (New York: Harper & Row, 1985)

Michel, Henri, *The Shadow War*, (New York: Harper and Row, 1972)

Miller, Edward, *A Dark and Bloody Ground: The Hürtgen Forest and the Roer River Dams, 1944–1945*, (College Station: Texas A&M University Press, 1995)

Miller, Nathan, *War at Sea: A Naval History of World War II*, (New York: Scribner, 1995)

Moorehead, Caroline, *Gellhorn: A Twentieth Century Life*, (New York: Henry Holt, 2003)

———, *Selected Letters of Martha Gellhorn*, (New York: Henry Holt, 2006)

Morison, Samuel Eliot, *The Invasion of France and Germany: 1944–1945*, (Champaign: University of Illinois Press, 2002)

Mort, Terry, *The Hemingway Patrols*, (New York: Scribner, 2009)

Neiberg, Michael, *The Blood of Free Men: The Liberation of Paris, 1944*, (New York: Basic Books, 2012)

Orwell, George, *Essays*, (New York: Everyman's Library, 2002)

Paul, Elliot, *The Last Time I Saw Paris*, (London: Sickle Moon Books, 2001)

Pyle, Ernie, *Brave Men*, (New York, Grosset & Dunlap, 1944)

Reynolds, Michael, *Hemingway: The 1930s*, (New York: W.W. Norton, 1997)

———, *Hemingway: The Final Years*, (New York, W.W. Norton, 1999)

Roberts, Andrew, *The Storm of War: A New History of the Second World War*, (New York: Harper Perennial, 2012)

Rooney, Andy, *My War*, (New York: PublicAffairs, 2000)

Rothbart, David, *A Soldier's Journal*, (New York: I Books, 2003)

Rush, Robert, *GI: The US Infantryman in World War II*, (Oxford, UK: Osprey Publishing, 2002)

———, *Hell in Hürtgen Forest: The Ordeal and Triumph of an American Infantry Regiment*, (Lawrence: University Press of Kansas, 2001)

Stein, George, *The Waffen-SS: Hitler's Elite Guard at War 1935–1945*, (Ithaca, N.Y.: Cornell University Press, 1966)

Vaill, Amanda, *Hotel Florida: Truth, Love, and Death in the Spanish Civil War*, (New York: Farrar Straus and Giroux, 2014)

Whiting, Charles, *Hemingway Goes to War*, (Stroud, UK: Sutton Publishing, 1999)

ANTHOLOGIES

The Paris Review Interviews, I, (New York: Picador, 2006)

Reporting World War II, Part Two, (New York: Library of America, 1995)

The 40s: The Story of a Decade, the New Yorker, ed. Henry Finder, (New York: Random House, 2014)

PERIODICALS AND WEBSITES

The Hour (Norwalk, Conn.)

Jewish Virtual Library website: http://www.jewishvirtuallibrary.org/

New York Review of Books

London Daily Telegraph

Watford Observer (UK)

National 4th Division Association website: http://www.4thinfantry.org/

Sydney Morning Herald (Australia)

Vanity Fair

Spokane Daily Chronicle

Foot-Pain-Explored.com

Royal Air Force website: http://www.raf.mod.uk/

INDEX